C000281718

RICKY
HATTON

To my mum and dad.

RICKY HATTON

WITH NIALL HICKMAN

THE HITMAN
MY STORY

EBURY
PRESS

First published in Great Britain in 2006

1 3 5 7 9 10 8 6 4 2

Text © Ricky Hatton

Ricky Hatton has asserted his right to be identified as the author of this work under the Copyright, Designs and Patents Act 1988.

All rights reserved. No part of this publication may be reproduced, stored in a retrieval system, or transmitted in any form or by any means, electronic, mechanical, photocopying, recording or otherwise without the prior permission of the copyright owners.

Ebury Press, an imprint of Ebury Publishing.
Random House, 20 Vauxhall Bridge Road, London SW1V 2SA

Random House Australia (Pty) Limited
20 Alfred Street, Milsons Point, Sydney, New South Wales 2061, Australia

Random House New Zealand Limited
18 Poland Road, Glenfield, Auckland 10, New Zealand

Random House (Pty) Limited
Isle of Houghton, Corner of Boundary Road and Carse O'Gowrie, Houghton, 2198, South Africa

Random House Publishers India Private Limited
301 World Trade Tower, Hotel Intercontinental Grand Complex, Barakhamba Lane, New Delhi 110 001, India

The Random House Group Limited Reg. No. 954009

www.randomhouse.co.uk

A CIP catalogue record for this book is available from the British Library.

Every effort has been made to trace and contact the copyright holders of photographs featured in the book. If notified, the publisher will rectify any errors or omissions in subsequent editions.

ISBN 9780091910853 (after Jan 2007)
ISBN 0 091 910854

Papers used by Ebury Press are natural, recyclable products made from wood grown in sustainable forests.

Printed and bound in Great Britain by Clays Ltd, St Ives plc

Cover photograph copyright © Mark Robinson, Punch Promotions

Acknowledgements

Thank you to Niall Hickman and Ebury Press for their hard work in putting *My Story* in black and white.

Thanks go to all my stablemates, past and present. There's far too many to mention all of them, but you all know who you are. In your own way you've all helped me along the way to getting where I am today.

Thanks to Kerry Kayes; I feel in the past few years when my toughest fights have come along you made me a better fighter. You opened my eyes to the importance of nutrition and strength training, and, let's get this straight, that was one part of 'Ricky Fatton's' game that was sadly lacking, but not any more through working with you, Kez.

Thanks to my right-hand man and great friend Paul Speak. Thanks for all the hard work you've done running me up and down the country and your help in taking the weight off my shoulders whenever it's needed.

Thanks to my amateur coaches Mr Paul Dunne, Mr Ted Peate and Mr Mick Lowan for setting me on the right road when I was no more than a little shit! You set me on the right road not only in boxing but in life in general, and I will never forget what all three of you have done for me.

Thanks to not only my professional coach but my very close friend Billy Graham. We have always had more than a boxing and business relationship. From day one to the current day you've been more to me than a boxing coach, you've been a real friend. In all the years you have trained me we've never needed a single contract, it has always been nothing but a handshake and that is the respect we have for each other, not only as boxing people, but as mates. You've been with me every step of the way on this rollercoaster, and what a ride it's been, and it isn't over yet! Words cannot describe how much you mean to me and how grateful I am for what you've done.

Thanks to my current promoter Dennis Hobson and everyone at Fight Academy. You came on board at the most difficult and lowest point in my career, and through my most difficult times, you've come up trumps, love!! You helped me make history with the fights you made against Maussa and Collazo. In doing that, it meant I won three world titles in three consecutive fights at two different weights. I'll always be extremely grateful. All I can say is any fighter under the Fight Academy banner is in the safest of hands.

And now to my family. My brother and best friend Matthew, we couldn't be closer, you're always there for me. I'm not the only one who has put our family name on the map. You're making me and Mum and Dad prouder and prouder with every win as you keep climbing the ladder, and I just hope it continues. I only wish everyone could be lucky enough to have a brother like you.

Last but certainly not least, to whom I dedicate this book, Mum and Dad. Thank you for all the time and effort and for putting yourselves out when I first started. If you hadn't put yourselves out and taken me to the gym, and made a gym in the cellar of the pub and all the other little things like that, I wouldn't have lasted five minutes in this game and I wouldn't have everything I have today. A lot of people get praise for my wins and what I've achieved but nobody sees what you have done as parents for the past 28 years. You tell me when I'm right and you tell me when I'm wrong (even if I don't like it!); that's what has kept my feet firmly on the ground throughout my career and throughout my life. If I can be half the parent to Campbell that you are to me, I will be doing well. In the last few years we've had ups and downs in my career and at my lowest point in boxing, what you did for me, Dad, was nothing short of legendary and I owe every belt and every win to you. Words cannot express how much you both mean to me. I love you both and hope to keep making you, and Campbell, the best son a man could have, proud.

Niall Hickman would like to thank, in no particular order, Ray, Carol and Matthew Hatton, Billy Graham, Kerry Kayes, Dennis Hobson, Gareth Williams, Paul Speak, Dave Jarvis, John Matthews, Paul Branagan, Barry Pearce, all at Team Hatton and the BetaBodies gym in Denton, Ed Robinson, Mike Allan and Adam Smith at Sky, my sports desk at the *Daily Express*, many of my fellow boxing writers in Britain who have given unlimited and much appreciated advice, occasionally even when sober! My partner Lynn, who has shown immense patience and consideration. All at Random House, in particular Andrew Goodfellow, without whom this book would barely be started, let alone finished, and Verity Willcocks. Finally, Ricky himself. The most entertaining, thrilling, determined and dedicated bundle of fun who ever walked the planet!

Contents

A note from Ricky

I decided to get involved with this book in the summer of 2005, it is due out in the shops in September 2006. That is just before the date scheduled for the hearing of legal claims Frank Warren has made against me. I have tried to set out the facts behind our dispute truthfully and explained our position as honestly as I can. Many of you will be reading this when the result of the court case is available and will therefore be in a position to find out for yourselves whether the court agreed with us or Frank. I will in any event update my website at www.rickyhitmanhatton.com with the outcome.

THE FRIENDSHIP OF MR GUINNESS AND MR DOM PERIGNON

Six months after the day that changed my life, I got a phone call. It was from my dad and he sounded pretty chuffed about something. He had every right to be. I had just become the first boxer from Britain to win *The Ring* magazine Fighter of the Year award.

In over 60 years no British boxer had ever succeeded in being voted the best by the bible of the sport in America. I had changed that statistic with my win over Kostya Tszyu. In plain terms, it meant I was now the International Boxing Federation's light-welterweight champion, but, more importantly than the belt around my waist, I had beaten the man who had held the unified 10-stone title and had never lost it in the ring.

Tszyu was a legend. A magnificent all-time great in the sport. And he had lost. To me. On that barmy night in Manchester, in the early hours of 5 June, he had retired on his stool at the start of the 12th and final round.

Ricky Hatton had arrived. And I intend to stay. Because I was born to box.

* * *

It was more constant pain without ever really shaking me up. It was round after round and me thinking to myself, 'Fucking hell, what is going on here?' but because it was my chance, my opportunity, it washed over me. Because almost everybody, all the experts, thought I was going to get knocked over, I didn't allow any other thoughts to come into my head. I flushed out the pain. People said I was over-hyped and hadn't fought anyone of any real quality and that definitely spurred me on. I fought like a man possessed against Kostya Tszyu that night.

When you get shaken up you are more in shock than anything else. It does hurt when you get clubbed by someone like Tszyu. Every time he hit me I thought, 'Oh Jesus,' but your heart keeps you in it. Your heart doesn't allow you to feel so much pain. A lot of that is down to conditioning and preparing yourself properly. Somebody from the street, a normal Joe, would be on the deck if they got walloped like that, but when you train as a fighter you condition yourself to taking the pain. Biting on your lip and swallowing it.

Taking shots is something you get used to over the years. You learn to take it and accept it will happen. If you made your pro debut and got stretched you would probably think, 'No, thank you very much,' but over a course of time it is something you deal with as part of the job.

As the fight got nearer everyone was tipping Tszyu to win in four or six, yet I was always supremely confident I would win it. Sometimes when you read things there can be doubts in your mind, but not on this occasion. Whenever I put on the DVD of Tszyu's fights, I always realized he was one hell of a fighter. It took me about a nanosecond to work that out. But I backed myself and I will do the same until the day I hang up my gloves.

It was definitely the most nervous I have ever been before a fight. Confident yes, but nervous, definitely. From the moment he turned up at the first press conference I was a little bit in awe of him. He had been the No.1 for so long. I was oozing confidence before he turned up in Manchester, but when I met him I remember thinking, 'Fucking hell, Ricky, this is the real deal. This bloke is a class act and he wants to take your head off.'

I've never had a problem with confidence. I'm not a cocky bloke or anything like that, but I am confident of my own ability. In the dressing room I was saying to myself over and over again, 'Come on, Ricky, this is your time. This is what you have waited the whole of your career for. Don't blow it now. This is why you first laced up a boxing glove, for this moment.' Different things went through my head. I recalled my days as an amateur and then I thought about my son Campbell and how much I loved him. This was the moment it had all come down to.

I went to the pre-fight press conference and normally my conferences are quite busy, but, blimey, there were more people at this one than there used to be at some of my fights. I thought, 'This is something different. This isn't exactly a Friday night in Wythenshawe.' Instead of three or four cameras, there were a couple of hundred.

It was unbelievable and everywhere I looked all I could see was a sea of faces. This was the big time and you know what? I loved it.

The press were calling it the biggest fight since Nigel Benn–Gerald McClellan. It was being classed with Jose Napoles–John H. Stracey, or Barry McGuigan–Eusebio Pedroza. And there was me, at centre stage. These people were my heroes and I was following them.

My nerves on the night were all over the shop, but I just kept talking to myself. This was where I wanted to be. This was why I had put in all those endless hours in the gym. This was why I had taken all the pain. This was the gain. This is what I had lived all my life for. For this moment. This was the one day I had been waiting for. I had told myself for years I could be the best in the world and now I had my chance. My shot at the title.

It was where I had wanted to be for such a long time. I said to myself, 'Don't let your arse go now, Ricky. Don't fucking be a bottle job. Show you've got real balls.' Loads of things went through my head that I had never thought of. Songs and situations I hadn't remembered for years.

People are talking to you all the time, but my way of dealing with it is to just block everything out. You have to work some things out for yourself and this is my job. This is what I do. Billy Graham always talks to me during fights, often saying things which are right on the button and I think, 'Shit, you're right there, Bill.' It'll be something he has spotted but I haven't.

In the changing room before the fight, Billy was saying do this and do that, but to be honest, he could have been telling me anything. I wasn't listening to him. It just went over the top of my head. You do all your tactics and your talking in the week leading up to the fight. In the changing rooms it is just about holding it all together. Nothing else. There are TV crews there from Sky and from America. There are 22,000 people in the Manchester MEN Arena. And all I have got is Billy chuntering in my ear. I said to him, 'Billy, shut the fuck up! We have been talking about Tszyu for the last 12 weeks. I know what I have got to do and I know what is coming. Just leave me for a bit.' But that is his job and that is what he's like. It is the way his nerves come out and I wouldn't want it any differently.

I love my mates coming round too. All my pals from years back come into the dressing room and we have the music blaring out. I didn't want it quiet so that Billy could rabbit on to me. I wanted it loud, the way I have always had it.

If a fighter needs reminding what he has got to do when he is in the dressing room before a bout, he is beaten already. When you go into the changing room, you should have it all in your head already. Talking tactics a few minutes before fighting is a recipe for disaster because you can clutter up a boxer's mind. For me, anyway, the only way is to stay in a little world of my own and get the job done.

The music started getting cranked up. Oasis. Red Hot Chili Peppers. James. I stuck on some rock, which I like just before the fight, then the last song is always the same. 'Crazy Crazy Nights' – I don't even know who it is by, but it just says it all for me.

My mate Paul Speak always puts it on before fights. When I think about it, my life is crazy. When I am in training I live like a monk, but then when I am out of the gym I put on weight and everyone knows I like a few pints with my mates. Out of training I just do what normal blokes do.

It is one of my favourite songs and I always play it in the changing rooms before coming out. I just thought it would fit the occasion because it was crazy and my life as a boxer is crazy. Making your living fighting in the ring isn't exactly normal and in years to come, when people ask me what I did when I was younger, I'll just tell them it was nuts. Crazy is the best way to describe it.

My dad always calls me and says, 'You are fucking crazy,' but if my song didn't go on I would be all over the place. It is now a tradition and it won't change.

All my mates come in and I get strength from them. Don't get me wrong, some of them had been in the bar and had a few, but I told security, like I always do, to make sure these blokes can come in. You could tell Steve and Wes had enjoyed a few scoops, but I love them being around just before I fight. These are mates I went to school with and they all get access to the dressing room. You could see they were nervous, possibly more nervous than me. They were saying, 'Come on, Ricky, we know you can do it.' I was pumped up. I didn't go into the ring crying, but there were definitely tears near the surface.

When it came to Tszyu, I remember thinking I had to stay in control. Think Eamonn Magee. Magee taught me a lesson. When I boxed him I didn't really rate him. He was bad-mouthing me before the fight, saying he was going to break me up and I was a wimp. And a chicken. The red mist came on a bit and when I fought him I took him too lightly. He was a lot better than I had thought, but the crucial thing was this: I wasn't in control. He dropped me on my arse and hurt me in the second round, causing me lots of problems. Magee can fight, believe me. I was playing to the crowd at first, but as soon as I relaxed and started boxing naturally I beat him all ends up.

Against Tszyu I got in the ring and bellowed out, 'Come on!' to the crowd, but while I was nervous and focussed, I wasn't overly angry. I was determined not to get too hyped up, like I had against Magee. I always get myself going, but against Tszyu I was in control and I owe that to Magee. I was in the ring thinking, 'Remember that little Irish fucker.' Don't make the same mistake again because this fella will knock your head off.

It is one of the differences between being a pro and an experienced pro. If Eamonn Magee had not done that to me I could have gone through my career playing to the crowd and getting too wound up. You have to be psyched up in boxing, but not to the extent that you forget your game plan and your tactics. I did that against Magee and I have not done it since.

If that hadn't happened against Magee, maybe I wouldn't have beaten Tszyu. You have to be cute and clever at the top level of boxing because one mistake and it can be goodnight. The step up is sharp and you have to deal with it.

* * *

Just before the fight I started recalling the first time I had Tszyu in my scopes. He was always regarded as the best light-welterweight in the world and arguably the best pound-for-pound fighter in operation after blowing everyone away. He won his first world title as far back as 1995 when beating Jake Rodriguez for the IBF light-welterweight crown, the belt I was to take off him ten years later, strangely enough. He had beaten top operators like Rafael Ruelas, Julio Cesar Chavez, Zab Judah, Jesse James Leija and Sharmba Mitchell in numerous world title fights. He was brilliant.

We first talked about Tszyu with Frank Warren about a month before I fought Ray Oliveira in December 2004 and Frank asked me, 'Who do you want next?' There was only one name in my mind: Kostya Tszyu. I wasn't interested in anyone else. I was getting increasingly disillusioned by not fighting the top men in the division and I told Frank the big fight had to be made or we would see if another promoter could get what I, the fans, and the media wanted.

I had always fancied my chances against Tszyu. He was a naturalized Australian, complete with the Aussie accent, but had been raised in Communist Russia and had even joined the Red Army when he was a kid. Like his name, Tszyu looked a bit of a funny bloke and he admitted to me after we fought that he had Cossack blood in him. I asked him if he could do that funny dance the Cossacks did, with their arms folded and their legs flinging in the air, but strangely enough he declined! His background was incredibly poor, but after breaking through to world level in boxing he made a bolt for Australia and had stayed ever since, so that he is now a fully registered member of the Pommie-hating society. In other words, an Australian.

Tszyu had certainly earned the right to be considered one of the all-time greats and he had stayed at the very top level for over a decade, but the thing that puzzled and surprised me about Kostya was that, despite this, he never sought out a rematch with Vince Phillips. Big, tall, gangly Vince had been the only fighter to have beaten Tszyu when he stopped him in 1997.

I was a bit thrown by this because the first thing I would want if someone beat me would be a rematch. I'd go bananas until I got another chance. It was a real head-scratcher because Kostya is not scared of anybody, he's far too good for that. He proved he has got the heart and the bottle of a true champion, so I could never work that one out.

Phillips was definitely up for another shot at Tszyu to prove his first victory was no fluke. It's not as if Vince didn't call him out either, because Vince said he wanted a rematch roughly every five minutes. It would be really disrespectful to say anything negative about Kostya, but I still cannot fathom it.

I watched Tszyu–Phillips on tape many times and the way Vince beat him was similar to me in many ways. Vince fought like a man possessed and after ten brutal rounds he stopped the 'Thunder from Down Under'. Vince had had his problems with drugs and when he came out of jail I gather he thought he was in the last chance saloon against Tszyu and that can make any fighter very dangerous.

But it wasn't just a case of Phillips getting lucky in his victory. As anyone in boxing will tell you, when he put his mind to it, Vince was a very good fighter. Apart from Tszyu, he gave me my toughest fight and he hits like a mule. It's a shame because you wonder what he could have done with his career if he had stayed clean and out of trouble. Even at this late stage of his career, he still managed to do a number on Kelson Pinto. Vince hit me harder than any other fighter has ever hit me. Tszyu's punches were more sustained, but the one punch Vince caught me with went down to my socks. Vince shook me up and Kostya never did that. Tszyu's punches hurt, but they never had the same instant effect.

I believed I was a champion, even if it was only the WBU, and I didn't and still don't have any fear of anybody. At the time Frank said, 'You don't have to fight Tszyu as there are loads of other opponents out there. You can still bide your time.' Me biding my time was over by this stage. I got the impression Frank wasn't too keen on the idea. However, Frank did a great job getting Tszyu for me. He delivered. I've got no argument about that. I didn't want to spend my career facing B-list fighters or, in the case of Dennis Holbaek Pedersen and Carlos Vilches, D-list fighters.

I didn't want my career to go the same way as others. Fighting for years and never getting a big name in the ring. I'm a massive fan of Joe Calzaghe's boxing talents. He's a terrific bloke as well and I get on really well with him, but I didn't want to be hanging around like he has. Joe has fought the likes of Charles Brewer and Byron Mitchell; good fighters but not what you would call defining opponents and in his early days he took the title from one of the biggest names of all time – Chris Eubank. But who can honestly say he has fulfilled his dreams since then? He was 33 when he faced Jeff Lacy and just look what he did to him. That shows how talented he is, but why wait until that age to prove it? Joe knows it because I have spoken to him about it enough times in private. He has been frustrated and I wasn't going to let the same thing happen to me. I was impatient and I wanted it now. By the time I fought Tszyu I was 26 anyway and had had nearly 40 fights, so I wasn't exactly wet behind the ears. I was ready and I wasn't willing to put up with any more delays.

I deliberately went to the press boys and told them how pissed off I was. I had reached a plateau in my career. Crowds were dropping off a little. I was supposed to be fighting Vivian Harris, which I was massively up for because I would have walked through him and taken his then WBA title, but instead I got Pedersen. Then it was supposed to be Sharmba Mitchell. I was told a deal was agreed, then I got Vilches. There were too many of those things happening and my performances starting stagnating. I got totally fed up with the sport and the politics of it all.

People had started talking. Instead of them saying Frank Warren didn't want the big fights, they were saying it was Ricky Hatton. Nothing could be further from the truth. All boxers say they would fight anyone and some of them even mean it. I mean it. I would rather get a right beating by the best than skirt around the sides. Bollocks to that. I think it might have stayed that way if I hadn't complained bitterly about fighting in Manchester against B-list stuff. So the pressure was on Frank Warren to deliver the fight because for some time I had been on a fight-by-fight deal.

* * *

I was so switched on and focussed when I came out of the tunnel to 'Blue Moon'. I looked around and the roar went up. It was a sound like I'd never heard. I took a deep breath and blew it all out. I have watched myself on video and have a laugh about it now. At the time all I was thinking was, 'Fucking hell, Ricky.' I knew then I could do it. Didn't have any doubts. But the crowd made the hair stand up on the back of my neck.

Thankfully, Kostya didn't try the age-old boxing tactic of eyeballing his opponent before the start of the fight. He isn't really into that and neither am I. I can't see the point because it is just old hat. Muhammad Ali wound up his opponents because he was a great talker, but then all of a sudden all these fighters started to think they were Ali and began trash-talking their opponents. Don't get me wrong, I didn't want to give Tszyu a kiss and a cuddle, I wanted to take his head off, but I wasn't going to stand in front of him, or any fighter, and pretend to eyeball him just for the cameras.

That sort of thing doesn't bother me in the slightest; in fact, when fighters have done it to me, I find it funny more than anything else. Playing the hard man is all well and good, but only when the bell goes do you find out who has really got balls and who is pretending to have them. Ben Tackie tried it as well, giving me the eye all the time and threatening to do this and do that, although most of the time I didn't understand a word he was saying as his English is pretty basic. I can vouch for the fact that he knows the words 'pussy' and 'bastard' because he kept calling me that throughout our scrap. Tackie is a high-class fighter, but he should drop that act. I suppose if it works for him, fair enough, but it didn't do anything to me and no amount of eyeballing would have the right effect. If my future opponents think it will get to me, then they too will find out I think it is a load of utter bollocks.

In all my pro fights and 80-odd bouts as an amateur it has never worked yet, so I think it is fair to say I am not going to be fazed by somebody trying it on with me. Thankfully, Kostya didn't, but then you find the very best fighters don't really need to.

Remember when Kostya fought Zab Judah? I went to the

bout in Las Vegas with Billy Graham and laughed my nuts off when Zab gave it the full eyeball works before the fight, telling everyone what he was going to do to Tszyu. Tszyu knocked him over with a cracking right hand, left Zab wobbling on his feet and the ref stopped the fight. Fair enough. Judah then threw a chair at the ref in a fit of anger. Unbelievable. Throwing a chair at a ref! Nothing more needs to be said other than what a complete joke.

I intentionally show no real emotion at all. My face before a fight is a bit of a blank canvas. I will be focussed and determined, and you can see that etched on my face, but nothing more.

The start of the fight was amazing. In a press conference beforehand, Tszyu had said my punches would bounce off him, and you know what? He wasn't wrong. I thrashed away at him and fired some excellent stuff but he didn't seem to flinch. Then he would have a go back and he hit me with four or five decent shots in the second and third rounds. He could throw punches with real force and in the middle rounds I knew he was impressing the judges with his hand speed and accuracy.

The one thing you mustn't do after any fight is think about what might have been. No point, is there? After the bell has gone you can't do anything about it, so what is the point in whingeing about the result? All boxers who lose, unless it is by a wide margin, will go on about how they were cheated and in a few cases they are, but in general I think most judges get it about right. Occasionally you will get a stinker of a result, especially if you go to Germany where you have to knock your opponent out to win on points, but I don't have a lot of sympathy for boxers who throw a few decent punches in 12 rounds then complain.

Had Tszyu beaten me fair and square I wouldn't have moaned about it. I was in there with one of the all-time greats, but I never had any thoughts about losing. The only focus I had was on overcoming him. Trying to impose myself on him, not the other way around.

When I was dumped on my pants by Magee, I worked it out myself. I found a way to answer the questions. Against Magee I changed my tactics mid-fight and against Tszyu I used my brain. I worked out how to beat him. I had watched Tszyu on video and seen him live twice. He doesn't have a high work rate, never has had. He is so good he sits back and picks his shots. He picks the time to strike and then delivers. Against Zab Judah he sat back, took some blows, then wham. He stung. He KO'd Judah with his right-hander. Tszyu is at his most devastating when his right arm reaches its full extension and he connects. When he throws that punch he could knock out a fucking lion. I had to make sure that punch never landed and I did that by closing the gap between me and him and not allowing him the full leverage.

Also, I out-worked him. I swarmed all over him. He must have thought I was his worst nightmare because I threw so many punches he didn't know where they were coming from. For a slow-tempo fighter like Tszyu I am a fucking night-mare. I am the angel of death. The fucking bloke wearing a black cloak carrying a scythe. I didn't let him settle and get into his routine. I fought the fight at my pace and that is what you have to do with your opponent in boxing. You have to make them do things they don't want to and I knew Tszyu didn't want a fight at the kind of tempo I was talking about.

Tszyu didn't really know what had hit him. He was up against this Energizer Bunny and he didn't like it. Fuck me, though, can Tszyu fight, and in the middle rounds he out-boxed me. But I knew and Billy knew that he couldn't keep up that tempo, whereas I could. By the eighth he was dead in the water. He knew it and I knew it. By winning rounds, he had taken too much out of himself. Again, that's called using your brains. I'm not a stupid fighter. I work it out. I worked out what I needed to do against Tszyu and I knew high-tempo boxing, throwing literally hundreds of shots every round, wasn't in his game plan. It was in mine.

In my earlier fights, I was learning all the time. When I fought Jon Thaxton I got a cut requiring 28 stitches in the first 15 seconds of the fight and so I had to change my game plan to accommodate Jon, who is as tough as they come and a really top professional. I did that. I used my boxing skills, which are often underestimated, and I boxed his socks off, winning every round. I started moving around the ring, using my jab a lot more at a distance, instead of getting in close and brawling. By giving myself some breathing space, it allowed my cut to heal up. That is the learning process that you have to build on in this sport. Similarly, Vince Phillips shook me up badly in the fourth round and Magee put me down. In all those fights I had to think on my feet. I had to work it out myself because trainers, cuts men, advisors can do nothing in those moments. It is down to you, and only you.

In my career I have had to tick off various boxes. Can I take a punch? Can I recover from a cut? Can I recover from getting chinned by Vince Phillips, who landed the hardest blow I've ever taken as a pro? It is called facing up to the challenges. If my career had all gone perfectly and I had never had any challenges, Tszyu might have beaten me. I am very fortunate in that all the way through my career I've always had challenges put in front of me. You have to then sink or swim.

Everybody knew I was a good fighter when I was a kid. But there are plenty of decent prospects who have gone by the wayside. I was sometimes accused of being over-hyped. I read the reports and listened to people saying Ricky has fought nobody. And, to be fair, the performances I gave against Pedersen and Vilches were bloody awful. I had to agree with the critics. You would not have put ten pence on me beating Tszyu after those displays, but you raise your game in boxing.

Against Tszyu I found a way. When Muhammad Ali fought George Foreman they said he was going to get killed. Foreman had stopped Frazier and Ken Norton in double-quick time and was a monster. Ali was up against someone bigger than him, stronger than him and younger than him, and you know what? He found a way. His boxing brain did it for him.

Though the middle rounds definitely belonged to Tszyu, none of them went to him by wide margins. All I knew was this work rate I was keeping up wasn't helping Kostya at all.

He wasn't used to it. I had to keep up the intensity, the momentum. I felt if I could take the pain but give it back to Kostya twice over, eventually it would work.

Billy was going nuts in between rounds, telling me Kostya was hitting me every time at the start of each three-minute session flush in the chops. Looking back on the video now, I can see Billy was not wrong, but at the time I felt like it was the best way to impose my authority in every round. Stand up to Tszyu, take his best punch and carry on wading in. Not in a stupid way, but cleverly. Alright, I swallowed some punches, but not in lethal areas. I was closing the gap between us all the time and that was exactly what I wanted.

Because of his long right hand I had to be faster and busier than I had ever been. I knew that right hand could spark me out. The knowledge that he had such a devastating punch was helping my concentration, because if you get it wrong for a split second it's 'goodnight, thanks for trying'.

Something strange happened in the eighth round. As usual, we traded blows, although this time they weren't to the head or the body, but to the crown jewels.

Of course I intentionally punched him in the bollocks. One hundred per cent. He hit me with a low blow in the seventh, and then he did it again. When referee Dave Parris warned him for a second time, I thought, 'Hang on, this isn't going to happen again. Give him a taste of his own medicine, Ricky. Punch him in the bracket like he's just done you, because there is no way any referee would ever take a point away when he has just warned Tszyu twice. No way.' So I collected my thoughts, walked to him. No, in fact I almost sprinted and I went whack, there you go, sunshine, see how that feels in your boots. I said afterwards that boxing is no tickling contest, and you know what? I'd do exactly the same thing tomorrow. If a fighter punches me down there, he will get it back. I've no problem with that. You do what you can to win. You find a way.

I don't consider myself to be a dirty fighter, but I am a boxer who will do everything he can to win. If my opponent slips in a few rabbit punches or, as in Tszyu's case, throws one into my knackers, rest assured, I'll do exactly the same back, only harder. Against Tszyu, I didn't want him to gain a stranglehold on the fight. I needed to keep him where I wanted him, not the other way round.

By the eighth, I knew the fight was turning anyway. I knew I had him. Kostya is a legend in the ring, but you know when you have got your opponent on the run. Their breathing patterns change and their body language alters, and Kostya's body language wasn't the same. The look on his face was one of 'Fuck me, what have I come up against here?' I could see it in his eyes that he was wilting and the spark and snap that he had had earlier on in the fight had gone.

I carried on whacking away at him in the ninth, tenth and eleventh and I could tell by the crowd's reaction and my own thoughts that I was getting through. I was getting so close to the dream. 'Don't fuck it up now,' I thought. 'Just keep concentrating, because this Kostya character is a mean boxer who won't give up without the mother and father of all fights.'

After the eighth, I went into overdrive. He must have been

bushed, but make no mistake, so was I. As the last round approached, Bobby Rimmer went to take my gumshield out, but I had already spat it out on the canvas. That was just pure tiredness. I took massive gulps of air. Billy said, 'Come on now, Ricky, he has got nothing left. Nothing at all. Have you got three more minutes for me?' I said, 'Fucking right I have. Get some water on my neck.' As tired as I was. I knew my tactics had worked. I tried to suck the air in and at that moment Billy turned round and said, 'It's over, it's over, he's not coming out.' I don't think I had the strength to celebrate. I fell over with joy and fatigue. Billy tried to pick me up. I had had to work so hard, throwing so many punches. I took it to another level in that fight. I threw more shots than I have ever done in my life because I wanted it so badly.

During those later rounds, the gap was getting bigger. I knew it. Kostya knew it and the crowd knew it. Fortunately, Kostya's corner also knew it.

When his cornerman Johnny Lewis pulled Tszyu out of the fight it was the greatest moment of my sporting life. My tactics had worked. I knew Tszyu was tiring. I knew that by the way he was breathing. I knew I was going to win after about eight rounds. After round eight, I thought, 'I have got you now. I've worked you too hard.'

It came as a shock because I didn't think for a minute he would quit. Quit is a bad word to use for a warrior like Kostya, the 'Thunder from Down Under'. Let's just say retired.

I just collapsed. The pain seemed to drain away. There I am, in front of 22,000 people, trying to stand up and just falling over. Me and Billy rolled around on the canvas and hugged each other. We had done it. Billy and I. I had beaten the best fighter in the world and not only beaten him. I had stopped him.

After the fight I started to collect my thoughts and the first thing I did was jump out of the ring in order to give my mum and dad a hug. Then I saw Matthew and did the same to him. I was overcome with the emotion of it all and I wanted to show my family how much it meant to me.

My world had changed. In boxing terms I was now a real somebody. I knew that because beating Kostya left me bracketed with some of the best fighters Britain has ever produced. That thought dawned on me very shortly after the fight.

Kostya was his typical self after, despite the fact that we had spent 11 rounds blazing away at each other. He was a real gentleman and took his defeat in the same way I would like to take it, if I ever get beaten. He just oozed class. He thanked the crowd and thanked me and said I was the better fighter on the night.

I asked if he was going to continue his career and he replied he was going to spend some time with his family and then decide what to do next. I told him, 'If that was your last fight, I hope when I end my career I'll go out in a fight like that.' The way the fight was, you would have thought we were the worst of enemies. We just kept lamping each other, but we got on really well beforehand and afterwards, so much so, that I went to Kostya's hotel the next day to exchange some gifts and get him to sign my gloves which I do after every fight. I wished him all the best in the future and he gave me a little koala bear toy to give to my son Campbell, while I signed some photos for his kids. To get so much respect from someone like Kostya was a great honour and I like to think we brought a little bit of dignity back to boxing that night.

Then, of course, I made my comments about reacquainting myself with my two best friends 'Mr Guinness and Mr Dom Perignon'! Don't ask me where I got that from. People have said I must have thought about my winning speech before the fight, but, believe me, it was straight off the top of my head. I often say the first thing that comes into my mind and, being a bit emotional, that is exactly what I did that night.

The crowd went bonkers when they heard that one, even though it was about 3 a.m. and well past bedtime. I got back to my dressing room and every person I have ever known and a few others took turns to give me a hug. Even Russell Crowe came into the changing rooms to congratulate me on the way I fought. It was a wonderful gesture from one of the Hollywood's biggest stars, especially as he'd come over to support Kostya. I did the press conference where I just reiterated my game plan and then it started to dawn on me. I had beaten one of the all-time legends of the game. So guess what I did the next day after a few hours' kip?

I met my mates in the local as we had arranged a 'Shit Shirt' competition. All of us had to wear the worst shirt we could possibly find. Mine was a black and blue trimmed effort which I had picked up in Hyde market a few weeks before for a few quid. It was bloody awful, as was everyone else's. I didn't celebrate with Dom Perignon, but believe me, I did celebrate.

The pictures of me show my face in a bit of a mess, but Kostya's was worse. After the fight you could tell he was struggling to come to terms with defeat. He looked shell-shocked. Not so much physically, but emotionally. To be at the top for so long you have to have so much pride in yourself and when I got to know Kostya I realized this was one proud man who had taken his family away from a life of poverty and raised his kids in another country. He had made a huge success of his life, but, now, for only the second time, he had lost as a pro.

It must have been difficult for him to say so many nice things about me, but that is a measure of the man. When you are beaten, you know you are beaten. But, believe me, I would much rather it was this way around than me having got clobbered.

One day my time may come, but for the moment let's put it this way, I'm a lot happier winning than losing. Aren't we all the same, deep down?

THE THREE AMIGOS

I was born on 6 October 1978 at the Stepping Hill
Hospital in Stockport and from day one I think I had
fight genes in me. During labour, in the early hours of the
morning, a monitor showed I was in distress so the doctors
decided on a forceps birth, which bruised me around my eyes.
I was a whopper at nine pounds and four ounces and the
midwife called me 'a little bruiser'. Strangely enough, over
two decades later and at roughly the same time, 4 a.m., I sat
in my dressing room having just beaten Kostya Tszyu and
become the widely recognised light-welterweight champion

of the world. I came fighting into the world and years later I was still fighting!

I was heavily into Bruce Lee films as a kid. Don't ask me why, but there was something about him which drew me like a moth to a light bulb. I suppose all kids love playing Cowboys and Indians, but for me my whole world revolved around Bruce Lee. I wasn't particularly aggressive as a kid, but I just loved the way he wasted everyone in his films! I had all his movies on video and would watch them morning, noon and night. He was very much my hero, so I started going to kickboxing classes at the age of around seven, after pestering my dad for a couple of weeks. My mum, Carol, and dad, Ray, probably thought it was just a phase and I would get out of it as quickly as I had got into it.

Nobody in the family had ever kickboxed. We were very much a football family because my dad had played for Manchester City.

I first started going kickboxing at the Centurions gym in Hattersley and, although it was only semi-contact because I was still just a nipper, I loved it. I won a few and lost my fair share, but whenever I came up against another kid who was decent, I always lost. I am the short and stocky type – I have a body a bit like the old Manchester City great Francis Lee – which meant I had these very stubby legs which were not exactly ideal for kicking. My talent, I soon discovered, was in my fists and not my feet!

I used to try to get close to my opponent in order to use my fists, which just played into their strengths and, to put it bluntly, I was getting my head kicked in every week. I could not get close enough and because I was giving away height and reach, although I won most of my fights it was getting harder. So, for these reasons, I decided to give normal boxing a go too, where my shorter legs would not be a disadvantage. There was no eureka moment. It was just a gradual thing.

Unlike kickboxing, there are some boxing roots in my family. My great-uncle Spider Hatton was a very famous local fighter in the Manchester area in the days when there were shows all over the place. My dad also tells me that on my Irish side I have another relative, my great-grandad, who was called Daniel Slattery. He was famous across Ireland for his fighting ability.

When I first walked into the local boxing gym, the Louvolite in Hyde, immediately it just felt right and soon I was telling my dad I would prefer to carry on just with the boxing. It all started from there, just one little kid trying to copy his hero Bruce Lee, getting his head bashed week in, week out, deciding to give something else a try.

Ted Peate was my first coach at the Louvolite. To be honest, at first I just went there to mess about. There was nothing too serious about it, just kids mucking around. I would turn up with two of my mates – Stephen Bell, who went on to win ABA titles as a kid and is now a professional fighter, and another pal called Tony Feno. We never took it seriously, even though we used to go to club shows all over the country. To put it mildly, we used to just fuck about. In the van on the way down to a show we would be in the back singing and joking and flicking Ted's ears. We must have driven him bonkers. Then we would get to the weigh-in and we would go around nicking all the other boxers' dinner tickets. We called ourselves 'The Three Amigos' after the comedy film of the same name and we were just a boyish handful. The official in charge of the local shows was a bloke called Bill Bateson and in Blackpool it was Arthur Walsh. As soon as we walked in the room they would shout out, 'Here they are, the three amigos!' I would do a little skit, saying, 'Well, I'm Rickos.' Then Stephen would say, 'I'm Belos and this is Fenos. And together we are The Three Amigos.' All the other boxers in the rival gyms used to look at us and think, 'What a bunch of knobheads.'

So I didn't take boxing seriously at all at this stage and it was only after I turned 12, when I had been doing it for 18 months, that I started to think, 'Hang on, what have we got here?'

It slowly dawned on me that I was quite good at it and getting better. I had been at the Louvolite for a while when my grandfather Stanley suggested I have a look at another gym at Sale West, run by Paul Dunne. Paul and my grand-father worked together as security guards for Security Express and knew each other really well, so when it was suggested I go down to the gym I agreed. My dad and grandad took me and I immediately warmed to the place and to Paul, who was a cracking coach for me. Here the penny really began to drop. I was hitting kids and they were going down.

Sale West, just like the Louvolite, wouldn't have won any awards for cleanliness. The equipment was very basic and the gyms themselves very small, but everyone mucked in and I had some great times there. It was very much one big happy family. I started out by hitting bags and doing some very basic sparring and I found I enjoyed whacking away at a bag, so much so that I would do it for hours on end.

Very shortly after joining Sale West, at the age of 13, I won my first national championships. It was the Junior A schoolboy championships, held in Derby. I beat a bloke called Michael Beary from the Dale Youth boxing club in London and I remember there was a big fuss made of it because I had won every fight leading to the finals by knocking out or stopping each kid I faced.

I boxed very much like a little pro because Paul, who became my regular coach at Sale West, was an ex-pro. I kept overhearing people in Derby saying, 'Jesus Christ, Paul, you have got one for the future there.' Even at that age I was renowned for my body-punching and my aggressive style and I was beginning to get noticed.

As a present for winning the championships, Mum and Dad made me a little gym in the basement of the New Inn in Hattersley, the pub they ran and the place where I grew up. My dad was a publican for years before moving on to the carpet trade, which is what he does now. When I was born my family was living in Hayfield and we then moved to the Oddfellows Arms in Hyde. From there we went to the Bowling Green in Marple and before long, when I was nine, we found ourselves at the New Inn. It was a great move for Mum and Dad, as that is the area where they met as teenagers, so all the regulars were friends of theirs and people they had grown up with.

It was a good life for us all. We were never that flush – we didn't exactly buy a new yacht every year – but there was always enough to go round. Growing up in a pub meant that there was always someone for my brother Matthew and I to play with, and the darts board and pool table were always in use.

I used to train at Sale West on Tuesday and Thursday nights and Sunday mornings. A very close friend of mine called Mick Lowan, who was my dad's age, used to be a boxing coach at the Louvolite. He would come and coach me in the cellar of the pub in his spare time and I owe him such a debt of thanks for all the hours he spent with me.

I was the happiest kid in the world in my own private gym. It was tiny and at first glance looked a bit of a dump, but for me it was perfect. Dad would put all the beer kegs in one corner and there was just enough room for my boxing gear.

I go back there every now and again and it brings back great memories of pounding away at the bags for hour after hour, building up my strength and timing. Even now there are the holes in the ceiling where my speed ball and bags used to hang. I remember asking my dad if I could put up a few fight posters, just to make it look like a proper boxing gym. Once those went on the wall I was in heaven. It was very much my own little world down there and I squirrelled away, working on my skills.

The pub ran a pigeon club for years which would meet to load the pigeons on trucks ready to race in the cellar, where they would also keep the cages and clocks. Every Friday the regulars would come down to my cellar with their pigeons and clocks and time which bird had won. Thankfully, it only happened once a week. It was a scene straight out of the first *Rocky* movie.

Mind you, I loved it when the locals came down to watch me. Little did I know it at the time, but I was getting used to being watched, which I am sure helped me when I started fighting in front of proper audiences. Some fighters do their best work in the gym with no-one watching, but I love boxing in front of a crowd. And it all started in the basement at the New Inn.

The regulars would come down, half pissed, of course, and some of them would watch for hours. I think they were surprised by how hard a little boy could hit, but when you whack a bag for hours on end every day, you can build up a fair degree of power. Mick used to bring his pads when he came down to coach me.

I don't see enough of Mick now, but whenever I talk about my amateur career, I always bring up his name because he was wonderful for me. He taught me so much and not just about boxing. Mick was very much into taking your boxing lessons into the rest of your life and I am sure this has had an effect on me. As a fighter you have to be very dedicated and I find that, even outside of boxing, when I decide to do something, I am determined to get it done properly. Even when I was carpet-fitting for my dad years later, I always did an honest day's work and I know one of the reasons for that was the advice I got from Mick to use the skills I learned in boxing outside the ring as well as in it. You find many fighters are the same. They are generally strong-willed and I believe that part of my character was developed in my little gym below the pub with Mick.

Even as an amateur I was training very much like a pro, as I rarely got a proper day off during the week. I would go to school and race back home to train and often I would wake up early and do an hour or so in my gym before heading off for lessons. Like a lot of nippers that age, I had bags of energy. Thankfully, I had something to channel it into.

It's a fairly well-known fact that I am very much a follower of the blue half of Manchester. My team has been City from day one – and always will be. I can even claim to have spent some two years at the club's school of excellence. You could not have found a happier 13-year-old kid when I was spotted playing for my district side, Tameside Boys, and was chosen to train there. I did OK, without ever really hitting the heights. The Whitley brothers, Jeff and Jim, were the only two lads in and around my year who I know made it in the professional game and when I was 15 I was pulled over and told by the club it had to be football or boxing, one or the other. Boxing had pretty much taken over my life by then so it was never an issue. At the time I was KO'ing anything that moved in the schoolboy divisions and I was loving it.

Training with City was always on a Thursday and I remember it clashed sometimes with boxing. One eventually had to give and there was no doubt which one it was going to be. Boxing had just taken over and the only problem I was having was not finding enough fights. I had earned a bit of a reputation for knocking kids out, so I was really struggling at one stage to get any scraps against kids my age. Basically, no-one in my age bracket wanted to fight me. I was a nasty little bugger in the ring and I wouldn't stop until I had caned the kid opposite me. I was also learning to box correctly as well as brawl and I think even at that age I surprised a few people in the youth clubs with the way I could actually fight. Technically, I was learning all the time. I'm a good listener. When my coaches told me to do something correctly it wouldn't take me long to catch on.

When the time came for me to make a choice between boxing and football there was really no decision to make. I knew my real talent lay in boxing. I tried a few other sports when I was a kid and even had a couple of months when I wanted to do nothing but go fishing, but really it was just boxing for me. And the darts team in the pub, of course.

From an early age I would pester the regulars at the New Inn for a game of darts or pool and although I am no Phil 'The Power' Taylor, I am half-decent with a set of arrows. I certainly know one end of a dartboard from the other, but then, growing up in a traditional pub, I have had enough practice.

This was the period when I really started to think about boxing and, although I was a normal 13-year-old kid in every other respect, it started to take over my life. Other than football, especially when it came to supporting Manchester City, I didn't really have any other interests because boxing took up the whole of my time. It meant my energy was channelled into something worthwhile, which I think Mum and Dad thought was a blessing. I was never in any real trouble. I could be a bit cheeky at times, but then all kids at that age like to answer back.

I started to win national titles on a regular basis and when I got chosen to represent England in a schoolboy match against Russia I was the proudest kid you could ever wish to meet. I am very patriotic and the fact that I had an England shirt on made me feel like a million dollars. It was an incredible feeling and I travelled to Russia with a bunch of about a dozen boys with a big cheesy grin on my face.

We went to an industrial town in the middle of Russia which was clearly dead poor. There was no money there at all and everything was grey. I had been abroad before because Mum and Dad always managed to save enough to take us to Spain for our summer holidays, but this was completely different. The poverty was everywhere.

I fought their welterweight champion, which is funny because I am now only a light-welter. I was a big lad for my size, so even as a kid I never felt the need to boil down to get my weight lower.

I beat their best boxer, but because the food was that poor the whole team spent every minute out there moaning about the state of the nosh we were being served up. It seemed to be the same every day – watered-down cabbage soup and potatoes. Our coaches, quite rightly, were saying don't moan about it because that is all these people have got. But kids can be quite insensitive at times. I lost that much weight in the week I was out there, I went down to 65 kilos. After beating their welterweight champion on points, I was given the chance to face their light-welterweight champion because I had lost so many pounds. Again I beat the kid, this time a bit more convincingly, and when I got home from Russia that was when I really began to think I could make a career out of boxing.

Back then you'd always hear about how good the Russians were, especially at amateur level. I think *Rocky IV* was out at the time and when I was travelling out there I thought, 'Fucking hell, I am fighting a Russian. I am going to get fucking killed here.'

Whether it was because of my exciting style or the fact that I fought very much like a pro, even at that age, I don't know, but I could hear people talking about me. Kids pick up on these things and I certainly did. Not in a big-headed way. It just sunk in that I was a lot better at boxing than maybe I had been giving myself credit for.

At 15, I really began to fancy my chances at this game and I was knocking out pretty much every opponent I faced, certainly in England. At 16, Paul Dunne started to take me around some of the pro gyms and that showed me a whole different side of boxing. We started turning up at gyms all over the north-west, asking for sparring sessions with some serious pros. Men such as Pat Barrett and Robin Reid were regular sparring partners. Brian Hughes, another highly regarded boxing coach, was also giving me some very valuable sparring advice.

When I went in the ring with these blokes, seasoned pros and, in Reid's case, a world champion, I did well. It was around this time, at 16 years of age, that I started going to Billy Graham's Phoenix camp, which was then based in Salford. Billy's gym was, like all the other gyms I had been to, a bit of a shit-hole, but it was exactly right for me. There was stuffing coming out of some of the punchbags and the showers were none too flash, but that did not bother me. It was a proper gym with sweat and blood coming off the walls. In other words, just perfect.

I got some great sparring sessions in with the likes of Paul Burke, who was Commonwealth champion at the time. Andy Holligan was also a regular when he was warming up for his clash with Shea Neary. A lot of people don't know this but I was actually Holligan's main sparring partner for this fight and unfortunately in the build-up I fractured Holly's ribs with a body shot. It's a measure of how hard he is that he still fought Shea, and to this day, Andy never lets me forget the incident. Ensley Bingham was another regular. Bingo used to say to me, 'You keep at it, Ricky, and your time will come because you have got the talent. Don't be stupid. Knuckle down at this because you have got the potential to become a world champion.'

When people like Bingo say that to you, you do think, 'Fucking hell, maybe they are onto something here.' I started knocking around with the pros on a regular basis and I picked up the buzz you get from a proper boxing gym. These were real fighters, not amateurs who could barely throw a punch, and I loved being around them. It was then I really decided that this was the job for me. School was a bit of a dead end for me.

I never took an exam in my life and I left Hattersley High School with absolutely no qualifications. My primary school had been Mottram Church of England, where my little boy Campbell goes to this day.

The school gained a certain notoriety long after I'd left and for all the wrong reasons. Nobody in Hyde was unaffected by serial killer Doctor Harold Shipman, who secretly killed hundreds of his patients. I went to school at Mottram with one of his sons, David. We played in the same football team. He was a fairly small and quiet kid, but polite. Years later Shipman's crimes were revealed and it turned out five of his victims lived in Joel Lane, a stone's throw away from where I live. Thankfully, all my family kept the same doctor we used in Hattersley so my grannies and grandads were OK, but when the news came out about Shipman, it was all anyone could talk about for months.

People have asked me about my schooldays and the honest answer is I was never in any real trouble there at all. I used to do nothing. Simple really, I didn't work, but I didn't fuck about either. I just sat in class and monkeyed around occasionally, but all the teachers will tell you that when I was told to be quiet I would do exactly that.

There was only one subject I liked: PE. That was it really. I suppose I quite liked the sex education bits, but I mostly learned about that behind the bike sheds. In the back of my mind, I always thought I was going to be a boxer. I didn't boast about it or anything, it was just a feeling I had. It was almost as if I was saying to myself, 'Everything will be alright, Ricky. The future is mapped out for you already.'

I would be sitting there with a sum in front of me and I just could not be bothered with it, because in my mind there was always boxing. My attitude was summed up by the fact that some days I would not even take a bag to school. Unless I was doing PE, I would just put a biro in my top pocket and that was it. I think the teachers used to just look at me and say, 'Fair enough. At least he isn't a problem,' and for the most part they left me alone.

I can only recall having two fights the whole time I was in secondary school. I was fortunate in that in my first year I used to knock around with a lot of lads who were two or three years older than me. I used to play football with these older boys – Stevie Bell, who once trained in Billy's gym as a pro, and Alan Page, who as a fighter took on Carl Froch a few years ago.

So nobody gave me much trouble. The first time it happened I think I gave the kid a bit of a seeing-to and that was the end of that. I was 11 years old and we were both getting changed for PE, me and this other lad, whose name I can't even remember. I put my stuff on the peg in the changing room and this kid took it off and threw it on the floor. I proceeded to take his stuff off the peg and throw it on the floor. This went on about three or four times. I then went crash, bang, wallop and it was all over in a few seconds. That was it. He was a lot bigger than me, but I cracked him one and trouble never came my way again. I can't really remember the other fight I had. I only recall that it was over very quickly. A kid called me something and that was it. I can't even remember the other kid's name. I can only remember it wasn't even a fight. It was just bang, bang, bang – over with before it even started.

Since I first started going out drinking with my mates I think I have only ever been involved in one fight with them. So two fights at school and one down the pub isn't a bad record. I was about 18 when my mate got a bit of a dusting. He went down, but these lads didn't stop so I dived in there to stop it.

My brother Matthew and I never really find trouble. We're both fighters, so I suppose that doesn't sound very macho, but it is just the way we are. Matthew has always been the same as me – sport crazy. We both collected boxing and football videos from very early ages and we both lapped up all we could about the sports.

When we were kids we were pretty much inseparable. We would hang around with each other after school and have always liked each other's company. He knows me better than anybody and vice versa. If he wasn't my brother he would still be my best mate – that is how much I rate him.

Unfortunately, Matthew has one black mark to his name. For some reason, he decided as a kid to support the red half of Manchester. To this day I don't know why, except that if you tell Matthew to do one thing, he will invariably do the other.

Even though the whole family supports City, Matthew would not have it. I tried anything and everything to get him to change his mind, but he has stuck with United through thick and thick. I've told him he is a disgrace to the family, but it doesn't do any good!

When I started going kickboxing, Matthew would string along too and he was certainly good at it. We put on an exhibition show at our local nightclub when I was eight and he was six. It went down so well we were invited back the following week, only this time he knocked me over. There is even video footage to prove it!

When I started going to the boxing gym, Matthew followed me and he was a very promising fighter until he gave it up at the age of 12. He told everyone it was for health reasons, but when asked at one of my fights a few weeks later what these were, he replied, 'My opponents.' He wanted to concentrate on football, which he was also very good at. But when he turned 15 he decided to give boxing another go and he has stuck at it ever since.

Because Matthew went back into boxing at a relatively late age, he has had it much tougher than me. He only really fought for three years before turning pro at the same age as me, 18, but he had only 22 amateur bouts behind him, whereas I had over 70. That made it hard because he had to learn how to be a professional on the hoof. There was no learning curve for Matt, just straight in. I had it a lot easier.

Matthew suffered a couple of early losses in his career, which was hardly surprising in the circumstances, although in both defeats he was never in any trouble. The first was a points defeat in the back end of 2002 to David Kirk. It was very tight and, although I am bound to say I thought Matthew edged it, having watched the video of the fight numerous times I am absolutely certain he won.

The second loss, to David Keir at the start of 2003 was stopped due to cuts, when, I reckon, the ref should have allowed it to continue. I have had much worse cuts and been allowed to carry on, but the official called the fight off with only a few seconds left of the second round. Our cuts man, Mick Williamson, was outraged. So was I and even the doctor argued with the ref, saying it was not a bad enough cut to stop the fight, but by then it was too late.

Fortunately, it hasn't put Matthew off and he has now developed into a fine fighter. Under Billy Graham he is really coming on. He looks a lot sharper, stronger and fitter and he has now pulled off a succession of victories against high-class opponents. He must be close to a British title shot and his career is starting to take off.

Whenever I go out for a pint, Matthew will always be there. It is an unwritten rule that we always go out together. We even go on holiday together and we have pretty much the same circle of friends. I feel very comfortable in his company because he has been there ever since I can remember. I think the fact that we have been going out together for over ten years and have had only two fights says it all really.

I don't think Scotland's WBO featherweight champion Scott Harrison could say the same thing. Every time I have met Scott and his dad Peter they have been terrific and like myself, Scott likes a drink. When I heard he was barred from every pub in Glasgow I thought, what is this all about? In May 2006, his world title defence in Belfast was postponed when it was revealed a week before the scheduled fight that he had been arrested in a nightclub in the early hours of the morning. Only now are we aware that Scott has had a drinking problem, which I sincerely hope he can get over so he can get on with the rest of his life. Scott is an all-action, no-nonsense fighter which boxing needs.

To be honest, I am not remotely interested in fighting anyone just because they or I have had a bellyful of beer. I do my job in the ring, but that bears no resemblance to my life outside of it.

I have had people come up to me in pubs and occasionally, very occasionally, someone with too much beer inside them will say something daft. I just laugh. Nobody can really get my back up unless they say something really nasty, particularly about my family. If it was something like that I would react, but who in all honesty wouldn't?

At the age of 16, after leaving school with no qualifications, I started working for Dad as a carpet fitter. It's safe to say I wasn't exactly brilliant at it. While I was working, a bunch of travellers ordered one of the best carpets in the shop and I went along to fit it in their caravan. A woman said I would be paid when I arrived on the job, but when I got there she told me her husband would be down with the money any minute so I got started. I finished the job and she said her husband was on his way, so I should go and get some dinner. She gave me two pounds to go and get a pie and chips and guess what? When I returned neither the woman nor the caravan were anywhere in sight.

Dad would give me the odd day off here and there so I could spend time down the gym with the pros and I would love it. The alternative was five days a week on my hands and knees, cutting up carpets and getting blisters. I would nearly slice my fingers off every week. As you can imagine, going down a boxing gym instead was fantastic and it became all I really wanted to do, though I still thought the idea of being a boxer was ridiculous. Getting paid for doing something you loved didn't seem believable to me.

Because I was spending so much time with the pros and picking up valuable experience and information, when I fought other amateurs during this period I really began to feel I could not be touched in the ring. Working with pros was ten times more challenging because their attitude was so much better. Fighting was their livelihood, which meant they took it so much more seriously than some amateurs I knew, who loved going down the gym, but didn't treat boxing as anything other than a hobby. It sounds obvious, but what I really valued was the professionalism they showed. The absolute determination to be the best. Because I was doing well in the gym with the pros, my confidence grew.

Leaving the amateurs behind at 18 wasn't even a decision for me, it was just a natural progression, but I will be forever grateful for what it taught me and the fun I had as a youngster fighting for a meal ticket and a free pair of shorts or socks.

Of course, in recent times Amir Khan has lit up the scene with the success he had as an amateur.

Lots of boxing critics have got excited over Amir Khan, and who can blame them, as the lad has real talent. But I will throw in a note of caution from my own experience. Amir was a fantastic amateur and that is all well and good, but the amateur game and the pros are worlds apart. There is no real comparison, as we have unfortunately seen with Audley

Harrison. Sure, it is roughly the same sport, but the whole set-up for winning is completely different and they are getting even further apart. In recent years, the tendency has been for the amateur game to become more 'amateur', if you see what I mean. There is headgear in the amateurs, a points system based on landing clean blows, but not necessarily hard ones, and a 'safety first' mentality which doesn't really exist in the pros.

It is a massive achievement to win ABA titles and Amir went even further by winning an Olympic silver medal at the ridiculous age of 17, but that proves he is a terrific amateur fighter, not a pro. It means he has a chance of making it in the pros, but he is by no means a certainty. I am not saying this to be disrespectful, because I've met Amir many times and he is a great lad, but he has to know that the really hard work starts now. He has amazing potential, but that is all it is – potential. I hope he can prove to be one of the few fighters who does have a glittering amateur career and then goes on to do the same in the pros, because, believe me, they are few and far between. Remember Ireland's Michael Carruth? Exactly. He won medals galore in the amateurs and even in the Olympics, but he flunked as a pro. There is a statistic that says only three Olympic medallists since the war have gone on to win a world title – Richie Woodhall, Robin Reid and Alan Minter. Not much of a record, is it?

As for Amir's career at the moment, nobody will be expecting him to go in there with anyone of any real pedigree, as he is still very young and raw. Naseem Hamed and Joe

Calzaghe had great amateur careers – amazingly, I don't think Joe was ever even put on his pants as an amateur – but they started the same way as Amir and it is only right he learns his trade in the tried and tested way.

Amir has to keep ticking off those boxes. He has to learn how to take a few shots and deal with the professionals. There is rabbit punching and sly digs in the ribs in the pros which you would not get away with in an amateur ring. He has to learn to build up his stamina to be able to cover 12 three-minute rounds, not four two-minute ones. That is a big difference. But, above all, he has to add temperament to his obvious talent. He can do it. He can become a world champion because he has serious ability, but only if he adds all these other things to his natural game. One thing is useless without the other so Amir still has a very long way to go.

If you keep blowing away opponents you can build up a false sense of security.

This is not a criticism of Amir, it is just a fact. Every boxer who has ever got to the top has been milked on a few ropey opponents early in his career and Amir should know that. He is being handed a decent early record, but it is no more and no less than that. It is when he fights another hungry, ambitious, domestic fighter like Tommy Peacock that we can really start to assess where his career is going and how fast. Talk of world titles after blasting out the Vitaly Martynovs of this game is premature.

Frank Warren can out-talk anybody in the world, but records belonging to foreign opponents, especially from the likes of Belarus or Kazakhstan, can be a load of bollocks and Frank knows that. Amir has to be carefully groomed and nobody in the business is better at that than Frank.

I don't want to sound overly critical, because Amir took on a tough opponent in Laszlo Komjathy in only his seventh fight in May 2006, which I think was exactly what he needed. Komjathy took him the distance and shook him up a couple of times and that will only do Amir's long-term prospects good, because he has had a little insight into what it is like to take on a decent pro. The six rounds he got in against Komjathy will have taught him a lot more than his other fights and he also knows that not every boxer will fall over every time he says 'boo'.

Of course it is tough for Amir, because if somebody asks him, 'Do you want to be a world champion?', he is only going to answer one way and then the next day we will be reading about Amir saying he is going to beat the world. Sometimes, you just can't win. I appreciate the fact that he is still a young kid who has much to learn, just as I once was.

He will find boxing is a different ball game when he is in the ninth, tenth, eleventh and final rounds of a championship fight and his arms feel like they will drop off. This is a seriously gruelling sport and Amir has to adjust. The amateur game is all nip and tuck, but watch some of the best pro fights – they are wars. Your opponent is in it to pay his mortgage, not to look flash for a few rounds. It is his living, as it is your living, and that means professionals are prepared to do almost anything to win.

Amir got whacked in one of his last amateur fights and nearly dumped onto his pants, but that is no bad thing. All amateurs lose and well they should. For me, amateur boxing was all about learning and I had to learn what it was like to get shook up. It prepares you better for the top level. In the pros Phillips and Magee had me in trouble, so I used the experience I had gained in the amateurs to recover. I cleared my head and got back on the job.

Maybe that was always big Frank Bruno's major fault. A brilliant bloke and a very good boxer, but he always struggled to get himself out of trouble when he got hit on the chin with a big shot. You cannot take anything away from Frank as he won the WBC world heavyweight title, but what I am saying is some fighters are better at recovering than others. Take Chris Eubank, for instance. You could have hit him with a sledgehammer and he would have come back fighting. With Frank it was, let's be honest, sometimes a case of lights out when he got chinned.

It happened to me when I was 16 years old and feeling good about myself. At that stage I had earned a bit of a reputation as probably the best amateur in my weight class in the country, so I started going in with the pros. I sparred with Robin Reid and Pat Barrett and a few others in the Manchester scene and, like all kids, I got a bit excited. Barrett was the one who really opened my eyes to the damage body shots could do because in one session with him he dropped me like a stone. It hurt so much I wanted to know more and that's one of the principal reasons why I became such a dedicated body-puncher. My sparring with Reid started getting more and more like a real fight as I pounded away at him. He then obviously thought he had seen enough, so he started to let loose and boy did Robin chin me. It shook me up all the way down to my socks. I had ability at that age, but Robin gave me a real going-over. And guess what? I loved every minute of it. He had to open up on me. He started by taking it easy with me, but by the end it was a war in there and I am not ashamed to say he put me down.

As an amateur, the only person I can remember who managed to drop me was a German called Jurgen Brahmer who was a bit handy. He has done well in the pros and is widely regarded as the finest natural talent to have come out of Germany for many a year, but the fact that he has been inside for some time hasn't exactly helped his career. Brahmer has bags of talent, but maybe he just hasn't worked this bit out yet – being in prison for a road-rage assault can damage your chances. He wouldn't be the first fighter to throw it all away, or the last.

As I was saying about Amir, Brahmer, who lost a close decision to former world title challenger Mario Veit in June 2006, has all the ability, but unless you have the whole package you won't succeed at boxing. It might be called the sweet science, but, trust me, there is nothing much sweet about the ring.

THE PREACHER

When I was 18, I discussed turning professional with only two promoters, Frank Maloney and Frank Warren. They were the two leading promoters in Britain and when they approached my dad and Billy about me I didn't feel the need to look anywhere else. At that stage, Maloney had Lennox Lewis in his camp and I was impressed with him. Maloney is a what-you-see-is-what-you-get kind of bloke and I liked that. I am sure he has cut a few corners in his boxing career, but I didn't mind that at the time and I don't mind it now. He came across as very reasonable and very knowledgeable about the sport.

However, Frank Warren has an aura about him. He is very slick and very clever and he can make you feel like a million dollars. It didn't really take me long to make up my mind as Warren was, and still is, regarded as boxing's leading promoter, certainly in Britain.

Billy Graham had teamed up with Warren with a number of his fighters, people such as Ensley Bingham, Carl Thompson and Steve Foster Snr, and he said he had never had any major problems with Frank. Maloney offered me pretty much the same money as Warren, so it was decided on who I felt more comfortable with and in that respect I chose Warren. The fact that he had worked with a few of Billy's fighters was also a major consideration. At the time, Warren also had the Prince, namely Naseem Hamed, who was cutting a swathe through the featherweight ranks and threatening to become a real force in the sport. Warren promised me a slot on some of Naz's undercards and that was really the final clincher.

I felt that Warren was big-time and that is what I wanted. A promoter who could take me to the top in double-quick time. Get me the biggest fights and the best deals. In fairness, he delivered, certainly in the early days, and I was immediately off to America to fight at the home of boxing, Madison Square Garden, on the Naz–Kevin Kelley undercard.

Although it was pretty much empty, there was a very special feeling about the place. It is a huge arena, seating over 20,000, and maybe there were a few thousand in there scattered around, so it is fair to say there wasn't exactly a ripping atmosphere. But I knew I was fighting somewhere out of the ordinary because I love watching all the old boxing videos of the greats, many of whom fought at the Garden.

I was surprised how intimate it felt. The MEN Arena in Manchester is the same. It is a similar size to the Garden and the banks of seating are also very steep, so even though there are over 20,000 fans in there, they feel very close to the action.

Crowds don't really affect me any longer and when you are in there fighting it can be a few hundred or 20,000, it doesn't really make any difference. The only thing that made New York different was the venue, right in the middle of central Manhattan, which is just a sea of skyscrapers in all directions.

Being without Billy in New York was a bit strange and in the immediate run-in to a fight I am always like a cat on a hot tin roof. I wanted to get in there, get the job done and get home. I wouldn't say I was homesick, because fighting abroad doesn't really bother me, but I was close to it. Hyde isn't exactly Manhattan, is it? Everything is different over there, but the TV stations are just wall-to-wall adverts, so I didn't even do much television watching. It is basically very boring because you have done all your preparation. All you can do is sit and wait, go for walks and hang around the hotel, which can get very frustrating.

I didn't have any real nerves about the fight, because I was confident I would win, but bearing in mind it was at the Garden, it is fair to say I wanted to put on a show and that wound me up a bit, maybe a touch more than usual.

I also appeared in Atlantic City when Naz beat Wayne McCullough, the first fighter to go the full 12 rounds with the Prince, and I then went on to fight in a funny-looking theatre in Detroit, the Motor City, on the undercard of an Acelino Freitas fight. Warren had some sort of slice of Freitas and it was great to get another chance to taste what it was like in America again. I loved it and I will always be grateful for those opportunities.

It was great fun travelling to America to fight and, as you can imagine, all boxers dream of appearing at the Garden as it is the spiritual Mecca of the sport. It is where Ali fought Frazier in probably the biggest fight of all time. I feel lucky to have fought there, even as an undercard boxer.

Even though the Garden was pretty empty when I fought, there was still the feeling that I was fighting somewhere very special. When Naz fought Kelley, the crowd went crazy, not surprising when you consider there was a stack of knockdowns in one of the most amazing fights I have ever seen.

When the decision was made to turn pro, there was no question who would be my trainer. Billy Graham had been coaching me for a couple of years and we had always got on well, so it was a natural progression that we would work together properly after I turned 18.

Billy Graham grew up in Salford in the 1960s, which he always tells me was a different world from the one I enjoyed. It was certainly very working class and Billy is a product of that – very much a what-you-see-is-what-you-get kind of bloke. He first got into boxing by chance when he came into his living room one day and saw the former world heavyweight champion Floyd Patterson on the television. Like all kids, Billy used to have fights with the local boys, but when a gym was opened up near his home next to the local police station, he went along and was hooked. He learned to fight properly and, from what he tells me, he was in the gym morning, noon and night from then on in.

Billy was a decent professional and fought 14 times, but he has really made his mark as a trainer. The first boxer who he trained on his own was the former world champion Carl Thompson and, over the years, he has had stacks of high-class fighters. He says it was fate, destiny, call it what you want, that threw us together. All I know is that from pretty much the first day I met him I had a good feeling about Billy. He is also just about the only bloke I know who swears more than me, so we are perfect for each other!

Billy and I have a very unusual relationship in boxing. We have never had a contract between us and there will never be one. We don't need one. We don't really do anything by the book. We don't stay at home and behave ourselves at all times like some boxers and trainers. We both live life to the full. At the heart of our relationship is the fact that we are good mates. Simple as that. We like each other. I think the world of Bill and I know he feels the same way about me.

He has got rough edges, and you know what? That is exactly what I like about him. He's no bullshitter. He tells it to you straight. When we're in the gym, I will know if I am cutting corners, but Billy will know before I have even thought about it. He has seen it all. He has been a brilliant trainer for years, so he has seen stacks of fighters come and go. He knows the ones who are lazy and the ones who really want it and will do anything to get it.

Boxing for me comes very naturally. It will always be No.1 in my life. I like to party, but when it is time for training that is it. I live like the most boring bastard you have ever known. I have never had any gripes about that, because it comes with the territory. Like I said, this is no tickling game. It is the fight game and the fight game is nasty and brutal. Any weakness and your opponent will take you apart. Which is why I won't allow any weakness. When I am in training, me and Billy go at it. I can't cut corners, because when I am out of training I pile the pounds on. Some fighters might walk around half a stone heavier than their fighting weight when they're not in training, but with me it is more like two stone. It doesn't bother me, because it has been that way throughout my career. But it means I have to take training ultra-seriously and I do.

I will go in the gym for a few weeks and people will say, 'Where has it all gone? Where has all the weight gone?' It's because I give it my all when I'm in training. If I am feeling OK about the week's work I will go and see City on Saturday, but that is literally it. You won't see me in the pub or going out on the town or watching a movie or anything. I train, eat and go to bed. Train, eat and go to bed. That's my day. I am like a monk. There are times to let your hair down and times to be disciplined.

I have been boxing now for so long I don't know what life would be like without it and the idea that I will one day retire is a strange one. Boxing has meant everything to me. People say it isn't exactly the best thing for your health, but I would dispute that. Boxing has done so much for so many kids who would otherwise be on the wrong side of the tracks. I am not saying I would have gone in that direction; in fact I know I would have stayed on the straight and narrow. But, let's face it, boxing is not exactly polo, is it? And the people that frequent boxing gyms are usually pretty working class. I've never had a problem with that and I don't know anybody that does, but if I hear of anyone trying to ban it, they are usually talking out of their arses about something they don't understand. Having spent my life in gyms, I know from first-hand experience that boxing is a force for good. Always has been and always will be, in my book.

When people ask about my love of the social life, I say to them that they have got to realize that when I fight nowadays I do 12 to 14 weeks in the gym to prepare. That is over three months for something which could last only a few minutes. It underlines the fact that when I talk about going out and having a few beers, that is only a fraction of my life, because most of it is spent in the gym, where the hard work needs to be done. That isn't a chore for me, far from it.

When Paul Dunne was my amateur coach I knew the time was coming when I would have to change to a pro coach and I always felt most comfortable with Billy, talking boxing while he was tugging on his fags, sitting on the steps of his gym.

Make no mistake, Billy knows his stuff when it comes to boxing. He knows how to get his fighters fit, and, more importantly, he knows how to make them technically better fighters. Pretty much anyone who knows anything about a gym can get a fighter fit; it is the technical stuff which takes real talent and Billy has got that. He will tell me I am throwing a left hand too open and leaving my chin sticking out, or my right jab needs more snap. He will then point out why the jab was coming out slightly wrongly and often it is something I have not noticed.

Billy's Phoenix gym in Salford was famous for its spit-and-sawdust reputation and, again, I loved that. I tried to go to as many gyms as I could when I was a kid to get as much experience of other coaches as was possible. Paul Burke was always giving me good advice and that was one of the avenues he recommended.

Sparring with Andy Holligan as he trained to fight Shea Neary for the WBU title was a very special memory for me and made me realize how much work I would have to do to make it as a pro. It also made me understand how far off winning a junior ABA title was to winning a world title. There is no comparison, but it opened my eyes up at an early stage to what it would require to go to the very top.

At Billy's gym we always used the body bag, a massive pad which he straps to his body and allows you to pound away without breaking his ribs. It was made for me and my style of boxing and I am sure it is one of the reasons why I have become such an accomplished body-puncher. I think Billy's coaching style suits my style of boxing. I would never say anything disrespectful about the likes of Brendan Ingle, who has a 'limbo dancing' style unique to his gym, but that is just not me and never has been. Brendan's fighters are often much more flexible and bendy than I ever was. But the proof is always in the pudding and Brendan has helped create some brilliant boxers including Naz, Johnny Nelson and Ryan Rhodes, so it obviously works for them. I just don't think it would have worked for me, but, as I say, there is nothing wrong with different styles in coaching as there is no right or wrong way.

Billy is a firm believer that training in the gym should be as near to a fight as possible. I see other coaches with hand pads on, shouting out instructions in a very methodical way. Almost as if they want their fighter to box in that fashion.

Billy isn't like that at all. He barely says anything when I am whacking away at him. No opponent is going to stand there and let you punch away in a robotic style, so what Billy does is say very little and allow you to feint and move and choose your shots. To try and make it more like a fight scenario. Obviously, we will practise on certain shots that I feel need working on, but it won't be rigid. It won't be Billy saying, 'Throw the left jab, followed by a right upper. Do it again 1,000 times.' It is much more fluid than that. It is pad work, but is more like a spar session and therefore I find it much more realistic.

Billy is also clever about how much work his fighter should do. In training, I might work my bollocks off on Monday,

Wednesday and Friday, so Tuesday and Thursday will be a bit easier. It will allow my body to recover without pounding at it all day and every day. Rest is just as important to a fighter as work and you need to get the balance right. On a few occasions, I have walked into the gym with a heavy cold and Billy just tells me to go home. No ifs and buts, home. His reasoning is simple. Your body is telling you it is in need of repair. It needs some help. So what possible good could you do by burning yourself out in two hours at the gym? It will only make matters worse. You have to accept what your body is telling you. I do, but I know a few fighters who feel the need to prove themselves all the time. Runs at 3 a.m., chasing chickens and drinking raw eggs is for *Rocky* films. Trust me, it is total bollocks. The reality is very different.

What is the point in getting up before the fucking milkman just to prove you are the hardest nutter in the world? None, as far as I can see. It doesn't impress me or anyone I know in boxing. The whole point of going to the gym is to condition yourself to give yourself the best chance of winning a fight. So where does running at 3 a.m. come into that? At that time the body should be in bed, preferably on your own, although that is not always the case with me! The body needs to be listened to because it is your only weapon and if you get in a ring knackered because of your training you will have no chance.

The most important work you have to do is in the gym, so that is where I always start my training. The rest, such as weights and road work is secondary, so you leave those until later. I have only ever stepped into the ring once when I haven't felt the greatest, against Carlos Vilches. I ran out of gas, and guess what? My performance was shit.

In the early days with Billy I would do about eight weeks in the gym, working up to a fight. Now it is more like 12 or 14 and yet we use exactly the same system. On Tuesday and Thursday we will do more technical stuff and at other times I will work myself into the ground, with good recovery periods in between.

Billy had a reputation when I first joined him of being a great conditioner, but not necessarily a great boxing coach. But, like I said, he knows his boxing stuff. Many coaches can get their fighters as fit as a butcher's dog, but Billy is no fool when it comes to the technical side. He hasn't read all the books. You don't need to. But he has picked it up over decades in the gym and what he says works for me.

With one exception, I have always felt as good going into the last round as I have at the first. Don't get me wrong, my arms want to fall off, but I have always felt in peak condition.

There are always new ideas we have to improve my fitness and we are always looking at different methods or diets, but generally our preparation has remained the same over many years and I can't see it altering.

One aspect which I took on board the moment I became a pro was using weights. I had only really fooled around with them before, but they soon became an essential part of my training. There are old coaches who say weights can only do a boxer harm, that the muscle will turn you into a bodybuilder and not a boxer. I agree, to an extent. Frank Bruno looked more like a bodybuilder to me and I don't think it was any co-incidence that he struggled with stamina throughout his career. But, in my opinion, weights, done at the right time and the right amount, can only have a positive effect.

The old idea that weights slow you down because muscle requires more oxygen is pretty much a load of rubbish. Billy has always been pals with Kerry Kayes, a former British champion bodybuilder who knows everything there is to know about conditioning and fitness. Kerry put me on a course of weights and, from day one, they have made me a much stronger fighter without turning me into a muscle-bound lump.

Stronger muscle, in my eyes, means a more explosive puncher and that is what you need in boxing. I do weight training four times a week when I am preparing for a fight. There is lots of grappling and shoving in boxing and the weight training has helped me massively in that department. I also know that when I go in there with an opponent and he feels my strength the first time we come together, he is going to know he is in there with someone who means business. I know Tszyu, after the fight, told me he was surprised at how strong I felt and this was one of the fittest blokes ever to lace a glove.

I think my weight training has also made my shots a bit quicker and I owe a lot of that to Kerry. My legs are naturally the strongest part of my body and in training I will do 25 kg on the leg press, doing three sets of ten. I am sure my legs are stronger and I have become a slicker fighter because of the weights.

I now train at Kerry's gym, Betta Bodies in Denton, and although the staircase needs a lick of paint, the rest of the place suits me down to the ground. It is the perfect place for me to train. Very close to home and Billy's gym is round the back, equipped with a little ring and some pads. And Billy's pet iguana, Liston! Some people are surprised when they see the state of the gym, as it is not exactly plush, but that is the way I like it and I don't know any fighter who trains with Billy who says different.

You go up to the gym via two sets of stairs, which I am surprised haven't fallen down years ago, as there are bits of floorboard poking through everywhere. The main gym itself has got all the latest new-fangled gear. Billy's place is through a side door. There isn't much room, but I like the intimate feel. All Billy's boxers can work together, within a few yards of each other, which means we can all take the piss out of each other easily enough! The stereo system is always on full-blast and the heating is always up to the maximum, to try to replicate what it will be like in the ring, under hot lights.

Along all the walls are old boxing posters and dog-eared photos. In a little room at the back there is the changing area, which is about the size of a toilet. The showers are very powerful, which after a long session is exactly what you need.

It is a very happy place to work, with everyone always prepared to take the piss out of each other while winding down over a cup of tea.

While Billy is in charge of my ring work, Kerry is the boss when it comes to weights and diet. While I do believe in the old saying that you don't need to fix what isn't broken, I am always interested in new ideas and ways to improve and Kerry is also always on the lookout for new things. You can always push yourself to do a little bit better.

Kerry has worked on my physique and I am delighted with the shape I have when I step into the ring. It looks like a boxer's body and that is what I want, with the added muscle there to help. All the weights I do are for a purpose and when it comes to shoving an opponent, I am one of the best in the business!

We have a routine worked out that I will get down the gym at midday, do my ring and pad work and general fitness, such as jumping the bar and cycling, and then afterwards it is the weights. I'll finish about 3 p.m. and then do a four- or five-mile run in the evenings, usually around 7.30 p.m. or 8 p.m. Then I can settle down in front of the TV or play some video games before it is early to bed. At the weekends, I will wind it down and just do a couple of runs to keep the sweat coming off me. I live like that for 12 weeks on end, so you can see why I am ready to let my hair down when I have finished a fight. And, yes, I do get a bit thirsty!

If I was running at 3 a.m. and then going down the gym and then running again in the evenings I would be fucked in a couple of weeks. Gym work is where fights are really won and lost and that is where I concentrate most of my resources and time. That is why I will get a good breakfast down me a few hours before going to the gym so that there is plenty of fuel inside me.

The gym work sometimes has to be seen to be believed. We will do 12 rounds on the pads and body bag and nearer the fight it will be time for sparring. I am basically looking to make sure I am ready, fit and at top whack to fight 12 rounds before going in to do the real thing.

Sparring has to be used to sharpen up the edges a little and to introduce a little bit of competition into the proceedings, without going crazy. Some fighters do a lot of touch sparring but I don't really go in for that at all. I feel that it is daft, because that is nothing like a real fight, more a tickling contest.

When I spar, I sometimes make sure I get clobbered a bit, to make it feel as near to the real thing as possible. I want my body to get accustomed to taking blows, so often I will deliberately hold a bit back. I always start sparring about a month before a fight and I usually do ten sparring sessions before getting into the ring.

If I spar four rounds, I will do eight on the body bag, lumping away at Billy. If it is six sparring, it is six on the bag and so on. I never do 12 rounds of sparring. The idea behind sparring is to get my body revved up to taking a bit of punishment, but it is also there to try out moves which I know need improving. There is no way I will use combinations I know will work in sparring, because what is the point? What I do is work on those aspects I know are weak and need developing. It might be a particular shot or a combination or a feint or a bit of footwork which we have noticed hasn't been going too smoothly. I love to get my lungs working in the gym and sparring is great for that. You can also overdo it and I know plenty of fighters who have left their best work in the gym. Less can often mean more and I am always very careful about how much I do in the gym and how much I have got left in my tank.

It is also important in sparring to make sure you always lose. There is no point in sparking out a sparring partner and looking great. As I'm looking to improve aspects of my technique which are not working well, if I concentrate purely on winning then that is doing no good at all. I am not improving, which is almost the whole point of sparring. Unless a sparring partner starts to take liberties I will never try to knock them out.

There have been times when my sparring partner has gone a bit far, so I've given them something to chew on. If that happens you have to show the cheeky fucker not to push it any further. But it is understandable. I got carried away when sparring when I was a nipper, so I know what it is like. Basically, I have nothing to prove to a sparring partner and I am only using them as a means to an end. To give me a better chance on the big night.

I intentionally will not try to put too many miles on the clock in sparring because I want to be fresh and ready when the fight starts, not in a training session three weeks before. They say Muhammad Ali always looked shit in sparring and you can understand why. There is no point in using up all your best work in front of your trainer and a couple of old blokes looking on.

During the course of training, I will steadily drop in weight and I have never had any real trouble in making the light-welter limit of 10 stone. It has never been a problem for me, despite the fact that the *Sun* called me Ricky Fatton before the Tszyu fight. Lots of comments like these have been made about the way my weight goes up, but just as it goes up quickly, so it also comes down. For the weigh-in the day before a fight I always get down to 10 stone, although on the night of the fight I am always at 11 stone 2 lbs. I have found that is the weight I perform best at and, therefore, that won't change. I have fought at that weight all through my career, up until Luis Collazo.

Twelve weeks of hard graft lead up to a fight and in the week before I will wind down, just doing a few runs to get the sweat going. So far, this is a method which has always worked for me.

Sometimes I will want to do too much and that is where Billy uses his experience to say, 'Slow down, we need to get in the right gear.' It can be frustrating, because some days I feel so good I want to fight straight away, but those are the days you have to take your foot off the pedal a little bit. The whole idea is to make sure I am in the best possible condition when the bell goes and therefore it has to be a balancing act.

I wouldn't say for a minute that mine is the only way to succeed in boxing, because fighters, like footballers, are all different. I know some boxers who prefer to do things in other ways and that is their choice. Some fighters never leave the gym all day whereas I go down there to work. That is their way and this is mine.

Some boxers train three or four times a day and I cannot understand it for the life of me, but if that's what makes them tick, fine. If I ever go into coaching I will say to a fighter, 'Do what you feel comfortable with, but this is how I did it. You don't have to mimic me, but, just to let you know, this worked for me and it might for you.'

Some people are surprised I don't spend 12 hours a day down the gym and do a marathon run at night. They are surprised and say, 'Is that all you do?' All I can say in response is, 'Have you ever seen a fitter fighter in the ring than me?'

Again, less can mean more. My three hours down at the gym every day are put to good use, whereas I have seen fighters spend all day down the gym basically doing fuck all.

Training has got to be harder than a fight, because you might need those extra resources you have built up, but, just as you can work too little, you can also work too hard. There is no right or wrong system, but my emphasis is on building myself up to a peak for fight night.

I can't see any reason why I would ever want to work with anyone other than Billy, because we have exactly the same relationship now as we did when I was a teenager. Some boxers go through three, four or even five trainers. They are always looking for answers through their trainer, which I can't understand.

All fighters can have an off day, just as other sportsmen do. But some boxers look for a reason for it and they choose their trainer. Billy is the best trainer for me and that won't change, whether I win, lose or draw. It is not his fault if I have a bad night, it is mine. If things are not working well then, sure, re-assess your training methods, but making a scapegoat of your main coach is the easy way out.

If I ever lose it will have nothing to do with Billy Graham, but everything to do with me. I know he will always get me in great shape for a fight, so the rest is down to me, not him. Sometimes change is for the better and fighters who genuinely are not seeing eye to eye with their trainer have to move on, but the blokes who seem to change their coach every other fight are just finding excuses in the wrong place.

Nobody knows me better than Billy and that's why I could never see me fighting for anyone else. In fact, it is not even a question I have ever considered. What I would say is we have some excellent coaches in this country and none better than in the Manchester area, where we have the likes of Brian Hughes, Oliver Harrison, Bob Shannon. All of them have helped make Manchester a hotbed of British boxing. My old mate Anthony Farnell is also going into coaching and I am sure he will be excellent at it, as he loves the game and is very knowledgeable.

The future of boxing in Manchester is very safe in the hands of these blokes and I just hope we can continue to produce the big names.

I am a bit of a mixture when it comes to trainers and fighters. There are those who say boxers are born and not made, while there are others who believe fighters can only succeed under certain trainers. I don't know. I think some fighters definitely need more of a helping hand than others, but I can only speak from my own experience when it comes to this issue. I think we have got some fantastic trainers in this country – I've always been a big fan of Jim McDonnell and Jimmy Tibbs – and I think our record in the world of boxing is very good, bearing in mind the size of our population. America has so many more fighters than us, but we seem to do pretty well on the whole when we come up against the Yanks. They have a much bigger pool to choose from, so I don't think there is an awful lot wrong with the state of our coaching.

The big argument comes down to whether you believe a world-class fighter is God-given or produced through good coaching and, again, I will have to sit on the fence a little bit. I am pretty convinced I would have been a good boxer regardless of who coached me, but I am equally convinced that putting my skills together with Billy Graham was the perfect marriage. Billy has definitely made me a better fighter, no doubt about it.

How far I would have gone had he not been there we will never know, but I think I would have made a living out of the sport. Whether I would have become a world champion, I don't know. I think I just got lucky. I know it is the all-round package which makes the fighter. I don't think I would have got to the level of fighting and beating Kostya Tszyu had I had another coach. You need a team in boxing to win and me and Billy are definitely a team. Paul Dunne, Ted Peate and Mick Lowan set the wheels in motion and Billy finished it off. He taught me things about the pro game I never knew and fine-tuned my style, which was always more professional than amateur, anyway. I know I had natural ability, but so had a lot of boxers who never made it to the top.

Naz went to Brendan Ingle's gym and went on to become a top fighter. His style was made for Brendan, just as mine was made for Billy. Naz was surely a bit of a one-off, because some of the shots he threw in the ring were from ridiculous angles which no-one else could come close to copying. I am sure Naz learned things off Oscar Suarez when he changed trainers, but he was not the same again. Brendan was the right coach for Naz and Naz was the right fighter for Brendan. So there you have it. I don't sit on the fence over many issues in boxing, but I do on this! I don't go with the idea that fighters are born, although some of them must come close to it, like my hero Roberto Duran. But I didn't know him when he was a kid growing up in Panama, so I don't know how much of it was him and how much was good, proper coaching.

I know of very few occasions where a boxer has changed his trainer in mid-career and improved beyond all recognition. I suppose the nearest thing to that in recent years was Nigel Benn with his coach Jimmy Tibbs. Nigel had been through a few trainers and had lost crucial fights when he took on Tibbs. What happened next has gone down in boxing history. Nigel's original style, which I loved, was all guns blazing. He always brought the house down. But then he started losing. He went with Tibbs and, all of a sudden, the brawler turned into one hell of an all-round boxing machine. Nigel stopped diving in like a crazed lunatic and started boxing, with much better footwork, and the results were spectacular, not least when he went over to America and beat all the Yanks. They then sent over Gerald McClellan and, although the fight had tragic consequences, it was an amazing performance from Nigel and one of the greatest ever by a British boxer.

You cannot argue with the results and Nigel definitely became a far better fighter because of Tibbs. I think you could say the same thing about Lennox Lewis when he dropped Pepe Correa and moved to Emanuel Steward. Pepe was a shouter and screamer, which, as anyone who knows him will tell you, is just not Lennox's way at all and, although Steward made Lennox a very cautious fighter, again you cannot argue with the results. Some people might have found his style a bit dull, but Lennox won the undisputed title so nothing more needs to be said.

I think Billy is simply the best coach for me. I honestly cannot think of a single weakness he has got. He is just so right for my style and my personality. Someone like Brendan Ingle would not have worked for me because my style is a lot more conventional, for a Mexican anyway! It would be fairly easy for me, with my conventional style, to change trainers, whereas I can only imagine what Oscar Suarez must have made of Naz the first time he worked with him. I would imagine he had kittens, because he would never have seen anything like it.

I think the days when you could basically just turn up, fight and win world titles are over. What I mean by that is that you need a team behind you these days in order to succeed. You need a trainer, a nutritionist, someone who knows everything there is to know about conditioning. You need a proper physio. You need all these things to succeed. Each person in your corner adds a tiny fraction to your chances of winning and nowadays you cannot leave anything to chance. The standard at the top is just too high. I remember being amazed when I first met Oscar de la Hoya, many years after I'd turned pro, and found he had a massive entourage of what seemed like 20 trainers. Everyone was in his corner bar his own hairdresser!

But in fact it was not for show. It can be the difference between winning and losing, because at the highest level you are dealing with small fractions. All the fighters are class acts so you need anything which can give you even the slightest advantage.

I wouldn't stop a good fighter changing his trainer, but I just think sometimes boxers alter them just because they are hoping the change will give them the added ingredient, the winning formula. When I boxed poorly against Carlos Vilches and, to a lesser extent, Dennis Holbaek Pedersen, I didn't blame my trainers in the interview I gave afterwards on the ring apron. I blamed myself. It was me in there not them. They had got me in great shape. It was me who fucked it up.

I am not a big fan of people who complain after the event. If you don't want to do something, it is quite simple, don't do it. I hate the idea of fighters blaming this and that when the blame lies with them. There is no use crying after the event and, no, I haven't got a lot of time for whingers.

I can certainly say I will never, as long as my career continues, blame my trainers. It is the fighter who is the only one who counts in the ring and spitting your feathers out after the event is just plain bollocks in my opinion. If I hear another fighter give an interview and blame his trainer I will throw something at the TV. It is such an easy way out.

Boxers often come out with all kinds of rubbish excuses, not just that their coaches are at fault. Some of them are true, of course, but a lot are not. I have had a few colds and sniffles leading up to fights, but some claim to have been so ill you are surprised they are even alive.

If I was properly ill before a fight you would not see me in there for all the tea in China. No way would I ever box if I was sick. I made one mistake in rushing my preparation and my performance suffered and I hope I don't make the same mistake again. It is my livelihood and I don't want to give my opponent a chance of beating me, so why would I possibly want to step into a ring if I should be laid up in bed? I would have no hesitation in calling off a fight. I would apologize to the fans, but I wouldn't box under those circumstances and I think you would be mad to expect any fighter to do so.

You have to be honest about these things, but thankfully I have no reputation for pulling out of fights because I have never done so. I'm lucky. I also know when I should train and when I shouldn't, if I have picked up a bug.

Also, if I have a few beers the night before I wouldn't dream of going into the gym. What does alcohol make you feel like in the morning? Apart from shit, it also makes you dehydrated. So what would be the worst thing I could do if I was dehydrated? Exactly. Go down the gym.

Some of the old-fashioned ideas about 'sweating out' a cold and fighting back when you are ill are just bonkers. When you are ill, there is only one thing to do. Go to bed.

The way I feel about my coaches and my relationship with them is best summed up this way: trainers make champions and champions make trainers.

THE GERMANS

I t's a fairly unknown fact that I very nearly made my pro debut in London in the summer of 1997. Minutes before I should have left my home to go to the train station I was telephoned by a British Boxing Board of Control official who told me they'd discovered an irregularity with my heart during my medical. I was broken up as boxing is all I live for. My mum and dad comforted me and Dad quickly made an appointment to see a top heart specialist at the Alexandra Hospital in Cheadle. I had every test in the book and was given the all-clear, but it was a worrying few days. Essentially, my heart was beating too fast when I got over-excited but under further tests it was shown to be no problem. So instead it was in the decidedly unflashy surroundings of the Kingsway Leisure Centre in Widnes that I made my professional debut, on 11 September 1997, against Colin 'Kid' McAuley, a decent enough opponent. The fight was designed to give me a few rounds to earn my spurs in the paid ranks.

The bill was topped by Robin Reid against Hassine Cherifi and I was a 'floater'. That means you hang about waiting for your chance. If there is a quick knock-down in one of the main fights, the promoter will throw you in for a four-rounder just to keep the live action going.

The 'Whip', namely Ernie Draper, a terrific fixer who works for Sports Network, told me I would be on at about 8 p.m., so I was all set and raring to go. The only problem was that every fight was going the distance. Nobody got filled in, so by the time I got on it was nearly midnight. The main event involving Reid had just finished, so we came out and got in the ring. But then suddenly the paramedics around the ring legged it into the changing rooms and the message got through to me and McAuley that Robin had collapsed from dehydration.

The paramedics weren't there, so, although we were ready to go for it, we could not start the fight. What a start to my pro career! There I was, ready to go to war, and yet I couldn't because there was no medical cover. We sat in the ring for about 20 minutes, like a couple of lemons, before the fight could start. Kid McAuley was sat on his stool while I was shadow-boxing to try to keep loose and warm and by this time of the night everyone bar a few hardy souls had already gone home. The 50-odd fans from the New Inn that had come to see me could sense I was nervous as hell. It was my first time in with the big boys and all I could think of was those bleeding lights roasting me. Professional lights are far brighter and more powerful than those used in the amateurs, especially if the fight is on television, and I was getting a sun-tan under them waiting for my fight to begin. The delay was killing me, so much so that I felt I was going to be the second person to collapse that night.

At last, the scrap started and I got down to business straight away. The first proper body shot I hit him with he went down. McAuley looked outside the ring at his manager Nobby Nobbs and the fight was promptly called off. McAuley then sat down on his stool, put his head between the ropes and threw up outside the ring.

It was a killer body shot. You could hear the slap of it from the back of the hall. It was a good one. Your pro debut is something you dream of when you are in the amateur ranks, so for it to go so well, despite the delay and the blinding lights, was a great way to start. I felt I had at least shown I was someone not to be messed with, although I was under no illusions – this was only the beginning.

To put in a performance like that made me feel on top of the world and I was the star of the New Inn. I always had a coachload from the pub at my fights, even when I was an amateur, and it was magical going back with them after winning on my debut. Friends and family all slapped me on the back, but little was I to know at the time that eight years later I would be drawing 22,000 supporters at the Manchester MEN Arena, selling out the venue in a couple of hours.

Next up was Robert Alvarez three months later. Unfortunately, Billy Graham couldn't come with me. He was in Ensley Bingham's corner that night, back in England for his British title fight with Nicky Thurbin. He had to give priority to Bingo, who was fighting for a title, whereas this was only my second scrap. I went to the weigh-in and saw my opponent for the first time. He looked massive to me and was covered in body hair and tattoos – so much so that I didn't know whether to fight him or read him. I phoned Billy in a bit of a state. He told me to calm down and that my training had gone brilliantly. He said if Alvarez was really good he wouldn't be fighting me. I said, 'Thanks a bunch, Bill, you've been a great help!'

Again, there was hardly anyone in the crowd, but there was a difference. The small matter of the fight being held at New York's Madison Square Garden, the undisputed Mecca of the sport. I was on the Naseem Hamed–Kevin Kelley undercard, which turned out to be a right rollercoaster, with both boxers going down several times before Naz found a devastating finishing punch.

I had gone over to America with Danny Williams and Ernie Fossey. Ernie, God rest his soul, who worked as Frank Warren's matchmaker for years, used to say the same thing every time he got any fighter an opponent. 'Hey, Ernie,' I would say, 'have you got me an opponent yet?'

'Yes,' would come the reply, in his broad cockney accent, 'I have and this bloke you are taking on, he can't facking fight.' Every single opponent, it would be the same. 'This kid can't facking fight. He's facking rubbish. If you can't facking beat him, then hang up yer facking gloves. I could beat this fella. He can't facking fight for toffee.' You could have fought Floyd Mayweather, or Rocky Marciano, for that matter, and still the same Ernie down the phone line: 'This facker, he can't facking fight.' It's not straight out of a textbook, but essentially Ernie was saying the right thing. If you can't handle this opponent, don't blame me.

Ernie died recently and is still sorely missed by anyone who ever met him because he was such a decent bloke, but ask him for his assessment of a fighter and he would always give you the same opinion. That and a liberal sprinkling of 'facking's.

So Danny and Ernie and I went to New York and trained in the famous Blue Velvet gym while waiting for our fights. Now, Danny is the nicest kid in the world, but in terms of personality we are about as far apart as Hilda Ogden and Elle Macpherson. We trained every day and it used to get on my nerves that Danny could go and get a McDonald's afterwards, whereas I would be eating budgie food. Being a heavyweight he could eat whatever he wanted and was happily troughing anything that vaguely resembled food, while I was on fucking salads. If it was green, I ate it.

I get on so well with Danny. He is a lovely lad, but, like I said, you could not have two more different characters than the pair of us. You could say I believe in God, but I am not a religious person by any stretch of the imagination, whereas Danny takes his faith very seriously. He prays a lot and gets a lot of strength from that, which is absolutely fine by me. It is just that I don't have the same feelings.

After our fights, we were standing in Times Square and I was rubbing my hands in glee, saying, 'New York, Danny. The world is our oyster, let's go out and paint the town red.' Danny just looked at me with his lovely big smile and said, 'I'm not one to party, Ricky. I'll just go back to the hotel room and get some sleep. I am not one for nightlife. I just want to pray and get my head down.' I have to stress again that I haven't got the slightest problem with that, because life is all about horses for courses, but there I am in the biggest, brashest city in the world, thirsty for a drink and some action and I am on my own.

I was hanging around the Garden, wondering what the fuck I was going to do now, when Richie Wenton walked past me with a bunch of his Scouser mates. Wenton would later get beaten by Marco Antonio Barrera. At the time he was seeking a fight with Junior Jones or Naz, and Jones had been on the Garden bill against Kennedy McKinney.

Richie walked up to me and said in his Scouse accent, 'Alright, Ricky lad? This is Joey, this is Stuey, this is Peter,' etc, etc. He said, 'What are you doing here, lad, on your own?' I replied that I had no-one to go out with. Richie immediately took over and said, 'Right, we will walk you to your hotel, chuck your bags in and you can come drinking with us.' I was only 18 but I went on the piss with them until about 5 a.m., even though you have to be 21 to drink in America. We had a great time. Those Scousers I met were still getting tickets off me for my fights years later, which just goes to show what a terrific night we had.

Danny has a lot of confidence now and, after beating Mike Tyson and Matt Skelton, he should have. But before that night at the Garden he was a bag of nerves. I get nervous before a dust-up, but it's nothing compared to Danny. The nerves that he had in his early career have largely gone, but at that time he was all over the place. I went down to breakfast on the morning of our fights and I am sitting there eating anything I can get my hands on as I have already been weighed in. Danny, on the other hand, can't eat a thing. His insides are coming out. Next thing, he is saying he doesn't feel right. He said, 'I have got a bug. I feel sick.'

I always thought to myself, 'For someone with your ability, Danny, you have got nothing to worry about, because you are a class act.' But he was sitting there unable to eat a thing, which was great for me because whatever he left I quickly hoovered up.

In the fight, which he won, he looked like a million dollars and I thought, 'What have you been worrying about?' Afterwards, he said the same thing and we laughed about it. You meet a lot of nice people in boxing and Danny is right up there with the best of them. The nickname gentle giant could have been invented for him.

I was so chuffed when he beat Tyson in Louisville. The criticism doing the rounds in boxing was that he always left his best work in the gym. How he lost to Julius Francis earlier in his career I will never know. I don't think even Danny could explain it, because in terms of natural talent, with due respect to Julius, Danny is in a different class.

I won on points against Alvarez that night by the fairly comfortable unanimous margin of 40–36, 40–36, 39–37, in what was a really good, testing fight. We got to the weigh-in and I came in at 9 stone 13½lbs, whereas Alvarez weighed 10 stone 7½lbs. Because of the weight difference, the New York Athletic Commission official was not going to let the fight go ahead, so I had to go down and have a meal, while he went for a run. He put on a sweat suit and came in two pounds lighter and I weighed two pounds more and the official then decided it was OK. He was still four pounds heavier than me and was a natural welterweight. During our fight, I hit him with everything except the kitchen sink, but I could not knock him out. He was a hard kid and a typically tough New York circuit fighter. It was a terrific fight for me, because in the early days you don't want to be knocking people over inside a round all the time. What I needed was some proper work against a decent pro and I got that against Alvarez.

You don't want every fight going the distance because it adds extra miles to your clock, but by the same token you don't want to be walking through fighters. I learnt a lot against Alvarez in that I knew my power was good, but decent pros take some knocking over. Maybe if the fight had been more than four rounds I would have got to him in the end, but I improved by getting in some great ring work.

As for Madison Square Garden, where do I start? I have got literally thousands of fights on video and some of the greatest were from the same venue that I fought in as a spotty 18-year-old. Perhaps the biggest and most eagerly anticipated fight of all time, when Joe Frazier fought Muhammad Ali for the first time, was there. The name alone means so much to fighters. So many great boxers have never fought there, so for me to be there for what was only my second fight was an amazing experience and one I have Frank Warren to thank for. Even if I had not had another scrap from there on in, it was something I could always tell my son and my family about, that I boxed at the Garden.

I can point to the video footage and say, 'There is your dad at the Garden, being announced to the crowd, if that is what you could call it, by none other than MC Michael Buffer.' There wasn't much of a crowd, but that did not make a blind bit of difference. Having said that, I remember looking around before the bell and noticing that the British press were all in attendance, so they were obviously interested in me.

George Foreman was working for HBO that night and he shook my hand afterwards and said well done. Little did I know at the time that we would be meeting again soon.

* * *

Wins number three and four came over David Thompson at the Whitchurch Leisure Centre in Bristol and Paul Salmon at the Telford Ice Rink. Both came in the first round and both my opponents went down from a succession of blows to the ribs. Neither had particularly good defences, which meant I could get under their guards fairly easily, and after that it was all over pretty quickly. If your defence is suspect in the pro game it will be found out and I was never in any danger. Neither had great records, but by stopping them in a round I showed I had some power. I especially remember the Thompson win, as I put together a series of combinations only to finally catch him with a big body shot.

A month after beating Salmon, I boxed Karl Taylor in my fifth fight at Manchester's Nynex Arena, on the undercard of Naz against Wilfredo Vasquez. It was a night I'll never forget, as I met George Foreman again, only this time we had a proper chat.

I knocked out Taylor in the first round, which was no easy feat at the time. I had KO'd Thompson and Salmon, but had to settle for a TKO win over Taylor, as the ref came in to stop me. But, in all honesty, the official did a good job, as Karl was just about ready to go after I had nailed him with a beautiful left hand. Nobody had stopped Taylor like that before and, as I walked out of the ring, I had one of my proudest moments. George shook my hand and said, 'You carry on going the way you are, son, and you will be up there with Naz in a very short time.' I swear, I could hardly get my head out of the arena that night, I was so happy, grinning from ear to ear at everybody and everything.

The word was starting to spread. Nobody got carried away after that fight, because I think everyone knew I had a long way to go and a lot to learn, but all the people I chatted with out there in the fight game said pretty much the same thing at the time: 'You don't box like an Englishman. You box like a Mexican or a Central American.' I was on the bottom rung of the ladder, but people were saying that I fought like a Central American, like my hero Roberto Duran. A few comments were knocking around about the frilly shorts I wore in those days as well. I had the piss taken out of me something rotten as they talked about this albino Mancunian who goes around wearing a grass skirt and can fight like a dirty Mexican.

The shorts have been around since those days and, basically, they are there to represent the opposite of my character. I'll explain. I think I am a fairly ordinary bloke who is more beer and skittles than pink gins. The shorts, what with their tassels and bells – OK, not the bells – are there to express the other side of my personality, which is that I am a bit of a showman. I feel like a Jekyll-and-Hyde character sometimes, because I love the mundane things in life, but I also love being on a stage, which in my case is the ring, showing thousands of people what I can do. That's why I insist on the daft shorts. As for the predominantly light blue colour, I don't think I have to explain why I chose that.

After five wins in a row inside the first round I was on fire, but I knew my next opponent would be a different ball game, as I came up against Mark Ramsey, who had serious talent.

To be tackling the likes of Ramsey in only my sixth professional fight showed that I was being developed very carefully by Frank Warren and Billy Graham. Ramsey may have been a journeyman, but if there are three different types of journeyman, the ineffective, the decent and the dangerous, he was definitely the latter.

Ramsey could box. He had previously drawn with Junior Witter and Bobby Vanzie and had gone the distance with the dangerous Justin Juuko in the fight before ours. He might not have the ability to knock me over, but Ramsey had a very tough chin.

I stuck him on the canvas twice, but, in fairness to him, he got up both times. I know now that Mark is a tough bugger who can take a shot, because I caught him with everything I had and he still came back for more.

At the time I thought, 'How has he got up?' It was a great learning fight for me, because Ramsey was switch-hitting and taking a lot of my best shots. If I had not been on my game I could have been in a lot of trouble, but I won it on a six-round points decision and there was never any doubt about that result.

After Ramsey, I had another points win over six rounds against Anthony Campbell in Sheffield, before I went to Germany and blew away Pascal Montulet inside two rounds.

That trip became famous in the Hatton and Graham households and even to this day it gives me a chuckle.

It was my seventh fight as a pro and I was suddenly a bit flush. But I was also pretty good at spending it, so I didn't exactly have a lot of readies on me when I travelled to Germany with Billy and checked into a hotel in a place called Oberhausen, right in the middle of nowhere. To put it bluntly, we got there and neither of us had a pot to piss in. We always tried to make sure we got paid the minute I got out of the ring, as we never had any ready cash.

We got to the hotel three days before the fight and on the first night we went down to the lobby. Billy had a lager and I had a cup of coffee. Billy was just about to pay for his beer, when the hotel staff said, 'No, no. You are part of the boxing show.' They said we just had to sign for the drinks and then settle up when we left. We signed for them and they put a little piece of paper above the reception in a little box. Me and Billy thought to ourselves, 'This sounds alright. We don't need to get any money out.' For the rest of the week Billy carried on signing for his beer and I did the same for my coffee. All is well and good so far.

The fight came along, which I won easily enough, and we both went to the after-fight party at the hotel. Now, the Germans know how to throw an after-fight party and this one was a belter. At the party we spent a few quid and just kept signing these little pieces of paper. Oh dear. There was also the small matter of a nightclub situated inside the hotel, which again was bad news for us.

The one thing I do remember with some clarity was the fact that the Germans are the worst dancers you have ever seen. They are bloody awful. They dance like robots and Billy and I spent most of the night on the floor, laughing our nuts off.

They had a cocktail named after the former light heavyweight world champion Dariusz Michalczewski, as his father had something to do with the hotel. It was called 'The Tiger' and it had a bit of a kick. We kept asking everyone if they wanted 'The Tiger' or just a beer and I could feel that these birds were thinking, 'Blimey, these English blokes must have a few quid.' The little pieces of paper kept piling up behind the front desk.

Then it was up to the hotel room where we raided the mini bar and stuck the porno channel on. We carried on until the early hours and woke up the next morning feeling a bit rough. We went down for breakfast and I said to Billy, 'I think we should get hold of Frank Warren to sort us out with some cash to settle these bills we have been collecting.'

I went over to reception and asked for Frank. This was where the trouble really started. They said, 'Frank Warren has already checked out.' I then asked for Andy Ayling, Frank's No.2 at Sports Network. 'He has checked out as well,' they said. They had all left. I asked if they could put me through to anyone from Sports Network. The receptionist said that everybody from the boxing show had checked out apart from us. We were due to leave the next day, the Monday, 24 hours after everyone else, because our flights were heading back to Manchester, not London.

I tried to stay super cool and not panic or anything, but I realized we were in the deep shit. I said to the receptionist, 'We don't check out until the early hours of Monday morning, so can you just tell me what my bill stands at now.' He looked at the big pile of chit sheets we had been collecting and gave me a figure. We worked out that it was something like £300 for me alone. Billy's was worse. His was something like £360.

I said, 'Right, OK, no problem.' I went and sat down next

© PUNCH PROMOTIONS

© PUNCH PROMOTIONS

above: In the lido at the Lakeside café at Prestatyn aged four. Even then I had a taste for flashy shorts.

top right: Coming out of my corner at about 18 months in the front room at home. The yellow number is a shocker and what about the slippers.

right: On my first bike, note the stabilisers, with Matthew in tow.

© PUNCH PROMOTIONS

© PUNCH PROMOTIONS

above: At a national kick-boxing championship aged nine, complete with steely look in my eye.

below: Representing England at amateur level all over the world was a real thrill and a great learning experience for a young lad. Here I am on the medals podium in Sardinia.

right: Richard "Spider" Hatton, my great uncle, was famous for fighting in the Manchester area. He was my Grandad's brother and apparently had a fearsome wallop. As did my Grandmother Eileen Slattery's father, Daniel, reputedly one of the best bare knuckle boxers in Ireland.

© PUNCH PROMOTIONS

© PUNCH PROMOTIONS

© PAUL SPEAK

above: Hitting the punch bag at Billy Graham's gym, just a few months before turning pro. A certain Naseem Hamed is keeping a close eye on me.

left: The fighting Hatton brothers with Billy in between us. I am 20, Matthew is 18.

© PAUL SPEAK

© PAUL SPEAK

above: Padwork with Billy. He's never been one for fashion but his lucky white Levis are a disaster. Then again, I can't talk.

© PAUL SPEAK

above: Billy with pork pie hat. Only now are his skills as a high class boxing trainer being fully recognised.

© PAUL SPEAK

BILLY "The Preacher" GRAHAM'S
PHOENIX CAMP
in association with
BOBBY RIMMER

left: Whacking away at the body bag at Billy's "The Preacher" gym in Denton. Only a few minutes by car from my house in Gee Cross, Hyde.

© PAUL SPEAK

right: With two of my biggest boxing pals from Manchester, Anthony Farnell and Michael Gomez, now both retired. The night Gomez beat Alex Arthur in Edinburgh will forever remain in my memory, especially as I was working his corner.

© PAUL SPEAK

© PAUL SPEAK

above: Proud dad – with Ray picking up a couple of boxing writers' awards.

left: Looking pretty happy with myself and four of my belts. I am patriotic and the fact that I won them for Britain as well as myself makes me immensely proud.

© TOM CASINO SHOW TIME

left: Hugging my No.1 boxing hero, the great Roberto "Hands of Stone" Duran. By the look on my face, I still can't quite believe it's him.

below: At the oche with Phil "The Power" Taylor and John Gywnne. Phil has become a really close friend and we try to see each other in action as often as possible.

© PAUL SPEAK

© PAUL SPEAK

above: Amir Khan has the talent to go all the way. Only time will tell if he has the full package, but like everyone else, I hope so.

left: After the Vince Phillips fight, City boss Stuart Pearce came to pass on his congratulations. Great bloke and nothing like his "Psycho" image on the pitch.

right: Kevin Keegan did great things at City, until it all went a bit sour. But he was a terrific supporter of mine and a charismatic personality.

below: With the City team at their training ground. Note how I am towering over Shaun Wright-Phillips! City have always been very good to me and I will never forget their support over the years.

base of page: Another Manchester legend. Me and Bernard Manning sharing a cup of tea in our big pants at his place. Don't ask.

© PAUL SPEAK

© PAUL SPEAK

© PAUL SPEAK

© PAUL SPEAK

© PAUL SPEAK

© PAUL SPEAK

above: Eamonn Magee was an incredibly tough fight for me. I underestimated his talent and paid the price as he knocked me to the canvas, the only opponent to have done so in the paid ranks. Our faces tell the story of the fight, as Eamonn prepares to get stuck into a well-earned can of cider.

left: The bruises I suffered the night against Collazo needed about a fridge full of ice.

right: Ben Tackie had the hardest head I have ever known. Throughout our fight, even though he claimed not to speak English, he offered a steady stream of expletives.

to Bill again and I must have looked like a ghost. 'I didn't think we'd spent that much, Bill.' To which he replied, 'You what? You were buying every fucker in the room a drink last night. Not just the girls, but everyone.' I thought, 'What is the first thing you do in a crisis?' so I went over to the bar, got another two lagers in and signed for them as well! We were in shit street, that's for sure. I asked Bill how much he had on him and he told me £80.

I said I had got £50. He looked at me and I looked at him and at the same time we said, 'Fuck, we are knackered here, aren't we?'

We were there for a whole extra day and we had no cards on us, so we carried on doing the same thing, ordering drinks from the bar and signing the little sheets of paper. After about five pints we were both a bit tipsy and Bill said, 'Ricky, we are going to have to do a runner from here.'

We then started plotting. I didn't know what the hell we were going to do, as I had never done a runner before in my life, nor have I since. Billy's plan was to get an early alarm call in the morning, at about 4.30 a.m., and just walk out. I said we couldn't get an alarm call as the hotel staff would then know we were checking out. 'True, true,' Bill replied.

'I tell you what,' he then said. 'I'll get my missus to ring me on my mobile then I'll call you on your mobile and we will meet on the landing and sneak out.' I thought this was a good plan, so we were set on it. We then got chatting about what we were going to do all day in the middle of Germany and Bill said we might as well fill our bellies because we were going to do a runner anyway. This made sense, especially after five beers.

We went out on the town and spent what little money we had on us, leaving about £20 between us for the taxi fare to the airport. Unfortunately, when we got back to the hotel the nightclub was open again, so we went out on the piss once more. The bill at the end must have been about £500 apiece, because yet again we started buying everyone drinks.

We owed the hotel about £1,000 and we had £20 on us. After another terrific night, Bill phoned me at 4.30 a.m., slurring his words, and the plan was set in motion. We arranged to meet near the lifts. We got down to the ground-floor reception and I stuck my head around the corner. The German receptionist was standing there, at 4.30 a.m., staring straight at me. We looked like a couple of tramps, with Bill in his flat cap and shaggy bum-fluff on his face and me looking distinctly the worse for wear.

I said, 'Oh fuck, Bill, what are we going to do now?' I glanced at the receptionist again and the bloke was looking down into a set of drawers for a second so I shouted, 'Run, Bill, we have got to do it now.' We legged it out of the lift and bolted for the main door. Bill was still that pissed that he ran straight into one of those metal ashtrays you get in hotel lobbies. It went crashing to the floor and the noise was unbelievable. The receptionist twigged what was going on – it wouldn't have been hard with us two clowns. We kept running for the door, grabbed a waiting cab and shouted, 'Airport, mate, sharpish.'

He stepped on it, but it was a round exit road, so we had to drive past the hotel entrance again on the way out. Billy was going nuts in the back seat shouting, 'Take us to the fucking airport, not the front door again.' The taxi driver must have thought he had picked up two nutters and the receptionist was standing there in the entrance, none too pleased. We got out of there and made it to the airport. For months afterwards we kept on getting bills from the hotel, but I just put them in the bin and I think the German promoter eventually paid it.

I was getting good money when I first turned pro, so I've got no excuse. Bearing in mind I'd won three national championships as a schoolboy, two junior ABA titles and a bronze in the world juniors I think I was fairly hot property. For my first six fights as a pro I was on £3,000 each, which was not bad at all.

When I first left school and worked at my dad's carpet shop, I was earning £75 a week, so £3,000 was a fortune to me. This was before Dad started looking after my money, so I would put £3,000 into my bank account and think, 'Fucking hell, I'm the richest bloke in Manchester.'

I was a bit of a ten-bob millionaire, but, rest assured, by the time I next fought the £3,000 would be gone. All of it. I just spent it. I must have made £50,000 in my first two years as a pro, but I was still driving around in a clapped-out Mini Metro because I blew all my money. That little car was knackered and on its last legs. My mates used to have to bump-start it all the time because it just wouldn't get going, but instead of buying a decent car, I just blew my money away. My dad sat back and watched me do it to teach me a lesson, and when I was skint he finally laid down the law and took control of my finances. He still does to this day and thank God, otherwise I would not have a pot to piss in.

THE ANIMAL

So we had a right laugh on that trip to Germany and the laughs continued in October 1998 when I faced Kevin 'Dog Pound' Carter in Atlantic City on the Naseem Hamed–Wayne McCullough undercard. The main fight was memorable, as it was the first time anyone had gone the full 12-round championship distance with Naz, but my scrap against Carter was somewhat different.

Once again, when I got in the ring there was no bugger in there. I think they had just opened the doors and the only people in the arena were the old blokes sweeping up from the night before.

Robin Reid was in my corner along with Billy because we needed another second and the only people I could see in the crowd were Glenn McCrory and Ian Darke, who were doing the commentary for Sky Sports. The ring announcer got in for what was the first scrap of the night. It must have been his first day on the job, because he was on another planet.

He asked us both for our names then got hold of the mike and bellowed out, 'Atlantic City, are you ready?' Then he said it again: 'Atlantic City, are you ready?' I thought it was some sort of joke and he was some random bloke who had got in there, so I started off a Mexican wave in the ring, to let him know he was going way over the top. There couldn't have been more than five people watching our fight and this bloke was announcing it as if it was an Ali–Foreman rematch.

I managed to stop laughing before the bell went and with my first punch, a fairly nothing jab, I nearly knocked Kevin Carter out. I thought, 'Jesus, easy night here, Ricky.'

It was only my second time in America, so I thought I had better showcase my ability and keep this kid in the ring. I don't want to knock Carter or his 'Dog Pound' nickname, but I could have blown him over at any given moment. I didn't want to do that, so I started taking it easy, dropping my hands and having a look around. That sent Billy potty. All I could hear was Billy effing and blinding in our corner because he knew full well what I was up to – he can spot me showboating from a mile away.

In the end, Carter finished the fight quickly by hitting me with a couple of good shots. I thought to myself, 'Hang about,

I don't like this,' and Billy shouted, 'Stop fucking about, you little shit.' He was going ape and was almost getting in the ring. Anyway, I was thinking it was probably time to stop messing about, so I whacked him with a body shot. He got up. I hit him with another in the basket and that was that. Kevin Carter was back in the dog pound.

Billy and I had a good night in the famous Irish Pub, just off the boardwalk in Atlantic City, which anyone who has ever been there knows is the only pub to drink in, mainly because it is the only pub in Atlantic City. As far as the nightlife goes there, everywhere else is either boarded up or full of old grannies betting nickels and dimes.

The Irish Pub feels like the kind of pub you get in the non-touristy parts of Dublin. It is dark, a bit tatty and made for serious drinking. In other words, perfect for Bill and me to get stuck in. We had a cracking time, chatting with the bar staff and the fight fans who had come over for Hamed versus McCullough.

It was about 4.30 a.m. when we decided to go back to our hotel, Bally's, which was on the boardwalk. We found the boardwalk alright but were walking around for about an hour, pissed as newts, before we actually managed to find the hotel.

We decided to grab something to eat and went straight to the breakfast room. Hedgemon Lewis, who famously fought John H. Stracey many years ago, was there – he was doing some coaching in the area at the time. Billy and I sidled up to him, saying, 'It is Hedgemon Lewis. The Hedgemon Lewis.'

He must have thought we were from another planet. Two Mancunians who had just fought the night before and were having breakfast at about 6 a.m.

He was a great bloke. We said, 'Hello, Mr Lewis, can we sit down and join you for breakfast?' He may have been thinking who in fuck's name are these two jokers, but he was brilliant company and we talked boxing for hours before hitting our pits with the sun already high in the sky.

Just before Christmas 1998, I embarked on my next fight, against an altogether classier opponent, Paul Denton, Mark Ramsey's brother, at the Everton Park Sports Centre in Liverpool. Paul had started off in boxing as a real prospect, reeling off a stack of early wins, including a knock-out victory over Ross Hale, who was good enough to become a British champion. When we met, he was starting to lose more than he won, but almost always went down on points, as he had such a strong chin.

I will never forget my fight with Denton because I got cut in the first round and that was when all my cuts problems began.

The cut was stitched up after the fight, but fight after fight the same cut kept reopening. The right eye kept slicing open, often with only the merest whack. I eventually got it sorted after fighting Jon Thaxton for the British title many years later and the surgeon opened me up. He probed around inside the cut and was astonished to see there was loads of Vaseline inside there which had gone black and hard. Consequently, every time I got hit on it, it would reopen. It could have ended my career – plenty of fighters have had to jack it in because of bad cuts.

So I got a reputation for suffering from cuts and it is only in relatively recent times that things have changed for the better, even though against Carlos Maussa years later I looked like an extra from *The Texas Chainsaw Massacre* after the fight.

I thought it was strange at the time, because the bloke who dealt with me after the Denton fight did not put an injection into the cut, but used only TCP. At the time it was my first cut and I didn't know any better. I thought it was the norm to put TCP in it and get it stitched up. I winced because TCP hurts like hell.

When I got cut regularly during the next few fights, the doctor used a needle and I started to think that maybe TCP wasn't the answer. It was when Thaxton came along and the cut above my eye opened up after ten seconds that we decided we had to deal with it properly and it was only then that I found out about the wodges of Vaseline lodged in my face.

Denton caught me with a good few digs and, again, I learnt a lot from fighting a very good boxer. I got tagged a couple of times and leant into him the wrong way, so my cuts were rubbing against his shoulders. Now I wouldn't dream of doing anything like that, so it served as a useful part of my learning curve. I don't leave my head on anyone's shoulder if I have a cut, because one movement of my opponent's head and it can slice open a big tear. I went in there a bit careless when I got cut and it taught me a lot about being patient. I learnt you have to bide your time occasionally.

The bell went for the start of the sixth round and three seconds later he was on his arse. I came out and burgled him, as they say in the trade. I caught him with a cracking left hook, a little bit like the punch that finished off Maussa. I took a bit of a run-up to get to him and whack, and it landed like a peach on the end of his whiskers. He was a bit off-guard, but he bravely got up before Brendan Ingle threw in the towel. But Paul Denton was another very decent journeyman, a bloke who, unless you were in great shape and up for it, could cause a surprise.

I think Denton and Ramsey taught me that I might be heading for big things because nobody had knocked them over like I had before. They were two tough fighters and yet I had nailed them both and I think it was then that I started to believe I was capable of going a lot further because of the way I was beating them. They were not close points decisions, but genuinely good shots which they couldn't handle.

People started saying to me, 'If you are knocking over the likes of Karl Taylor, Ramsey and Denton then you have got something a bit special.'

Despite the cut I suffered against Denton, it was only two months later that I had my first title fight, a British Central Area light welterweight clash against Liverpool's Tommy Peacock at the Oldham Leisure Centre, just down the road from where I live today and where I was brought up.

I think this was the performance that made even more

people say that I was a real find, because he was unbeaten and I was unbeaten and yet I made short work of him. It was the first time I came out of the journeyman bracket.

I remember sparring with Peacock many years before that, when we were both amateurs. He was a full England international and I was a young England international. We went at it hammer and tongs at Crystal Palace and I never forgot it. He was being built up on Frank Warren's shows as a potential star in the making and was getting a few headlines. He was definitely a decent young talent.

I got him on the ropes and everyone knows that is where I love an opponent to be, so that I can slip to the side, go upwards, go down and around and basically throw everything in the book at him. I did exactly that with Peacock. I hit him with 13 unanswered body shots and threw combinations galore by going side to side and just whacking away. I know everybody was thinking, 'Fucking hell, what have we got here?' I got voted the Boxing Writers' Young Fighter of the Year after the Peacock scrap and I knew then that I could go a lot further.

It was that performance, a TKO stoppage after two rounds, more than any other, which raised a few eyebrows. Peacock was being touted for the top and he deserved it as he was a decent fighter. Even now, when I watch those combinations going in, I am impressed with my work. Usually I am always nit-picking, thinking that I could have done this or that even better. It was one of those nights where everything I tried came off. I have watched it countless times on video and I still don't get bored of it, because, as anyone who loves boxing will tell you, it looked absolutely blinding.

At the level I am now, I probably would not get as many unanswered shots in, but I can look back at it and think that I put those combinations together very nicely. After what I have achieved now, I sometimes wonder when I first started to really believe I could live with and beat the very best and it all stems from the night I boxed Tommy Peacock in Oldham.

There was only one downside to the night and it was truly tragic, as a lad fell under one of the coaches outside the venue and died after some sort of fight broke out. He was taken to hospital, but did not make it. It was terrible because it was just a small boxing show the kid had gone to. I don't know what went on outside because I wasn't there, but I won't ever forget what happened. It was a terrible shame, because the atmosphere that night was fantastic. My Manchester pals Anthony Farnell and Michael Gomez were also on the card that night, so the place was going bananas.

I can't remember a better small-hall atmosphere. At the time, all Tommy's supporters were in there wearing the Harry Enfield 'Calm Down, Calm Down' Scouse perms and false moustaches. It made for a great occasion and the boxing that night was brilliant, but I will remember it for the death of one unfortunate boy who was in the wrong place at the wrong time. As for my performance, it was, up until then, the best of my career.

I nearly ended up not fighting at all that night, because at the time Billy Graham and Frank Warren were having a bit of a disagreement. It was more than that, actually, it was a verbal war, because Billy was sponsored by Naseem Hamed's Prince Promotions. Naz had left Frank Warren to set up his own promotional company and Billy turned up at the show with a T-shirt on displaying the words 'Prince Promotions'.

Anyway, 15 minutes before I was due in the ring, a message came through to the dressing room that Billy could not go into the auditorium wearing the T-shirt, especially as the fight was being televised on Sky Sports. Billy stood his ground and basically said, 'Fuck off, I will wear whatever I want.' My head was in bits. Andy Ayling from Sports Network came in the dressing room and he and Billy started rowing. I was getting a bit cheesed off with this, as I was the one supposed to be doing the fighting. Ensley Bingham sat down with me and said, 'Calm down, Hitman, it will all get sorted.' In the end, the fight went ahead as planned and I did the business, but Billy had to put a tape over his T-shirt to hide the Prince Promotions logo.

Naz was forking out some decent money, but I got caught in the crossfire 15 minutes before the fight. I was told the fight was off, then it was going to go ahead but not on Sky. Eventually it all got sorted, but it left a nasty taste in my mouth. There was a lot of anger inside me before getting into the ring and I think that came out in the fight, as I went in there like a man possessed and tore into Peacock.

Incidentally it was after my sixth fight against Denton that I sat down with Sky and we decided I needed a nickname. Up until then I had been known as Richard Hatton, which my mum and dad call me to this day. Friends of mine have always called me either Richard or Ricky, so I said to Sky I could also use Ricky.

They were of the opinion that Richard Hatton didn't really have much of a ring to it. I like the name, but it is not exactly fearsome is it? More like a fucking librarian's!

Sky and I decided we could revert to Ricky and so it just stuck. We also talked about a nickname and I always loved Hitman. I don't remember who first suggested it, but it just sounded so right and still does to this day. With my surname it fits perfectly and I am very proud of it. It was one of the names I discussed with Sky, along with a few others, but it was always going to win the day because I felt it sounded the best. One of the reasons was also my respect towards Thomas Hearns, one of the all-time greats in boxing and the original Hitman.

A few years later I was lucky enough to meet Thomas when I fought in Detroit. I was introduced to him and I asked him before the fight if he minded me using his nickname. He said he had no objections at all. I still remember Tommy saying if I was an average fighter, he would mind, but because I was special he would consider it an honour. What about that! Coming from Hearns that was really something.

Over the years I have met Tommy a few times and he has always joked with me to look after his nickname. I think I have done my best to do so. It is a cracking name and I am very proud of it. In fact, some of my pals even call me Hitman, as opposed to Ricky or Richard, which is not the worst thing in the world I have ever been called!

* * *

By this time, I had appeared at some diverse venues: from New York's Madison Square Garden and the Convention Centre in Atlantic City to Oldham Leisure Centre and Widnes's Kingsway Leisure Centre, but my 12th professional fight was to be London, my debut in the capital.

I was up against another of manager Nobby Nobbs's fighters, Birmingham's Brian Coleman, at the Royal Albert Hall. Again, Brian wasn't the best, but he was a very good journeyman who got dumped onto his pants only very rarely. His record wasn't much, but he was difficult to stop at the time I boxed him – he had gone the distance twice with Junior Witter and neither Jason Rowland nor Jon Thaxton, both high-class fighters, could stop him.

We were walking through London after having had a big breakfast on the morning of the fight. I always gorge myself at the nearest greasy spoon immediately before a fight, followed by a long walk to try and get rid of the food sitting in my stomach. At the time the South Park song 'Chocolate Salty Balls' was all the rage, so me, Billy and a few of the other fighters, including Ensley Bingham, walked into HMV and asked them to put the song on.

I was singing away, thinking what a great song this was. And, there and then, I decided this was going to be my ring entrance number. I bought the CD and told Bingo of my plans. Bingo, who thinks I am nuts anyway, was doubled up with laughter and said I had finally lost what was left of my marbles.

He thought I was pulling his leg and didn't believe for one second that I would use the song for my ring entrance in such plush surroundings as the Royal Albert Hall. 'How much will you bet me, Bingo?' I asked. We had a tenner bet and so, in those magnificent surroundings, the patrons were treated to the sounds of 'Chocolate Salty Balls'. As I was walking to the ring I could see everyone in the crowd pissing themselves laughing.

When it got down to the fight, I knocked Coleman out with a couple of body shots, one of which nearly cut him in half. It was the undercard of the Danny Williams–Julius Francis fight and, again, I knew I was causing a few shock-waves by consistently knocking over blokes who, while not top-class, knew how to handle themselves in the ring and were difficult to stop.

My next opponent, in the summer of 1999 in Halifax, was Dillon Carew. It was for my first 'world' title, the vacant WBO Inter-Continental light-welterweight title. I knew absolutely nothing about Carew, not even his ring record, other than the fact that he was from Guyana. A week before the fight, I discovered he was a southpaw and had boxed in the Barcelona Olympics. I saw him at the weigh-in, but there were no tapes of him, so it was the blind leading the blind that night in Halifax. I should have been a bit more worried about Carew than I was, because he had just achieved a draw against

DeMarcus Corley, the former WBO light-welterweight world champion.

The changing rooms at the venue, the North Bridge Leisure Centre in Halifax, were squash courts, so immediately we hatched a plan. One of Billy's friends, 'Boxing' Andy, who used to drive Billy to shows back then, said he would go on a scouting mission. I said to Boxing Andy, 'I have not seen this opponent fight, so can you try to get into his dressing room and see what he is like when he is shadow-boxing?'

Andy tried everything to sneak his way into Carew's training room, but the doormen blocked his path, so I said, 'Look, these are squash courts, right? Which means they have all got viewing balconies. Go up to the balcony above Carew and have a look-see. Go up the stairs and have a sneaky look over the balcony.' Boxing Andy runs off and hunches down, walking up the stairs until he gets to the balcony, and sticks his head over the top. Carew's people immediately spot him and go bonkers. Poor Boxing Andy runs back down the stairs and, breathless, insists he isn't doing any more capers. It was an early attempt at spying on the opposition camp and it failed miserably, but it just showed how innocent we were back in those days.

I needn't have worried, because in the fight I blew Carew away in five. He was decent, but I kept hitting him with those trademark body shots and eventually they caught up with him. It was my 13th straight pro victory, despite my lack of knowledge about Carew.

Next up was Mark Ramsey again, this time at the

Doncaster Dome. It was a strange night, because before the fight there had been some suggestion that I would be fighting a Mexican, but as we had no tapes of him in action, Billy and I turned it down flat.

Anyway, I was now facing Ramsey, so all my preparation went into dealing with him. On the night of the show I was walking around the Dome and all I could see was Nobby sitting there at the back of the hall with Paul Denton. I am watching them both and still there is no sign of Ramsey. Eventually, I sidled up to Nobby and said, 'Who the fuck am I fighting tonight?'

Nobby, in his thick Brummie tones, said he didn't know. All he knew was that Ramsey had called him on his red phone to say he was injured (Denton would always call him on his blue phone, as, being brothers, they both had exactly the same accents and that was the only way Nobby could tell them apart). On this night, Nobby seemed as confused as everybody else. Anybody who knows Nobby will tell you he is a great character and a real lifeblood of the sport because of the way he will always supply last-minute fighters for desperate promoters, but trying to pin him down about which one of his fighters I was facing was impossible.

On my way to the ring, I was still none the wiser, but, eventually, from out of nowhere, Ramsey appeared. I smacked away at him for six rounds, but Ramsey was so versatile and he did not budge. I could not stop him. I had him in plenty of trouble and there was never any doubt when Mickey Vann raised my arm, but, once again, it showed what a decent fighter Ramsey was at the time. Mickey gave me the fight 60-56, which was about right, as Ramsey had shown all his ring craft to the full.

* * *

I knew it was going to be a tough night when I did battle with Bernard Paul, a multi-talented banger who had a fearsome right hand and was a former Commonwealth champion. Bernard, whose ring nickname was 'The Punching Postman' due to the fact that he used to work as a postie, was known for being able to hit, but his stamina was a touch suspect. A few years before he faced me, he had knocked out a then unbeaten Jason Rowland in the first round, which underlined his fearsome punching ability.

Sure enough, that night at the sold-out Bowler's Arena in Manchester, Bernard came at me like a crazed lunatic and kept trying to unload his big right hand, which everyone knew could knock over a speeding train.

I used my skills to keep out of his firing line and by the end of the third, I could see Bernard was beginning to struggle and I was starting to gain the upper hand. The fourth round was carnage, as I threw the kitchen sink at him. Bernard was in real trouble and at last I thought it was my turn to dish out a bit of pain.

At the end of the fourth I had him in desperate straits. So much so that Bernard pulled out. His corner stopped the fight and in the dressing room Bernard came up to me and said he had damaged his hand. I was annoyed, because I had weathered the storm and my tactics had worked perfectly, only for Bernard to pull out when I was on top. I had taken it, but just as I was preparing to give some clobber back, Bernard had thrown in the towel. Afterwards he said to me that I would be a world champion if I showed the same amount of heart throughout my career as I did against him.

I accept that fighters do hurt their hands during the course of a bout. I certainly have, especially when I fought Ben Tackie. But it is very rare that I have spoken to a fighter and been told they had to pull out because of their hands. When you are in there, you can hardly feel a thing anyway, because the adrenalin is pumping so much.

It is really only after a fight that they start to swell up and hurt. We spend all day and all night hitting bags and sparring, so it makes sense that the chances of getting a really bad hand injury and feeling it during a fight are pretty low.

Joe Calzaghe suffers from painful hands, but then he has won all his fights, and to his credit, has never pulled out during a fight.

I was back at the Everton Park Sports Centre in Liverpool again just before Christmas 1999, this time against Northern Ireland's Mark Winters, who had been the distance with James Hare and drawn a ferocious scrap before I got in the ring with him. In his other previous fights, he had also gone the distance with Junior Witter and Jason Rowland, but it was business as usual when he faced me and didn't last long. I KO'd him in the fourth at the packed sports centre, which again underlined my status as a rising star in the division.

Winters was a competent fighter and I felt I was learning a lot as I took my time before cutting him in half with a body shot.

Needless to say, the Millennium New Year was the same as pretty much every other New Year I have ever enjoyed, although with a fight coming up at the end of January, I tried to keep the celebrations as low-key as possible.

Throughout 2000, I was kept busy, fighting six times in that year. Frank Warren did a cracking job by giving me some experience against decent foreign opposition, all of whom I beat quickly enough. The names won't necessarily mean anything to you, but I learnt some valuable lessons about different styles in getting past Leoncio Garces, Pedro Alonso Teran and Ambioris Figuero in double-quick time.

The Garces fight will forever stay in my memory, as I appeared on the undercard of Mike Tyson's British debut, when he stopped Julius Francis in front of 22,000 fans at Manchester's MEN Arena.

I didn't get much chance to speak to Mike, but to this day it gives me goose pimples to think that I fought on a Mike Tyson card. I was just another young upstart, but I gave the massive crowd a big lift when I stopped Mexican Garces, who had a decent record, in the third round of a one-sided contest. The thrill of fighting in front of such vast numbers was incredible. It showed that I wasn't fazed by big crowds when I went to work against Garces and finished him off in style with a thunderous body shot. Garces barely laid a glove on me and was not in my class as a fighter, but it was still a terrific stoppage which had the crowd on its feet.

I watched as Tyson ripped into Julius, who never stood a chance. Tyson was on fire that night and Julius was a brave man just for getting into the ring with him, however it came as no surprise when he was stopped inside two rounds. When big attractions like this came along you could see how much the British public still loved their boxing. Obviously I didn't know it then, but five and a half years later I would be packing out the MEN Arena with my own fans for my battle with Tszyu.

After beating Teran and Figuero, both in four rounds, at Liverpool and Warrington respectively, my unbeaten run almost came crashing around my ears when I travelled to Detroit, home of the original 'Hitman', Thomas Hearns, who achieved so much in the sport. If I can achieve half of Thomas's amazing successes in the ring, I will die a happy man.

It was a great honour to fight in his home town, but I came to Detroit in totally the wrong frame of mind.

I have never been ashamed of my past, and I am not going to start now, but there was a period, when I was between 18 and 22, when I had a few relationships. I wasn't disrespectful to women, but it is fair to say I liked to try a few out! One of the relationships I had at that time was with Claire, a local girl who I went out with for a while. We enjoyed ourselves, but eventually split. There was no animosity and we went our separate ways still very much friends.

Anyway, about three weeks before the fight in Detroit, Claire rang me up and said she had to see me. It was then that she told me she was expecting. It felt like my world had collapsed around me, as I was still very young and so was Claire, but there were no real arguments about it. It was just something we both had to accept and be responsible about.

I told Claire I was going to Detroit to fight. While I was out there, I was forever moping around. I had things on my mind and my dad knew it. He kept asking me if everything was alright and what was wrong. He knew, as any good father would, that something was up. But I kept saying I was OK. I didn't want to tell him, or Mum, before my fight. I just wanted to bottle it up. Don't ask me why, because I cannot really explain it. I think I just wanted to get the job done in Detroit and get back home.

In the end, everything turned out OK. I have a beautiful boy now and obviously a lot of what I do is focussed on him, as it should be. He is the most important person in my life and I want him to have a great start. Even though his parents are not together we both have one priority in common and that is Campbell's welfare and happiness. He doesn't go to some posh private school, because I want him to have the same upbringing as me.

I suppose having a child has made me think more about the financial side of the sport I am in, but I certainly haven't become obsessed with money overnight. I regard it as a by-product, albeit an important one, of my career. In a sense, boxers have to try and cash in when they can, because, with very few exceptions, they are past their best by the time they are in their mid 30s. Then they are yesterday's goods.

I am aware that if I look after my finances properly Campbell won't ever have to work, but it won't be like that. He will have to earn his bread, like everybody else, and when he grows up he will be under no illusions that his dad will just solve any problems for him by throwing money at them. That won't happen.

Campbell won't be handed things on a plate because, let's face it, is there anything worse than a spoilt kid? We all know the sort. He won't be like that at all, I am sure of it. I want him to make his own way in life and make his own mistakes, just like I did. On numerous occasions, so my mum would tell you.

He won't live his life relying on Daddy's money all the time, but I am not going to turn into Scrooge either. My parents worked their socks off when Matthew and I were kids and we always had foreign holidays every summer, unlike a lot of the nippers where we lived. We knew we were fortunate and we knew how hard our parents worked. Mum and Dad are not exactly stuck-up; in fact, they are the absolute opposite. Matthew and I never clapped our hands and got whatever we wanted. We were a very close family and we all got on well with each other. There were the usual rows, of course, but nothing too major. I think I was brought up correctly and I know that is the way Claire and I will bring up Campbell.

Claire and I deal with everything that comes along to do with Campbell as well as we can. We were only an item for a short time, but we have a good relationship, which I think is very important when you have a kid. You don't want to be bickering all the time, because kids pick up on that. We both fuss over him like mad, but that is only because we both love him so much. Claire's family and my family found it difficult at first but they accepted the situation and I think their feelings on the subject are the same as mine. As long as Campbell is treated well then everything is fine. We all agree that we've been blessed with a wonderful little boy.

In the early stages, when Claire was pregnant, her mum felt we should try to make a go of it. Maybe she felt her daughter had been rejected or something like that, but, to be honest, it was never really going to happen. Claire and I both knew that and since Campbell was born we have got on with our separate lives as smoothly as we possibly can.

My relationship with Claire is so good that I can see him as often as I want, and I would like this opportunity to say that Campbell could not have a better mum and he is a credit to her.

Campbell and Claire live ten minutes down the road and she is always popping in or dropping Campbell off. She has now got a boyfriend who is a great lad and we get on fine. Both of them come over to pick up Campbell when he stays with me and we are all agreed that Campbell is the most important thing in our lives.

If I am in training, then he won't stay over, but other times he comes over a couple of nights a week and I see him as much as I possibly can. My mum and dad also have him on a regular basis and I can pop in to see him whenever I want as they are only a few seconds away from where I live in Gee Cross.

I feel like the luckiest man in the world when I am around Campbell, as he is a lovely little kid. He is very even-tempered and is well behaved and polite when he meets people. He finds most things hilariously funny and, unlike Kostya Tszyu, he loves a good tickling contest!

My mum and dad, after the initial shock, have been incredible with Campbell, as they always have been with me and my brother. They are always there to help and nothing is too much bother for them. Mum does my special dietary needs when I am in training, all of it set up by Kerry Kayes, my conditioning coach. As my parents are so close by, I always go round there for my lunch and dinner when I am in training.

Mum and Dad are the reasons why I am who I am and I have them to thank for my success as a fighter as well. They have driven me to countless shows, only getting back home in the middle of the night. I am not big-headed at all, which I get from them. Mind you, as Mum always says, I might still go off the rails when I grow up!

I feel both Matthew and I were very lucky nippers. We had our moments when we were kids, but the fights, be they verbal or handbag stuff, were usually over and done with pretty quickly and we soon got back to being friends. Campbell will be brought up the same way we were. I want him to be polite and not plummy. I don't want him looking down on people and I am sure he won't.

I had a very happy childhood and I want Campbell to have

what I had, although when we were living in the pub in Marple when I was eight years old I do remember coming down the stairs one day with my suitcase packed, ready to do a runner. I suppose I was a bit like Jack Dee when he put his flat cap on in the Big Brother house. I told Mum and Dad I was leaving home and said my goodbyes. They said, 'OK, son, be good. Let us know when you've settled in where you're living.' I asked Matthew if I could borrow his bike and he said, 'Yeah, take it.' I think I lasted barely half an hour! That was the only time I ever remember running away and to be fair, I wasn't exactly successful at it.

We had some fantastic times in the pubs we lived in and by the time I was about 15 years old I was already nicking the odd pint here and there. My granny and grandad used to come down regularly and on Fridays and Saturdays we would always have a singer on. Sometimes they were good and sometimes bloody awful, but great fun all the same and after a few pints no-one seemed to care.

One Saturday, when I was about 15, Dad closed up at about midnight and got rid of the last of the stragglers at about 12.20 a.m. I was in the kitchen with a friend and saw a couple of lads outside, hanging around Mum's car. They looked a bit shifty. Next thing I know, I am watching them as they are trying to nick it.

Dad and I went outside to sort these kids and get rid of them. I took with me a little leather cosh which we kept behind the bar and Mum whispered to us to be careful. Dad and I confronted these lads and he shouted, 'What the bloody hell do you two think you are doing?' They took off and we went chasing after these two thieves, me going one side of the houses and my dad the other. Neither me nor my dad were the fastest people in the world. I chased one lad into a garden and the security lights came on, so the place was lit up like Wembley Stadium. Imagine my surprise when I caught up with him and saw he was on crutches. He was trying to nick my mum's car on crutches. My dad then came around the corner and bellowed, 'Oi, you lot! What the fucking hell are you doing?' This bloke on crutches said, 'Please don't hit me. I'm a cripple. I was just trying to nick the radio.'

We asked where he was from and he said the multi-storey flats nearby. At that point the police came so I tossed the cosh into a bush. The coppers knew my dad by name and said, 'What's up here, Ray?' He told them that we had spotted this lad and his mate trying to break into my mum's car. The cops asked how much damage they had caused and Dad said it was about £200, as the car door was knackered.

Dad said to the thief, 'I want £200 off you tomorrow morning.' Sure enough, the bloke brought the £200 around the next day and I went to school feeling like King Kong as I had just tackled my first thief.

The New Inn wasn't a particularly rough pub and there was only the occasional scrap. Usually it was over as soon as it started and always it was over a few beers. My dad wouldn't have any regular troublemakers in there. If you wanted to fight, you wouldn't do it in the New Inn.

If I got in trouble I got smacked on the arse, but I wasn't

a difficult kid to bring up. I just had too much energy and as soon as I started boxing it was all channelled in that direction.

Dad was more the quiet type, although when he had a go you would know about it. Usually if there was a fight in the pub, Mum would be the first to go over there and sort it out. She called anybody small a 'little shrimp' and belted a few around the head, knowing full well they wouldn't dream of answering back. They were both well respected in the area and ran a decent pub, so the police got on with them very well and knew there would be no funny business going on in the New Inn.

It all changed when I turned 16, as they got rid of the pub and Dad started in the carpet trade. He bought two shops, in Gorton and Hyde, and all his energies went into that. Running a boozer can be very long hours and I think they just decided they needed a change. My Uncle Ged and Uncle Paul had been in the carpet business for years and I think they had always tried to persuade my dad to go into it as well. As Dad and Uncle Paul were very close, it was only a matter of time before they got their way.

Dad was a very good footballer and was on Manchester City's books for years. He has still got an athletic physique and, even now, you can tell how quick he must have been just by looking at him. He was just starting to get going at City, playing for the reserves, when he got a bad achilles tendon injury which basically finished him off in the pro game. Whether or not it would end a player's career now I don't know, but it was certainly enough to end his dream of making it as a professional footballer.

Everyone I have spoken to said Dad could really play and he was just unlucky. I suppose it is where I get the strength in my legs from. After coming out of Manchester City he went on to play for years for the likes of Stalybridge Celtic, Glossop and New Mills. And he finally played for his pub team at the age of 41. He worked for a while in Chapel-en-le-Frith making brake linings as well as running a market stall selling china. Strangely enough, he was never a boxer. I think he might have laced a glove a few times when he was a kid, but he never took it any further than that.

Mum has got a short fuse when she is in the wrong mood, whereas my dad is much more laid-back. Like with most father and son relationships, we have our ups and downs. He can be bloody annoying and we have had some belting rows over the years. We do argue quite a bit, but it is almost always knockabout, bickering stuff. He calls me Flat Nose and I tell him he knows bugger all about boxing. Then we smile about it.

Dad is not a big one for smoking or drinking at all. In fact, he gets pissed about once a year and has never smoked, whereas Mum likes the odd fag with a drink, although she is not a big smoker. When we were kids, Matthew and I used to creep into the house after a night out and he would be sitting there, watching television and keeping an eye on things. He would just watch as we fell into the house, pissed as newts. I would go straight up to bed, but Matthew would go up to Dad and say, 'Go on then, say something.' That is just the sort of thing Mum would do and Matthew is very similar to her. He is far more confrontational, whereas Dad and I would rather settle for the quiet life. Mind you, when my dad did say to Matt, 'Just get up the stairs,' he would do as he was told and didn't need telling twice.

So you can see how great my parents are and how much respect I have for them, but still, before that fight in Detroit, I didn't yet feel able to tell them about Claire's positive pregnancy test.

I went into the fight like a zombie and the Costa Rican Gilbert Quiros, whose boxing nickname was 'The Animal', took full advantage. He was a pretty big lad, about 5 ft 11 ins, and he knew how to box. Before facing me, he had only lost twice, although much of his record was compiled in Costa Rica, so the standard he was facing could have been pretty poor.

In the first round, he beat the shit out of me and I was in bits. I knew I was going to lose and I could not handle it. Then I got cut. It was a bad one and I knew it was curtains for me. The only thing I had on my mind was Claire and the fact that she was pregnant with my child. That and the fact that I had not told anyone. I am sure everyone there who knew me could sense something was going wrong as I was getting beaten up in that first round.

At the end of three minutes, the ref came over to our corner and looked at the cut. The eye was almost entirely shut, so I was boxing with only 50 per cent vision. He said he would give me only one more round, because it was too bad to continue. I was nearly in tears and felt like I was on the verge of a nervous breakdown. All I had ever dreamed of was going up in smoke, in some city thousands of miles away from home, against some bloke I had never seen before who was enjoying beating the crap out of me.

It was at that point that Billy stepped in. My definition of a good trainer might differ from other people's, but this is what I believe. The best trainers know what to say and when to say it. When a fighter is on top, it is easy peasy lemon fucking squeezy, but it is when you are down there in the trenches that a trainer really earns his money.

Billy just happened to say the first thing that came into his head and it was exactly the right one. He could see I was nearly crying and he could see I was about to lose the fight, so he countered by saying, 'It's a terrible shame, Ricky. I thought you were different. I thought you were going to be a world champion, but here you are snivelling like a little baby at the first sign of trouble. You've blown it. You've swallowed it. You've gone down in my estimation. Champions don't do that, so I was wrong, wasn't I?'

It did the trick. I saw the red mist and went bananas after Quiros in the second round. I hit him like a rabid dog. He must have wondered what the fucking hell was going on here. In the first round he had me all but beat, then in the second I wasted him. It started with a left hook, then the body shots were raining in from all angles and one of them went straight into his guts and almost came out the other side. He was doubled up and that was that. It was the first time I had been pushed to the limit, but instead of bottling it I had come out the other side. It showed that you can be the greatest fighter in the world, but sometimes you need someone to help you out and, in my case, that was Billy. He knows how fiercely competitive I am and he knows the last thing I ever want to do is lose in the ring.

Basically I was building up an excuse for myself, albeit a pretty decent one. And that is what fighters and sportsmen do. We have all heard it. When a football team loses, the manager comes out and says the ref did this and that and lost us the game. In boxing, it is no different. A fighter will lose then say he felt unwell leading up to the bout. He had the flu. He was worried about his fucking pet budgie. It is usually, although not always, absolute bollocks. Fighters often get beat because something is preying on their mind, maybe in their personal life, and they use it as an excuse. That is what I was doing. Of course, it might have been easier if I had told my parents or Billy, because what is it they always say about a problem shared? But I left it inside me with the result that I nearly lost to a fighter who I knew I could beat.

Billy came up to me in the ring afterwards and said, 'No offence, Ricky,' with a big smile. I was still feeling a bit sorry for myself, with one eye shut and a secret I had to get off my chest. It was the only fight as a pro I thought I was going to lose. I couldn't see any way out until I was woken up by Billy's words and my inner rage took over.

I would not change anything about my life and that

includes the relationship I had with Claire, because it led to our beautiful boy, Campbell, who is the most loved kid in the world. I am so proud of him, I have a tattoo of a pair of boxing gloves with his name written next to them, alongside mine. In fact, he gets the best of both worlds as my family are all over him like a rash and so are Claire's.

But at the time, there I was in Detroit, thousands of miles from home, and I was miserable. I had to tell Dad. I burst into tears in the changing room and just said, 'Dad, there is something you need to know.' At first he called me a silly fucker and said it was about time I learnt a lesson, but he is a good bloke and a great father and, like all good dads, he knew he had to do and say the right thing. He said, 'We will work it out. It is not the end of the world and we should be happy there is another little Hatton coming into the world.'

We got back to Manchester and had some meetings with Claire's family, who are all very decent and caring people. There were some rows about this and that, but essentially we worked things out between us.

* * *

Next up, for fight number 21 at Bethnal Green's York Hall, was Giuseppe Lauri, who had a terrific 19–1 record when I met him in September 2000. The fight was not only for the WBO Inter-Continental light-welterweight title, but also the WBA International light-welterweight title. Although it was a terrific night for me, yet again there was some violence outside the ring, none of it caused by my supporters, who know how to handle themselves but have never started a fight in their lives.

The brawls outside were due to the fact that Spurs had played Manchester City earlier in the day at White Hart Lane. My supporters, many of them City fans, went to the game before coming to see the fight and a fair few Spurs supporters came along too. After the fight and a few ales, it started cracking off and by the time I got outside it was mayhem, with scraps all over the place. It was like a fucking war zone on the streets, so I decided that the best course of action was to go to the pub. There is a terrific little boozer right next to York Hall on the main road, so I ran in there and ordered myself my usual post-fight Guinness or three.

That decision may surprise some people, but I have never had the slightest interest in fighting in the street with some-one I have never met and am never likely to meet again. Almost all of it is beer talk anyway, so why bother? I was just settling down to my pint when the landlord came over and said he was closing the doors and shutting the curtains. I asked him what it had been like during the day and he said he could spot my fans a mile off, what with their *Coronation Street* accents.

He insisted my supporters had been drinking in there all day and had been both polite and as good as gold. That was fine with me, as I would hate to attract the wrong kind of follower. He said we could all carry on drinking and that we were welcome in his pub any time. There was still a bit of friction going on outside, but none of us cared. We were in the warmth of a nice boozer, supping away.

As for the fight, I had finished Lauri off in spectacular style. It was my York Hall debut and anyone who loves boxing loves the famous hall in the heart of London's East End. It is not exactly the most prestigious of venues, with its faded wood panels, but it is the heartbeat of boxing in this country and when you get a ringside seat for York Hall, you are literally by the side of the ring, as it is so small and compact. When you watch boxing there, you can see what the fighters have had for dinner, you are so close to the action.

Italy's Lauri was a real contender at the time and, as well as bringing an outstanding record to the fight, he was being talked about as a potential spanner in the works for my plans.

He was certainly hungry and brave and, even though I kept banging away at him with my body shots, he just would not go down. He would have made a good poker player, because although I caught him with some terrific blows to the ribs he didn't flinch at all. He made no sound, whereas usually fighters react with a sharp intake of breath.

I was beginning to think his ribcage was made of metal when finally I got through in the fifth. One body shot too many landed and this time Lauri went 'Urgh' and dropped to his knees. I know when a fighter has had enough and Lauri was spent.

As well as keeping my WBO Inter-Continental title, I had now added the WBA International light-welterweight belt to my collection and was becoming a name in the division, with some analysts suggesting I was now in the top 20 or so in the world.

I stayed in the pub for a few hours with my mates, before making my way to the coach and a load of beers on the way back to Manchester, getting in at God knows what time in the morning.

I think it is fair to say at this stage that Frank Warren had handled my career superbly, as I had just the right degree of opponent. I'd started with a few straightforward fights, but before long I was in with the likes of Ramsey and Denton, no mean boxers themselves. I had shown that I had something extra.

I always feared the worst as a fighter – I suppose being a Manchester City fan I had every right to be a pessimist! – and that built up in me a burning desire to prove people wrong. I knew what people were saying, that I was the latest boxer from Sports Network to be served up a succession of easy wins in order to boost my record, but I think if you look at who I fought in those early days you will agree that I didn't have it like that, and for that thanks must go to Frank Warren.

What I mean by fearing the worst is this: while I always expected to win, I always hated the thought of losing. I never had any problems with confidence, but throughout my career, at the back of my mind, there has always been the horrible thought that one day I will lose, and that I cannot stand. Even now, after having won over 40 fights, I get the same feelings. I suppose it is the fear of losing which is one of the things that drives me on to this day.

Everything was rosy in the Ricky Hatton garden after beating Lauri so convincingly and my record and reputation were improving. A month after the Lauri fight, in November 2000, I was handed the one I really wanted, a crack at the vacant British light-welterweight title and, boy, was I chuffed to bits to get a shot so early in my career, just three years after turning pro.

Frank Warren did a fabulous job in getting me Jono Thaxton for the British title. It was brilliant for my development. The timing was right, as I was hungry and wanted it badly. I was the right age and Jono knew he was in for a tough time. Mind you, so did I, as Thaxton can dig. Some people have described the punch that knocked out Paul 'Scrap Iron' Ryan a few years ago as the best single shot they have ever seen and I would certainly rank it very highly. Ryan made the mistake of hanging his chin out to dry and Jono basically took it off its hinges. It was a cracking punch and so I knew I was going in there with someone more than decent.

I had been suffering from cuts ever since the Denton fight and it didn't take long for Jono to find that weakness – about ten seconds, in fact.

The first dig he had at me and the opening sliced. Claret was pouring down my face and I was furious. I knew it was a bad one and in the end I had to have 28 stitches in it. I was getting a bit of blood in my eyes, but it was nothing too serious and I certainly wasn't hurt in any way.

Jono got excited about seeing me cut, as you would do, and went after me hell for leather. I would have been a superb name on his CV and I knew that, so instead of going out all guns blazing I turned on the boxing skills.

I have been dismissed as a brawler by some experts and I can brawl with the best of them, but I also have technical skills and in that fight I needed them. I used those skills to choose my shots and keep Thaxton at bay and I think I won the fight by a distance. The referee gave it to me by four points, but I have watched tapes of the scrap and I believe it should have been wider than that. However, I have the ref, Paul Thomas, to thank for keeping me in there.

Paul showed his experience and ring knowledge to full effect, because a lesser ref might have called the fight off due to my cuts, especially as the main one happened so early in the fight. But Paul had a good look and let us carry on, for which I am forever grateful. I think he did the right thing because it would have been criminal to have stopped such an important fight at such an early stage. Jono Thaxton would not want to win a title like that and I know I wouldn't either. If you boxed the ears off your opponent for eight rounds, got a bad cut and had to be pulled out, you wouldn't feel you had lost. Equally, if I won a belt I had been losing in the ring because of a cut I wouldn't be celebrating. No chance. You win fair and square and you lose the same way.

In fairness to Jono, I never heard him moan once about the result. Paul Thomas gave my cuts man, Mick Williamson, by some distance the best in the business, time to work on the tear and by the middle rounds it had all but healed up. That was probably because I had lost so much blood there wasn't anything left to come out, but well done to Mick, who has saved my bacon a few times in the ring.

Thomas is an example of a good referee and we are blessed in this country to have some of the very best in the world. Paul is a high-class official, as are the likes of Mickey Vann, Dave Parris, Ian John-Lewis and, in the not too recent past, John Coyle. All of them exceptional refs who know the fight game inside out and who pride themselves on the job they do.

Thaxton has made a decent comeback as a lightweight and I can see why. He has lots of upper-body strength, can punch and is a fitness fanatic. He is one of the good guys in boxing and I could not have won the British title against a more deserving opponent. I think he has gone on record saying he is not blessed with a great deal of natural talent, but he can dig and he has always shown amazing dedication to himself and to the sport.

I caught him with some terrific shots, but Jono is a tough man to knock down and he took some heavy stuff from me, especially in the later rounds when it looked as though he was about to cave in. Even in the latter rounds, he still had some power in his hands. For me, that fight was part of my learning curve as it was the first time I had gone beyond six rounds. I proved to the public that I could keep up my work rate for championship-length fights. I never had any doubts because, for years, I had done it and more in training, but it was great to get a 12-rounder under my belt.

After our dust-up, Jono and I were in the dressing room getting our cuts seen to. It was like the Hammer House of

Horror in there, as blood was covering just about every surface. Dominic Ingle was with Jono and they both thanked me for a great fight. I returned the thanks, but then Jono asked when are we going to do it again. The only reply I could think of was, 'Fuck off, no chance!' I had seen enough of Thaxton and wanted to move on, as I believed I had beaten him fair and square, despite such a big early setback, and the referee's scorecard, which had me winning by four rounds, said as much.

* * *

Talent is a strange thing. Natural ability can only be fully developed by good old-fashioned hard graft and those who have been blessed should work even harder than those who haven't. If you are lucky enough to have been given special gifts, then it is a crime to toss it all away. There are thousands of kids in all sports – whether it be boxing, cricket, football or whatever – who work hard and get very good but have never had an ounce of natural talent. It is the ones who have been given that opportunity who must try all the harder to seize the moment, because they have been so fortunate. I was lucky, simple as that, to be given boxing skills and natural strength, but I have worked at it until I have dropped.

My home may be a shrine to Manchester City, but it also has two Manchester United players on the walls. I have signed photos of both and I wouldn't want any other players from Old Trafford on my wall. George Best is there because he was a genius who worked exceptionally hard at his game before he suffered from alcohol problems later in his life. He used to get into training before anybody else and work at it non-stop until he became the complete package. The other is Wayne Rooney. Now, I've only spoken to Wayne a couple of times, but I know genius when I see it and he has been touched by it.

Earlier in his career, I thought he would self-destruct, just as our last soccer genius, Paul Gascoigne, did a generation ago. But he has really matured on the pitch and I suspect that might be down to his Old Trafford manager. Rooney has so much talent it is frightening, but if he starts bad-mouthing refs and getting himself sent off for daft challenges he has got only himself to blame. Recently, I have been impressed with the way he gets clobbered, gets up and gets on with it. In one match he got fouled, picked the ball up and immediately stuck it in the top corner – the perfect response. I don't know how hard he works on his game, but I would guess he is a football addict, because you don't get that level of ability from not practising.

When I was a nipper, I played football with players who could run rings around me and I thought, 'These lads cannot fail to make it.' Unfortunately, we know what happens to a lot of boys when they turn 16. They find they can walk into the pub and get served and they also find out what the bit between their legs is for. Don't get me wrong, I loved it when I could order a pint and I loved it even more when I found out what the thing hanging down there does, but I was always so in love with boxing. Boxing was the be-all and end-all for me and so whenever I was in training for a fight I would live like a monk. Then, of course, in the few days or the week I had off, it would be time for the pub and the girls, just like any other normal kid.

I hope City fans don't mind me admitting my love for Best and Rooney, but I think I am first and foremost a Mancunian. When my team plays United there is only one side I want to be victorious, but that doesn't mean I can't appreciate talent in others and if you can't appreciate Best and Rooney, then God help you.

THE TERMINATOR

I was expecting to take on Londoner Jason Rowland next for the vacant WBU light-welterweight world title. After vacating the title, he had asked me for first shot at it. He's a great bloke and I was happy to oblige, but unfortunately he had to pull out after one of his Rottweilers bit his hand.

Instead, I faced the formidable skills of Tony Pep for the title in March 2001 and everything I knew about my opponent suggested it was a step up in class.

Pep, a Canadian, was a former Commonwealth champion who had been in there with some big names, so it was always going to be a tough one. I expected it to be my hardest fight yet. This was a bloke who had previously gone the distance with Floyd Mayweather and was an experienced pro, having stepped into the paid ranks in 1982.

Tony wore his nickname, 'Kid Fire', on his shorts, but the only fire in that fight was from me. I stopped him in four one-sided rounds, but only after I had suffered another bad cut, this time in the nick of my left eye, following a stiff jab. The problems I had suffered previously had been mainly with my right eye, the one with the wodge of Vaseline in it, but this time it was the left and during the fight I remember thinking, 'Here we go again.'

However, it didn't stop me pouring forward and, in fact, made me all the more determined to get the job done quickly. Pep is a tall lad, well over 6 ft, which made him a perfect target for my body shots and I let one go which knifed him in half. It took a couple of seconds for the left-handed body shot to register, but, once it did, you could see the pain on his face. He went down on one knee and took a standing eight-count and just before the end of the third he was in bits as I tore at him. He did remarkably well to survive the round and, seconds before the bell, I caught him with a right hand to the body which would have finished the fight had there been time.

I thought the break might give him time to recover, so I bolted out of the stalls and went bananas again. This time Pep had had enough and he went down on one knee after another combination of body shots with my left hand. I heard Tony saying, 'No, no,' so I knew the fight was over even before the ref called it off.

Billy grabbed hold of me and we both lost our balance, so Sky television viewers and the thousands there in person were treated to the sight of the two of us, me half-naked and Billy wearing his favourite pork pie hat, rolling around on the canvas. I dusted myself down and felt on top of the world.

Afterwards, Tony said he fully expected me to slow down in the third, but was amazed when, if anything, I upped my work rate. He had no doubts about my ability and said so to the cameras. In the dressing room he told me to keep knuckling down because I had the talent to become the best in the division. He asked how I managed to keep up such a frantic pace and I told him that before every fight I do 15 rounds with Billy in the gym. By the end of it I feel fucked, but no-one could ever question my stamina.

Tony was telling anybody who would listen that I was a future big name in the sport. I asked him if he was serious and he replied, 'Deadly. Like those nasty punches you keep throwing to the body.'

It was great to hear from someone of his calibre. As well as going the distance with Mayweather, he had also won a version of the world lightweight title by beating Louie Espinoza. I wouldn't have said he was at his peak when I met him, but he was a fighter still to be respected and when he said I had it in me to dominate the division, I took notice.

As events transpired, I would make 15 defences of the WBU belt I won that night at London's Wembley Arena and I will always contend that a title is what you make of it. In my case, the WBU belt was a stepping stone to what I would achieve later in my career by beating the best 10-stone fighter in the world. At this stage, I was still ranked outside the world's top ten, but I was getting closer with every fight. Pep wasn't a nobody in the sport, so I was raising a few eyebrows. When I won the WBU belt, DeMarcus Corley was the WBO champion, while Tszyu held all three of the main titles, underlining his supremacy in the division.

The WBU title has been slagged off by all and sundry, but I look on it this way: it was only a few years ago that the WBO belt was regarded as a joke and now look at it. Joe Calzaghe has been the best super-middleweight in the world for years and up until recently he only had the WBO crown. I considered myself a world champion when I won the WBU title and I still do now. Fair enough, some of my earlier opponents when I was defending the title weren't world class, but towards the end they certainly were. Fighters like Vince Phillips, Mike Stewart and Ray Oliveira had been in with the best and in Phillips's case had beaten the best, namely Kostya Tszyu.

I'll accept that some of my earlier defences weren't in that league, but when I won the WBU belt I was satisfied that I could tell my son I was a world champion. Now I have gone on to prove I am a unified world champion.

One of my few regrets in boxing is that I didn't earn a Lonsdale belt, which is given to fighters who defend their British title three times. I have cheated in that I have now bought one, but it would have been great to have won it legitimately. Lonsdale belts are a real something in boxing and I missed out on one by not defending my title, but money talks more than anything else in the fight game and turning to the WBU title meant I was able to make fights which were to my financial advantage. While the British title was a great honour, it didn't pay the bills, whereas the WBU title did.

I know fans get pissed off with the stack of belts now on offer and they have every right to be, because sometimes they get the shitty end of the stick. It is true that in the past boxing supporters have been cheated and no doubt this will still go on in the future. I think the amount of belts on offer is great for the fighters, because it helps them make more money, but, of course, it is not so great for the fans of the sport who hark back to the days when there were only eight weight divisions and one world champion in each. In those days every sporting-daft schoolkid could name the eight champions, whereas now they have got no chance.

It would be better for the sport to have only one world champion, but these days I take my lead from *The Ring* magazine, the undisputed bible of boxing. They have had me at No.1 in the light-welterweight division since I beat the man who beat the man, as they say. That is surely right. There should be a rule brought in which makes fighters unify the titles, but will it ever happen? I doubt it. I know the TV companies in America have become very big on unification battles and fights between the best, regardless of belts, and that can only be good for the sport. I know in my career there is no way I would just sit back, stay in Manchester and defend my titles against lower-risk fighters. I want to test myself to the full in what is such a short career.

The silly thing about boxing is the fact that I could be ranked in the top three with the WBO, IBF and WBA, but not even in the top 15 with the WBC. Any boxer could be in the same position. That is ridiculous, so I would tell any boxing fan who wants to know who the best is to buy *The Ring* or Britain's *Boxing News*, which is also well respected, because, although they are not perfect, they are the best guides out there and are pretty much impartial. When I won *The Ring*'s Fighter of the Year in 2005 it was the second biggest honour in my career, only coming second to beating Tszyu by a short head.

I grew up watching Nigel Benn, Naseem Hamed, Chris Eubank and Barry McGuigan. All of them great fighters, but none won *The Ring*'s top title, which makes me incredibly proud. One of my favourite framed pictures on my wall at home is *The Ring* front cover with me on it, proclaimed as the best fighter in the world for that year. To this day, I nearly cry when I look at it. My mates think the whole thing is ridiculous. Their pal from Manchester, the best boxer on the planet.

Unfortunately, with the way boxing is, I can't see anything changing in the near future and now there are more world titles out there than ever before. It doesn't make them any less worthy than the big ones, but, generally speaking, the best in the world hold one of the four main titles.

* * *

Pep was a class act, both in and out of the ring, but I knew I then had to defend my newly won title against Jason

Rowland, who was trained by Jimmy Tibbs, one of our very finest boxing coaches and had only been beaten once before he met me. There was no contract between us – I was adamant that this should be my next fight. In some ways it felt more like a world title fight than Pep, because Jason had vacated the belt. At the time, although I was building up a big reputation, there were still people saying I hadn't met anyone as clever and ring-savvy as Jason.

Our clash was set for July 2001 at Manchester's Velodrome, a fantastic arena. On the night there were about 6,000 fans packed into it. I was headlining the card, with my fellow Manchester boxers Jamie Moore, Michael Gomez and Anthony Farnell also appearing.

It was a cracking atmosphere that night, but from the start things didn't exactly go according to plan and the omens were not good for me.

When I got to the venue I asked one of the security guards how Jamie had got on, only to be told he had been knocked out in the fifth round by Scott Dixon. He then told me that Farnell had been stopped in the first round by Takaloo. Not exactly what I wanted to hear – the Mancunians were going down like nine-pins.

Next up was Michael Gomez, and guess what? In his rematch against Laszlo Bognar he got dropped twice inside the first two minutes. I was beginning to think this night was jinxed, but then Mikey made a stunning comeback. When he won his fight it made me feel a lot better and all thoughts of luck being against me went out of the window.

I had known Rowland for years and respected him as a decent and very tidy fighter. He had been a pro since 1989 and in all the tapes I watched of him he looked a high-class, well-organized boxer with good defensive skills. He was a favourite with many of the boxing fans since he had stopped Jono Thaxton in five rounds on a cut, a sad way for any fighter to lose a contest.

He came into the arena in his trademark West Ham United claret and blue shorts. I caught him with a cracking left hook in the opening exchanges, but during the early stages Jason countered by hurting me with a couple of body shots. He has a textbook style and I was having a few problems with it. I think maybe I was a bit nervous that night, because I wasn't performing as well as I could, but then Jason delivered a stinging body shot and that did the trick for me. For some reason it woke me up and, although I sensed Jason knew he had hurt me, the fact that I felt under pressure had the desired effect.

No boxer has ever gone in the ring and not got some stick and I am no different, but, in this instance, the fact that I felt Jason was getting the upper hand made me react in the right way. I decided not to take a backward step and so I went after him. Because of the success he had had, Jason was adventurous. He changed his tactics and this led to his downfall as I saw a gap and went for it with a big left hook. Two more left hooks and I had him all over the place in the fourth round. I put him down with a belting punch which caused him to stagger back before hitting the canvas and about half a dozen black trilby hats were thrown into the ring.

Some of my followers had started wearing these 'gangster' hats in reference to my 'Hitman' nickname, and when I knocked Jason over a few of them landed inside the ropes. The referee Mickey Vann had to kick them out of the ring while trying to officiate the fight. Shortly afterwards, I feinted and caught Jason with a nasty left-handed body shot. I knew Rowland was not going to get up again. I could tell by the look on his face that all the fight had gone out of him. It was all over as Jimmy Tibbs threw a towel into the ring. He had seen enough and told me so afterwards.

I was chuffed to bits, as Jason had stopped Jono Thaxton, albeit on a cut. It meant yet another name on my record had been stopped and I felt Frank Warren was guiding my career perfectly, putting just the right amount of pressure on me.

Two months later, I moved to what was to become my second home, Manchester's MEN Arena, for my next test, against American John Bailey, fought under unforgettable circumstances. Coming only four days after the 11 September atrocities in New York, it was touch and go whether the fight would take place at all.

There was a lot of talk about cancelling the show, but in the end it was felt, rightly so in my opinion, that we had to try and carry on. What happened in New York appalled anyone with even the slightest bit of humanity in them, but I was all for carrying on. It sounds a bit corny, but if the world had stopped, then the people responsible for 9-11 would have won, wouldn't they? Politics has never exactly been my strong point, but I know the difference between right and wrong.

Why anyone would want to commit a terrorist outrage like that mystifies me. I mean, what has that got to do with any religion? I have always been told that religion is all about tolerance and understanding and loving your neighbour. Not killing thousands of innocent people.

Anyway, the decision was made to go ahead with the show, which, after nine weeks' training, I was all for. If they had cancelled it, fair enough, but I believed we were doing the right thing. I spoke to Bailey and Frank Warren and we all agreed we should use the show to try and help in whatever way we could. England and America would unite and we would show two fingers to the people who were prepared to murder so many.

We held a minute's silence and both Bailey and I held the American flag. It was very emotional, but both of us knew we had jobs to do so it was back to business when the bell went.

I have been told people thought Bailey was out of his depth, but I will let others decide on that. All I know is it was over pretty quickly and was never in doubt. I think boxing fans have to accept that fighters cannot have one test after another in a short space of time. Just as our footballers get hard games and easy ones, so it is true for boxers. You have to get the balance right and I have always tried my best to give value for money. I know boxing tickets aren't cheap, so I will guarantee to anyone paying to see me that I will never leave them short-changed. The nearest I have come was in beating Carlos Vilches many years later, when I took the fight at short notice. I was pretty crap that night, but I still gave it my all. It was just that there was less all to give than on previous occasions. I don't think a war followed by another war is necessarily good for any fighter.

The Bailey fight was over with very quickly after I floored him four times. I felt I could not miss him. He wore the nickname 'Macho Midget' on his shorts, but he left Manchester a thoroughly beaten fighter. In fairness to him, I thought he showed a lot of toughness before eventually going down for the last time, as I hit him with some massive shots, mainly to the body. I had watched Bailey on tape and noticed he didn't have much of a defence when it came to keeping out blows to his midriff. Suffice to say, that was good enough for me and so from the first bell I targeted that area.

The fact that Bailey went the distance with Mike Stewart, a future opponent of mine and a top-class boxer, shortly after fighting me underlined his decent chin, but towards the end of our clash he was all over the place.

The referee, Mickey Vann, called it off in the fifth and, as far as is possible in boxing, it was a straightforward win, as I don't think Bailey hit me with a meaningful shot. I now looked forward to my next challenge, from one Freddie Pendleton.

He was a big name, but had seen better days. In the past he had traded blows with some of the legends of the ring like Felix Trinidad, Frankie Randall and even Pernell Whitaker, and when I watched some videos of him when I was preparing for the fight there will be no prizes for guessing my reaction: 'Fucking hell, what have we got here.' Pendleton had held his own against some of the best fighters of the last two decades, so it was a case of 'Watch out, Ricky, this bloke is big league'. It was the first time I had ever been introduced properly to the American public as the fight was broadcast on ShoBox, part of Showtime, so I felt I had to put in a decent performance. It was all over inside two rounds.

About 10,000 people came to the MEN Arena that night and they saw me flatten Pendleton. Tony Pep was an experienced fighter, but Pendleton was in a different league and had been around even longer, turning pro in 1981.

The following I had started to generate was beginning to rival that of any other boxer in the world – thousands were flocking to my fights. That might have something to do with the fact that I always put on a show. Can't guarantee what will happen, but it will always be entertaining.

Pendleton creased up when I banged him downstairs. I was surprised how quickly I dealt with a former world lightweight champion, but the best part of it was the way the packed stands celebrated my victory.

Freddie had on a pair of flashy bright-red shorts with the word 'Fearless' emblazoned on them, but there was nothing very fearless about the way he folded as I whacked away at his body. He was a tall light-welter, just like Pep, and was therefore made for me. He was coming off a good first-round win over Horatio Garcia when we fought, but a left to the body followed by a solid right had him in real trouble early on. Another right to the body doubled him up and I went for the kill. I tried a looping right hand which missed his whiskers by a fraction, then, right at the bell, at the end of the first round, I caught him with another devastating body shot, again with the right.

Pendleton was saved by the bell, but it didn't take long to finish him off. Freddie's big weapon was his overhead right, which I was careful to avoid. He threw it a couple of times at the start of the second round in a desperate attempt to get a foothold in the fight, but two lefts to the body had him backing up again. The second blow had a delayed effect, but, eventually, after a few seconds, Pendleton went down and lay on the canvas and rolled over and over. There was no way he was getting up and Mickey Vann called the fight over. Another KO win. Pendleton never fought again and afterwards you could see in his eyes he was thinking about giving the game up. After nearly 80 pro fights I was the sort of opponent he needed like a hole in the head.

The same fans turned up again in amazing numbers only a few months later, just before Christmas 2001, although this time the action was back at Wembley Conference Centre, where I had won the British title.

Even at this early stage in my career, my ultimate goal was to fight Kostya Tszyu, but I had to be content with another Australian, Justin Rowsell. He came over with a big reputation and a very strong record, having lost just once in 34 fights. In his corner that night was the legendary Jeff Fenech, one of the giants of boxing who has now become a very handy coach. He backed his boy, even though I felt Rowsell was 18 months past his prime. He had been stopped by Lovemore N'Dou, a world-class fighter, three years before taking me on, which I felt was significant. And so it was to prove, as another quick-fire, two-round stoppage victory came my way. Basically, I knocked Rowsell clean out of the ring. At the weigh-in, when boxers are always literally weighing each other up, I looked at Rowsell and liked what I saw.

As a fighter, you look for weaknesses in the opposition. All boxers do it. Sometimes, of course, it is absolute bollocks. You will say to yourself, 'This bloke has got a gammy left jab which means I will win easily,' and it will turn out not to be the case. Boxers can try to believe what they want to believe and I am no different. Except this time I was spot on, as I felt Rowsell looked so fragile he would shatter the minute I went near him. Showtime were again relaying the fight back to America, so once more I felt a burning need to put on a decent performance. I needn't have worried, as I jumped all over him in the first round and knocked him down. It took very little of the second round to finish the job and Mickey Vann came to his rescue. Just as Pendleton never fought again, neither did Rowsell. I think in his heart of hearts he felt he was good, but just not quite good enough at the top level and getting whacked by me made up his mind for him.

Afterwards, Fenech admitted he had been surprised by how superior I was, which, coming from Jeff, was praise indeed and another major boost to my confidence. He took me to one side in the dressing rooms and said I had something very special. He also warned me not to waste it and a warning from him is taken on board.

In interviews with the American channels they kept referring to my Mexican style and I was beginning to think I should change my name to Ricardos!

I knew I needed to keep the momentum going and I did just that by facing my first widely recognized top-ten-ranked fighter when I took on Mikhail Krivolapov in the last days of summer 2002. And, boy, by the end of the fight I knew I had gone up a few notches as this bugger must have had the hardest head ever.

Krivolapov was ranked No.4 with the WBC, so I knew anything in the stoppage category would be a terrific night's work. He had recently lost a split decision to Oktay Urkal and had taken Kostya Tszyu the distance, so you didn't need to be a boxing genius to work out he was as tough as they come.

Apart from the two-round battle I had with Gilbert Quiros in Detroit, which was my own fault, Krivolapov was just about the first fighter to cause me real problems. Not in the sense that I was looking at losing, but over an extended nine gruelling rounds he just knew what he was doing a lot more than any other fighter I had faced. He soaked up punishment from me, then came back for more. Every time. I think Billy was beginning to think he was a bit superhuman and he wasn't the only one. I didn't leave him alone for nine rounds, but still he came back for more. At around the eighth round he started hobbling and I started worrying. This gnarled old Russian just would not go down.

I could see why others had struggled against him and, with just two losses to his name going in against me, I understood what a step up in class this was. He wasn't looking to survive, even though I was way ahead on points, but kept giving something back whenever I thought I had him nailed. Until the ninth, that is, when all of a sudden I got through. At last he couldn't take any more and Mickey Vann called it all off after one devastating combination, topped with a left to the head, which had Krivolapov dangling on wobbly legs. I think Mickey moved in more as an act of mercy than anything else, but it was the right time to stop the fight as he was a beaten man.

I had achieved one of my goals with the Krivolapov win, by breaking into the world's top ten. Krivolapov taught me so many lessons I don't really know where to begin. For a start, he was the first fighter to turn me when I was whacking away on the ropes. Up until then, any opponent I had managed to get on the ropes was in big trouble, as I would use my body shots from all angles to inflict some serious damage. Not with Krivolapov. He just turned me the other way and started banging at me himself. It was a completely new scenario for me and one which I had really not faced before. But boxing, like anything I suppose, is a learning curve and I was taking all the lessons in. He also had a cracking defence which smelt out trouble. It meant I often sized him up, ready to finish him off with my body shots, only to find he wasn't there any longer. In the end, he just took too much punishment, but after the fight I was very much aware that my future opponents would not be falling at my feet at the first sign of my power. They were good too, so it was another level that I was heading into and Krivolapov was the first to really teach me that.

By the end, I think I was more grateful than he was when Mickey stopped the action, but at least I had managed a TKO over him, better even than the great Tszyu.

* * *

If I learnt a few lessons in the Krivolapov fight, I learnt plenty more in my next outing – a battle which led to my first, and so far only, trip to the canvas.

In fact, the punch that Eamonn Magee delivered to send me to the seat of my pants wasn't painful and it wasn't particularly hard. It was more of a shock than anything. I know boxers always say the same thing when they are decked, so I will balance it out by saying that the blow I took in the second round from Magee went all the way down to my socks. Yes, that did hurt and a lot more than the knockdown.

When you get dumped, it is often more through shock than anything else and that was certainly the case with me. Basically, I got duped. I got angry and I paid the price for being amateurish.

Magee had spent the build-up to the fight in press conferences saying I was rubbish, over-hyped and too young to deal with someone like him. I felt it got a bit too personal, because he was just calling me all the names under the sun. If the plan was to get under my skin, it worked, because when I went into the ring all I wanted to do was knock seven shades of shit out of Magee.

That is a bad mistake if you are a professional boxer, as I learned that night in front of a full house at the MEN Arena.

All the trash-talking had got to me and, to make matters worse, I had watched tapes of Eamonn's fights and was none too impressed. I thought he was just very average and I couldn't believe he was talking to me as though I was the beginner. If anything, he looked slow and ponderous in some of his previous fights and I felt I could not lose when I went into the ring. I thought, wrongly as it turned out, that I could have picked a few old boys in my street and had a harder fight.

Eamonn revelled in his nickname, 'The Terminator', which I thought was hilariously over-hyped. Alright, he had stopped Thaxton just before facing me and had beaten a fading Shea Neary, but he had lost years before to Paul Burke for the Commonwealth title, so I was super-confident.

Magee had lost before and yet he kept going on about being stabbed in the street and lots of other macho stuff, so facing me would be a cakewalk. All the bravado left me angry, but I am glad to say that I know Eamonn a lot better now and can safely tell you that he is a different person from the one I experienced in the build-up to our scrap.

Boxers should never go on performances anyway. Sure, Eamonn had had some duff displays, but I have as well, against Carlos Vilches, and it hasn't done me any harm.

When you start comparing yourself you are in potential trouble, because one fight is never the same as the next. Some boxers would have terrible trouble against a certain type of opponent, but none against someone ranked considerably higher. The cream does rise to the top, as it does in other sports. If Chelsea lost to Stalybridge Celtic, you would be a bit surprised, but boxing is strange because styles often make fights. It is an old cliché, but it is true. Just look at the recent heavyweight clashes involving my pal Danny Williams. The match-up against Audley Harrison looked great on paper, but stank the place out and was, by some margin, one of the worst fights I have ever seen. Then, a few months later, his clash with Matt Skelton was a classic. There you go. It takes two to tango in boxing, because if you have good feet and a decent technique, you can spend all night running and even the best fighter in the world will have difficulty tracking you down.

Anyway, I went in with Magee with little or no regard for his ability and was also steaming inside. The result? I got knocked over.

A fighter who underestimates his opponent is heading for big trouble. As a rule I never do that. I think you have to have balls of steel to get in the ring in the first place. People tell me that this fighter or that fighter is rubbish and I laugh. How can they be rubbish if they have laced up a glove and are prepared to come out of their corner fighting? Have you ever put on a pair of boxing gloves? Ernie Fossey rubbished fighters all the time, but he was mainly doing it for effect and he also knew the game inside out.

I am not ashamed to say that I learnt a few valuable lessons that night against Magee. I came out in front of a huge crowd and to my right was the biggest Irish flag I think I have ever seen. Magee had brought a few thousand fans over, which just added to the excitement at ringside.

I looked at him and thought, 'Fucking Irish eejit, you're

gonna get some.' Then it all started to go badly wrong. I sprinted over to Eamonn in the opening few seconds and the next moment I was picking myself up off my arse. Because I was in a rage, I wasn't concentrating at all and threw a humongous left hook, with deadly intentions. Just as I was bolting it out of my shoulder, a short right landed on my whiskers and I fell down, more off-balance than anything else. The immediate feeling was one of embarrassment, because I knew I wasn't hurt. Whether the crowd knew that I don't know, but I do know that they went berserk.

I should have tried to calm down, steady myself and start boxing properly. Instead, what did I do? I decided to meet fire with fire, so in the second round I came out like a maniac again, throwing shots all over the place. The vast majority were missing by a mile and Eamonn was giving me a bit of a lesson as I piled into him. That was when I made my next big mistake.

Magee caught me near the ropes as I was going nuts yet again. This time it was flush on the chin with a brilliant left hook and this time it registered. I was in serious trouble and I knew it. Fortunately, we had got tangled up and my body had gone through the ropes, which meant referee Mickey Vann had to stop the action while I got back into the ring.

The break allowed me to start to use my brains rather than my bollocks and this time I responded by sticking to him like glue.

These moments happen in every fighter's career. There are times when you are hurt and you have to hang on in there, sometimes literally. Don't think for one minute that any fighter who has ever stepped into the ring has not had the same happen to him. You can include all the greats in that. It is how you respond that makes the difference between a good boxer and a truly legendary one.

The best know how to survive. How many times was Muhammad Ali in trouble in his career? Just look at a tape of him getting beaten to a pulp by George Foreman in Zaire. Or Joe Frazier when they fought to the brink in the Philippines. Or when he took a pasting from Ken Norton but still came through. But Ali invariably found a way to turn those fights around.

At the time I wasn't exactly thinking about Ali, but I was making up my mind that now was not the right time to be a hero. Now was the time to knuckle down and work for my money and title. The important thing in this situation is not to back off – that is the worst thing you can do. By putting some space between you and your opponent you allow them the chance to get some leverage behind their shots. Basically, they can then throw knockout punches, as opposed to dangerous ones. This I was determined not to do, so I wrapped myself around Eamonn and clung on for dear life.

Billy spotted as much at the end of the second and told me in no uncertain terms to stop fucking about and start showing how I could box. He also kept insisting that Magee was no good and would soon buckle if I started boxing properly. I knew I was three points down after two rounds, but I also knew that if I could clear my head there was still plenty of time to go.

From the third round onwards I changed my game plan. I wasn't going to dive in there like a dumb amateur any longer, but was going to pick him off. I started to move and to use my jab, and guess what? I won it. Not by battling it out with Eamonn Magee, but by out-boxing him. As a southpaw, Magee had caused me problems, so I turned the tables and started switch hitting, just to mess him up.

I felt the rounds were becoming wider as the fight wore on. I believe I showed that night that I could think on my feet and change my tactics, always a hallmark of a really high-class fighter, in my opinion. By the end, although I never had Magee in any real trouble as he took some great shots from me, I didn't have any doubts about the outcome and the judges backed me up in that, giving me the fight. Two of them had me winning by five rounds and a third by three, which shows that after the initial rounds I must have considerably impressed them. I have watched the fight on tape many times and I wouldn't argue with the judges. I thought I won comfortably and I was a little surprised Eamonn didn't try to come out with all guns blazing in the latter rounds, because he must have known he was losing. Frank Warren said as much after the fight and I agreed with him, but then maybe by boxing the way I did I had ruined Magee's plan and he didn't have much left to respond with.

Whatever the case, I know Eamonn a lot better now, having met him often on the boxing circuit, and I like him a lot. We are similar in that I think we are essentially both very honest people, but we are also very different people in other ways. Obviously Eamonn's career almost ended when he was involved in some sort of gangland battle which left him with terrible injuries. I don't know anything about that and don't really want to know. All I can say is that Eamonn has been in my dressing room a few times before fights, including the night I fought Tszyu, and he has always said he is rooting for me, which is great to hear. At the end of our dust-up we hugged in the ring and did so many times in the changing rooms. He said that all that stuff before the fight was just rubbish to try to get to me. 'It worked,' I told him.

Eamonn would make a terrific poker player, because I ripped some big shots into his body and he never flinched a muscle. The punches seemed to just bounce off him. At the time, I thought they had to be hurting, because, with the power I was throwing, they would have hurt me, but they seemed to have no effect on Eamonn. Right at the end, he caught me with a big right hand as if to outline the fact that, although I had won the fight, he was still standing.

Eamonn got roundly booed by the crowd when his corner lifted him onto their shoulders after the final bell, which I thought was a bit daft as there was never really any doubt about the result.

In the dressing room, we sat together, with towels wrapped around our waists, and I could see the damage I had done. Magee's body was just a collection of welts and bruises. I asked him if they had hurt and he told me that sure they had, but he just hadn't wanted to let me know. We laughed our knackers off at that.

I have the utmost respect for Eamonn, as he is a proper fighter and one who gave me the scare of my life. I remember we discussed afterwards how different boxing was from other sports. In fact, I would go so far as to say it is unique. In what other sport would you hate each other beforehand, then hug each other afterwards and have so much respect for each other?

At the Joe Calzaghe–Jeff Lacy show in Manchester in 2006, which I attended despite my problems with Frank Warren, who was promoting, I was chuffed to see Enzo Maccarinelli and Mark Hobson hug each other at the start of the 12th round, especially after they had spent the previous 11 knocking the crap out of each other. It is great to see and I wish other sports would take boxing's lead, not the other way around.

When was the last time you saw a boxing referee in this country questioned about his decision? It is almost never. OK, fighters, promoters and managers will all have a pop at a ref from time to time, but they certainly wouldn't do it during the contest. You are just told to get on with it and tough shit if the ref is not siding with your opinion. I know Zab Judah threw a chair at the ref after losing to Tszyu a few years ago, but he is very much the exception to the rule. I wouldn't dream of arguing with a referee, even if I disagreed with his decision. They are there to do a job and make sure the sport's values are upheld. I have seen a few fights which I think were stopped too early or too late by refs, but that is their decision to make, not the fighter's.

There are no prima donnas in our sport and I don't think there ever will be. I just wish I could say that about a few other sports, including football, which is now awash with players diving all over the place at the merest hint of a tackle. I don't want to put a downer on soccer, but isn't it embarrassing when one of your own players goes down, feigning injury? I don't like it and I don't know anyone else who does.

Mind you, my next fight, against Stephen Smith, my 30th as a professional, made headlines for all the wrong reasons and caused a massive split in the Smith family, with father and son no longer on speaking terms. A few months after Magee, I was handed the job of taking on Smith, who had a terrific 31–1 record when he took me on. Smith was nowhere near the top ten in any of the ranking organizations and had lost to Bobby Vanzie, so I was confident of victory, as long as I trained hard and didn't underestimate my opponent.

I took the Smith fight because I believed I needed something a bit more straightforward after Magee and Krivolapov. As I've said, boxers cannot go to the well every time they step into the ring. We didn't know it at the time, but the best we saw of Nigel Benn was when he fought Gerald McClellan. After that, by Benn's own admission, he was never quite the same again, although I would point out that his victory over McClellan ranks as one of the best I have ever seen in any ring.

Some fighters never quite reach their best level and I believe this is because they have done too many miles on the clock by the time they reach the top. Mind you, all fighters are different. I would fight ten times a year if I could, but I know that at the highest level you have to be in fantastic shape and that only comes through killing yourself in the gym.

However, I can see where many fans were coming from when they dismissed the Smith contest as a filler. Because even though he was a good fighter and was also a world title holder, most of his wins had come in small hall shows in Germany, against names who had disappeared from the sport. When I stepped into the ring that night in Manchester and hit Smith with my first decent punch, I knew straight away it was going to be a quick night because I was the naturally bigger man. If Magee was a master poker player and never showed his emotions, Smith was the exact opposite and from the first bell you could see from the back row at the MEN Arena that he was hurting.

Stephen was a class fighter but I feel it was only at a lower weight that he would have been more effective.

I was surprised because I rated him, but my shots were causing him all sorts of problems and, at one stage, I thought the fight would be stopped in the first round when I hit him with a perfect straight right which caught him flush on the chops. Smith walked into that punch and took an eight-count. As he was taking the count he looked at his corner, which, in my view, is always a big mistake. The minute a fighter starts looking around for help from outside the ring he is in big trouble. It also sends exactly the wrong vibes to his opponent. I saw it and thought, 'I've got him here. No problem.' I could see the look in his eye. In the ring you are in your baby suit. You are naked. The fighter who looks to his corner for help, in most cases, loses.

I worked in Michael Gomez's corner in Edinburgh in 2003, when he beat Alex Arthur in a shock win for the British title, and we knew Alex was in big trouble when he kept looking at his corner for inspiration. The same was true with Smith a year earlier. I knew I had him on the run.

It went into the second and I had Smith on the ropes in the first few seconds. I was blasting away and shipping nothing in return, but then the incident happened which caused all the headlines. As I launched into another right hand I missed him, but the force of my movement kept me going forward and my elbow clashed with the skin above Stephen's right eye. It caused a bad cut and the blood spurted out, but I can only give my honest account, which is this: it was never anything other than an accident. I didn't need to beat Stephen Smith by using my elbows and I am certainly not good enough to throw a punch and know where my elbow will land. It was pure chance, but his father and trainer, Darkie Smith, went bonkers and threw a towel into the ring, causing Mickey Vann to have no option but to disqualify my opponent.

Darkie jumped through the ropes while the fight was still going on and protested that I had head-butted his son. Then he tried to persuade the referee to disqualify me. To make matters worse, he even started grappling with Mickey. It was a disgraceful scene and one Darkie, I know, as a proud and genuine man, will still regret. Darkie, if you are reading this, you know any suggestion that I elbowed your son deliberately is absolute bollocks. We have now all seen the video of the fight and it was an elbow, as well as being completely accidental.

I can't think of any fight where I have been accused of deliberate head-butting, even though fighters' heads do clash occasionally in the ring. They are bound to, but I have never had a reputation for using mine in order to win.

Truthfully, I think Darkie just wanted his kid out of the ring and for that I cannot blame him. Stephen was getting a beating and any father would want to protect his son in those circumstances. I know mine would and I can't blame Darkie for that.

The real point is this, though. Darkie Smith cannot referee boxing matches and neither can Billy or I. Or my dad, for that matter. By going into the ring and behaving like that, he just made things difficult for Stephen. I don't really know Darkie, but if your son is a boxer you have to accept the highs and the lows. When Stephen was beating opponents all over the place, I presume his father was enjoying that. By the same token, you have to control yourself and you can't throw in the towel when your son is taking some heavy shots. It doesn't work like that in the fight game. If I got licked I would be furious if my dad tried to jump in the ring and save me. It is my job and you take the rough with the smooth.

Anyway, Mickey Vann had no choice but to DQ Smith.

There are a lot of father and son teams in boxing and surely they have to put to one side their own feelings and just get on with the job. If Joe Calzaghe got torn up in the ring, I am sure Enzo wouldn't jump in there. He would be protective if he felt his son was getting a right going-over and couldn't possibly win but I only hope as a father I'm never put in that position with my son.

Stephen is a terrific lad. I have seen him in my gym quite a few times, sometimes with his son, who, Stephen tells me, is a big Ricky Hatton fan. The last time we spoke, he was still not on speaking terms with his father, which I find difficult to understand. The fight is over now. Mistakes were made, but, as far as I'm concerned, that is history. The minute the ref stops a fight that is it for me. I hope they can get back together, because they are flesh and blood and although Darkie was wrong in what he did, he may have done it for the right reasons.

* * *

American Joe Hutchinson had just gone the distance with the great Arturo Gatti when I faced him in Newcastle just before Christmas 2002.

What a classic night that was. The place was packed to the rafters with sports-mad Geordies, plus what seemed like the whole Newcastle United side. Joe Calzaghe and I were headlining a bill and Frank Warren insisted we could have sold out the venue three or four times over.

The 12,000 who were in there had a cracking evening,

although I had to dodge Hutchinson's head, which was certainly better than Niall Quinn's. The reception I got was unbelievable and yet I started fairly carefully, as I was well aware of Hutchinson's swinging head and his unusual southpaw style.

Hutchinson had been around the block and was 32 when we fought, so I knew he had experience on his side, as well as a good chin and decent hand speed. It made me a little too cautious and after the second Billy told me, in no uncertain terms, that I was showing him too much respect. I started to wind myself up.

A right hand of mine got through Hutchinson's defences in the third round and I saw him wince. That was all the invitation I needed to pile it on. I banged away with my trademark punch, a left to the body, followed up by two lefts to the head. They all found the spot.

The left hook I delivered to the body in the fourth round was probably the sweetest punch I have ever thrown and Hutchinson crumbled. I left him writhing in agony on the canvas. It was a classic left under the ribcage which finished him off. Exactly the same punch which Paul Dunne saw me use as a 12-year-old kid when I stopped a lad a couple of years older than me and there I was, years later, still banging away to the body.

Having tasted a few body shots in my time, I know what it feels like. Getting hit around the head is different. Taking a big head shot can make your legs go and you feel sick. You are not in control at all and your vision can be impaired. But it is not real pain. It is painful when you get cut and even more so when you get hit on a fresh cut, but even that is nothing like the pain you get when hit with a proper body punch.

Aimed at the right place, just under the ribcage, a body shot can stop any man. There is no real muscle layer in that area to protect you, so if you manage to catch someone under their ribs, it can finish a fight. Just as it did with Hutchinson on that night in Newcastle.

Anyone who has ever had a broken rib knows the pain involved. Times that by about ten and you have got an idea what a great body shot can do. You cannot breathe or move and the only thing which will clear the pain is time. That is something you don't get in the ring, apart from a standing eight-second count.

I practise for hours on end at getting my feet in the right position to throw body shots, because you can deliver a cracking punch, but if your feet aren't right, then the impact will be minimal. If you are balanced correctly and have the right amount of leverage, that is when a body shot can be really damaging.

All punches start from the soles of your feet. You can be the biggest heavyweight in the world, but if your feet are wrong, you won't knock out a flyweight.

You also need to set yourself up to deliver body shots. There is no point in just winging away at the ribcage, because a fighter will soon work that out and drop his guard. There needs to be variety in your game plan, but at the right time, as I showed against Hutchinson, body shots can be devastating. I caught him perfectly, just under the heart, and knew the second I had delivered it that it was all over by the sharp intake of breath he took. I didn't need the ref.

Who are the best body punchers around? Duran was well before my time, but he was the all-time best. More recently, former two-time world champion Mike McCallum was a great exponent of the long left hook to the body. My left is a lot shorter, as it is thrown from a much closer range. I will often take a step to one side and then fire at the kidneys in the same movement and McCallum was a master at throwing the same punch, only from a greater distance, maybe because he was a much taller fighter than me and had a much longer reach.

'Irish' Mickey Ward, famous for his amazing trilogy with Arturo Gatti, also had a cracking technique when it came to body shots. Gatti once told me those punches almost cut him in half and when you watch it on video you can see exactly what he means.

After I finished off Hutchinson, the Newcastle fans went bonkers. I would love to fight there again, as the venue and the support were incredible. Joe Calzaghe then came into the arena wearing a Newcastle shirt, which went down magnificently with the locals, and, as usual, he did the business, with a brilliant early stoppage of Tocker Pudwill. Geordies are a bit like Scousers and I love them, because they bring so much passion to their sport. Afterwards, I met Kieron Dyer, Craig Bellamy, Gary Speed and Alan Shearer. The former England skipper struck me as about the most normal, down-to-earth bloke I have ever met. We had a few beers and laughed our tits off at each other. He didn't have a minder within 100 yards of him, unlike some footballers I have met, but, then again, who in Newcastle would want to start a fight with Alan Shearer? He is, rightly, a God up there.

Whenever I go out with my mates we end up taking the piss out of each other all night. My family and friends are the same – Mum is always on my case, telling me what I should be doing and why I am such a plonker.

When I am in the pub with my mates, I like to be treated exactly the same as everyone else. I don't put on any airs. When I walk into the pub there will always be a chorus of, 'Come on, Fatty, get the pints in.' And I like that. It is what I am used to and what I want from my friends. Usually we will then have a pretend argument about boxing or football or whatever.

Nobody who has ever met me thinks I am a big-time Charlie or anything like that. What is the point of acting like a tosser? I don't understand it. You won't have any real friends, just hangers-on. None of my pals are remotely interested in me for my money. I'll buy my round like everybody else, but that is it.

I am very lucky in that the friends I had as a kid are still friends with me to this day and they are always knocking on my front door for a cup of tea and a chin-wag. I can't really recall falling out with any of them, because what is there to fall out over? Nothing is that important. I have the same group of mates now that I did when I went to school. Nobody new has really come into that group, although you make good friends along the way in boxing.

I suppose the fact that I have now made some money and I have been on the front covers of magazines and newspapers has made me a bit more mistrusting of people I don't know that well. But with my friends, I will tell them everything. They like me for who I am as a person, and the fact that I am a successful fighter doesn't really come into it

It is very rare that I get someone wrong, because, like most sensible people, I have a radar for bullshit. I am not saying I get it right every time – far from it – but I would like to think I could spot a hanger-on a mile off. I am lucky as it has never really happened to me, though there have been one or two people who have done things to me that cheesed me off. But nobody is perfect. I certainly am not. Does it make me angry when people do things like that? Not really. It just makes me feel a bit sorry for them and I don't mean that in a superior way. It is just a disappointing fact of life that some people will try to take the piss if you are famous.

This may surprise people, but I cannot recall ever having had a single problem with one of my pals. I can't remember us fighting amongst each other or anything like that. We argue and row over footy and other things, but that is it. It is all playful stuff. Nothing to get too narked over. I like to think I am the same with everybody I meet, from the most famous person in the land to the window cleaner or binman.

I know fighters who tell all and sundry that they don't go drinking and go to bed every night at 8 p.m. and then there they are, in a nightclub at 3 a.m., quaffing more beer than Bill Werbeniuk. What is the point in that?

I love going out and I love a pint. There. What is the problem with that? If I went out every night getting sloshed I wouldn't be a world champion boxer, so I don't really need to say any more than that.

My stamina is not in question any longer, because everybody knows I can do 12 rounds standing on my head. So to anyone out there who feels they need to lie about what they enjoy and what they do, I would say don't bother. Blowing smoke through your arse isn't my way at all and I think the fact that I sell so many tickets underlines how the public sees me. I am the sort who likes being normal, who likes hanging around in normal places, not some stupid VIP lounge where everyone in there is looking over their shoulder for the next big star to come in the room.

What other fighter would go into his local after the biggest win of his career and have a 'Shit Shirt' competition? Not many, but I am convinced it is the reason why I sell as many tickets as I do. And I am not doing it for a gimmick. I would much rather be with my mates having a round of darts than anywhere else. I can't see Bernard Hopkins doing that, though, or Oscar de la Hoya, or Floyd Mayweather. That is their lookout, not mine.

I don't see me changing my way of thinking. I believe the people who have been around me all my life are good for me and they like me as Ricky the bloke, not Ricky the fighter. I know they are very proud of me and I am of them.

I have had one occasion when an ex-girlfriend sold a story to the newspapers about me, but that is just the price of fame,

I suppose. It didn't keep me awake at night, because yesterday's news is today's fish and chip paper. I didn't like her doing that, but so what? She dished the dirt on me and she has to live with herself for that.

I am not a shrinking violet who lives a quiet life. I go to some places where people don't expect me to be, but that is only because I don't shy away from going out at all. Why should I? When I am in training I live like a monk, so when I am not training I like to let my hair down, so to speak. I will go down my local pub or I might go somewhere in Ashton or Stalybridge with some pals. Sometimes people come up to me and say, 'What are you doing here?' as if I should be living on a different planet just because I box on television. I always say to them, 'Same thing as you, mate. Having a pint and relaxing with my friends.'

To give an example, for years, before every fight I have had in Manchester, I have always had the proper full English breakfast at The Butty Box in Hyde with my brother. The fry-up has become something of a tradition. It is not a put-on. I am not trying to prove anything. I am just saying pubs and greasy spoons is what I prefer.

It all depends on the occasion, but I love nothing more than going back to my place with a gang of mates, putting the karaoke machine on and nattering until the early hours.

Everyone gathers around and dances very badly, talking absolute utter shite. 'Suspicious Minds' is one of my favourites, although I am a bit of a dab hand at 'Brown-Eyed Girl'. It's a well-known fact around Hyde that I love to sing

Elvis songs. I think I'm excellent at them, but everyone says I'm crap. It doesn't stop me, whatever they say. One Sunday night I was out with my mates at the Ring O' Bells pub and they had their usual Sunday show on. The landlord sometimes lets people go up and sing before the professionals, so no prizes for who went up on this occasion. I had the place bopping – or so I thought. After my third song the landlord handed me his phone and my dad was on the line. He said, 'Get off the fucking stage and let the artists sing, you knob!'

The landlord had phoned my home and pleaded with Ray to get me off the mic. But if you think I'm bad, you want to hear Matthew when he hits some notes – you would be convinced that his balls have still not dropped. Whatever you do Matt, don't give up the day job. I am not the vainest bloke in the world and I don't mind making a fool of myself sometimes. I don't see anything wrong with it. Some people would never make themselves look an idiot in front of their mates, but I do it all the time. I don't think there is anything wrong with being able to laugh at yourself and I've never had any trouble on that score.

When I met Bernard Manning, one of the funniest blokes in the world, a few years ago, I had my picture taken wearing a big pair of underpants next to him. What is the harm in looking like a bit of a dickhead every now and then? In fact, I went round Bernard's house to do some photos and afterwards I asked him if he would sign the pants. He said he could do a lot better than that, so he fished one of his old pairs of pants out of the laundry basket, and signed those instead. All I can say is they had been well used. We had a great laugh together and, to this day, the picture makes me chuckle. It is up on the wall in the gym, so barely a day goes by without me seeing it. Some people cringe if a hair is out of place, but not me. That is just not me at all.

As I've said, after the Kostya Tszyu fight, we held a 'Shit Shirt' day in the local pub. All my family and friends had to turn up in the most disgusting shirt they could find. Great fun. I didn't want to go to some swanky restaurant or nightclub. I wanted the boozer with my pals all wearing shit shirts. That is my way of celebrating. The New Inn in Hattersley went bonkers that day and it was one of the happiest times of my life. The fact that I was wearing a glitzy blue shirt which you would never wear in a million years just made it even better. There are no airs and graces about my friends. They come from council estates like me and they are just good, normal people with girlfriends and wives and mortgages like 99 per cent of the population. They will never change me and I won't try to change them.

After the Ben Tackie scrap we had a fancy dress competition in the pub. I was interviewed on Sky television wearing Ginger Spice's Union Jack dress. Not the actual dress, of course, as Geri Halliwell is rarely seen in the New Inn! The only problem with that little number was that I had nowhere to put my cash. I was always putting my hands down my knackers because my pants was the only place I could keep my money. Honestly, I don't know how girls get away with it!

When the Sky interview started I remember the first

question was, 'Where would you like to go from here?' I didn't think about it. I just said, 'What I want, what I really, really want, is to win the world title.' Some people watching that at home must have thought I was bonkers, but that is the way I am. Of course, blokes in the pub kept asking me to come back to their place for a nightcap, so I just kept telling them, 'I have heard about guys like you, always trying to take advantage.'

I remember going to see Paul Smith fight in Liverpool and straight after the scrap we went and had a few beers. We got back to our hotel sometime later and these lads from Liverpool who were on a stag do recognized us. They all said we should come over and have a couple of beers. They seemed like a great bunch of lads so we joined them. The only thing was, they were all dressed up to the nines as women. All in dresses and looking a right sight. I sat down with a few of them and started talking boxing and football and, before you know it, we are getting stuck into the beers. I was getting a bit tiddly so I asked one of the lads if he had a spare dress. He said he did, so I got changed and the picture was in the *Sun* a few days later. I had never met these blokes before, but get a few ales down me and I always think, 'What the hell. Why not?' The fact that someone presumably sold the pictures to the papers would bother some people, but I didn't really care. I can't see the point, but if some lad made a few quid out of them, fair enough.

I had never met these blokes before in my life, but I bet when they woke up the next morning and told their pals they were drinking with the world light-welterweight champion who was wearing a dress, they would have been told to stop making stories up.

I was out with my pals once and we were having a game of cards in the city centre. One of the lads was cleaned out during the game. We absolutely murdered him. He didn't have a bean on him. He told us he was going home because he had no cash left, but we managed to persuade him to come out with us. I said to the lads, 'Any suggestions?' One of them mentioned this new posh restaurant in town which did great steaks and was full of nice-looking ladies. It was a tremendous place and was rammed to the gills. The lad who had no money had a bit of a problem when it came to paying the bill, so someone said that if he took his kit off, all of it, we would all chuck in a fiver each to pay for him.

My pal, who shall remain nameless, is the same as me. Up for anything. He was broke, so he didn't really have any choice. Anyway, he walked into the men's toilets and ten minutes later came out, in front of this rammed restaurant, wearing nothing. Totally naked. Actually he did have one item of clothing: the men's bog brush. Jaws dropped in that restaurant like you have never seen. He was waving the toilet brush around and saying, 'God bless you, sir. God bless you, madam,' and doing the sign of the cross, like a priest. Can you believe it? Next he said he was going to get some holy water from the toilets, but I think we stopped him there. Those of us that were still managing to stand up, that is. I was on the floor, holding my sides.

The funny thing was, everyone in the restaurant also laughed their tits off. Even if the police had turned up, they would have carried on laughing. Now, I wouldn't suggest doing this regularly, but as a one-off, it was just the funniest thing I have ever seen. All to pay off a stupid bill.

Another story revolved around Whitley Bay, the seaside resort near Newcastle, and a stag do. I was up there with my mates a few years back and, of course, it was pissing down with rain and about minus ten. So what do you do in Whitley Bay on a stag do? Have a few scoops. For some reason, after a few drinks, I decided, along with two of my pals, Steve Eaton and Sid Pickford, to go skinny dipping in the North Sea. All I can say is that it seemed like a good idea at the time. Now, anyone who has ever been to Whitley Bay will know that when the tide is low the sea is bloody miles away. What began as a good idea ended up as a total nightmare.

We all took our kit off and ran towards the sea. And kept running. And kept running. The sea seemed to be getting further away, but unfortunately for us, worse was to follow. After ten minutes of freezing our knackers off, running out to the sea, we turned round. Of course, no prizes for guessing what happened when we got back to where we'd left our clothes. They weren't there. Cue lots of hiding behind lampposts in the street and cupping our bollocks in our hands. Our B&B was on the seafront and, as we didn't have our keys, we had to persuade the owner to let us in. We all had to borrow clothes because, to this day, I still don't know who nicked our stuff. Probably some bloke from Newcastle who had seen it all before and thought, 'I'll teach these stripping Mancs a lesson.' And he did.

I have shaved the eyebrows off mates tens of times and had it done to me. Ralgex has been sprayed on every pair of bollocks my mates possess. And you know what? There is nothing I like more than going out with them and doing what is now called male bonding. I call it pissing about. As long as nobody else gets hurt, I don't think I will ever stop. Campbell is the most important thing in my life, but going out and having a good time with my mates is very special and is something I will always do, world champion boxer or not.

When I am not training I have got to unwind. I could not live like a monk the whole time. I would go bonkers. Without getting too philosophical, life is too short to be worried about what others think and if other fighters have a problem with my lifestyle, I can't do anything about that. All I can say is that in the ring I am always 100 per cent. I have never been anything other than in great condition. I know the rules and the rules say you cannot cut corners in boxing, so I don't. When it is time to knuckle down, the gym becomes my life.

The way I live my life is the way thousands of young men and women live theirs. They blow off steam after a week in the office or the factory by going out with their pals and having a good time every weekend. That is maybe why I have the following that I do. People can probably relate to me more than they can to some fighters who are never out of the gym.

When people come up to me and ask for my autograph, they often say, 'I hope you don't mind.' Why should I mind? It was only a few years ago that I was doing the same thing to my heroes at Manchester City. Waiting for hours after games at Maine Road just to catch a glimpse of the players and maybe get an autograph or two.

I go shopping in Tesco and Asda and get a few funny looks from time to time. But what am I supposed to do? Not shop? Go short of tea bags and bread just because I am boxing on the television? People put you on a pedestal, but where am I going to get a pint of milk from? I can't drive down to Harrod's.

Some people don't really understand what I am about. I would never dream of going to the front of a queue at a nightclub if I am out with my mates. There is no way I want people in the queue thinking, 'There is that Ricky Hatton. What a flashy knobhead, going straight to the front.' Generally speaking, the bouncers clock me these days and they will come down the queue and say, 'How many of you, Ricky?' I always say the same thing to them: 'Don't worry about it, mate. We are happy here.' I hate the fact that people might think I am getting too big for my boots, so I won't do it. Never have. We queue just like everybody else. The bouncers will say to me, 'What are you doing? Why won't you go to the front? We will let you in,' but I won't have it. I am not trying to make myself sound like a saint; I am far from that. But there are certain things I won't do and one of them is coming over all big-time and pretending I am something I am not. I have close mates who feel the same way. My reputation means everything to me and I will have to live in Manchester long after I am retired and there is some other new kid punching the lights out of people.

I like 70s music, Motown and pretty much a bit of everything when I go clubbing. I haven't got a favourite type of music and, yes, I am a shit dancer. But I enjoy it, so who cares? There are some decent clubs in Manchester and we will often go to places like the Sugar Lounge or the Printworks. There have been some legendary after-fight parties in there.

Every now and again when I am out there'll be some tosser, too full of beer, making a tit out of himself. They are just an annoyance, but are probably different people altogether when they haven't got a bellyful inside them. I am not remotely interested in fighting when I go out. Why should I be? The whole point of boxing is that it is based on mutual respect. You lock horns in the ring and belt the shit out of each other, then hug after the fight. That is what I love about the fight game. The fact that it is you, pitching your skills against those of another proper boxer. It is not a brawl.

The first time I met my all-time hero, Roberto Duran, was a few years ago at a sportsmen's dinner in Newcastle and I was nervous about meeting him. Now, Duran is a bit of a legend and not just for his ability in the ring. Let me put it this way, he likes to enjoy life, much as I do. I had heard stories about Roberto and when I met him I was not disappointed. He has always had a bit of a wild streak. After he had been given a standing ovation, just for walking into the room, the interpreter said, 'OK, who is going to ask Roberto the first question?'

I was sitting there, holding a Smirnoff Ice, when, all of a sudden, Roberto stood up and said, 'Look, first thing is first, where is my fucking beer?' The whole room collapsed with laughter. I handed him a spare bottle of Smirnoff Ice and Roberto looked at it, took a sip and said with a big smile, through his interpreter, 'This is good stuff. You don't get anything like this in fucking Panama.' He then gave me the thumbs-up.

Roberto is one hell of a character and after the do he wanted to go to a lap-dancing club in Newcastle, so we dropped into a place called For Your Eyes Only. We spent the evening talking about boxing and, after all that he had achieved in the ring, I was just humbled to be with him. What a great bloke. He signed anything for anyone and was fantastic company. I loved the fact that he got his priorities right. Look, I am not starting anything until I have got a beer. Top man. He signed some gloves for me and I had a night I will always remember with a real gent. We talked about his fight with Ken Buchanan at Madison Square Garden and he had nothing but respect for Ken. That is what I love about the fight game. Roberto lived on the edge and fought like a tiger throughout his career, but had nothing but good things to say about the people he fought.

They say you are always disappointed when you meet your heroes, but in Roberto's case nothing could be further from the truth.

Drinking a few pints with my pals after a fight has always been my way and, on one trip to Las Vegas, I managed to surprise even the great Marco Antonio Barrera. Marco has become a close friend now, but even before we met we had a mutual appreciation for each other.

I had turned up to watch him fight Erik Morales, in their second fight. I was standing at the weigh-in when a middle-aged lady came up to me and started talking through an interpreter, telling me how much she and her son loved to watch me box. It's fair to say I didn't have the foggiest idea who the lady was but I was polite nonetheless as she told me I was one of her son's boxing heroes. I was trying to watch the weigh-in, but then the interpreter said to me, 'You don't know who this is, do you? This is Mrs Barrera – Marco is her son.'

My chin dropped to the floor when I realised she was talking about one of my heroes. At the end of the weigh-in, Marco started gesturing in my direction for me to come forward and meet him. I thought he meant someone else but after a period of confusion I realised he meant me. I went up to him, shook hands and we've been massive friends ever since. He is such a cheerful character that we hit it off straight away.

Years later, I invited Marco to my fight with Carlos Maussa in Sheffield and he was very much our guest of honour.

By now he knew I liked a drink after a fight, but he was to get a bit of a shock. Marco and his family went to bed at about midnight and we all wished him a good kip. I said I would see him in the morning and I did. At 7.30 a.m. Marco got up and wandered down to the bar, where we were still sitting, necking beers. None of us had gone to bed. Everyone fell around laughing as Marco just could not believe it.

We had to tell him he was not in Mexico now, but the far north, capital of the drinking world.

THE SUPERSTAR

Showtime were now beginning to take a serious interest in my progress and so, after the relatively quick win over Hutchinson, it was decided that 2003 would start with a bang and I was pitted against the only person to have beaten Kostya Tszyu as a professional, Vince Phillips. The man I fought had major talent, even in his late 30s, which is when I met him. He had beaten good fighters throughout his career, but the big name on his record was Tszyu, who he had smashed to pieces in Atlantic City six years before we faced each other in the ring. He had a hell of a dig, as I was to find out.

But despite his talent, his career had gone badly wrong. He always seemed to be in and out of prison for various offences, most of them caused by his drug-taking. However, the Vince Phillips I got to know was a terrific bloke who just wanted the world to be his friend. By now I had gone through quite a few fringe contenders and decent fighters like Eamonn Magee and Freddie Pendleton, but Phillips was a different kettle of fish, a proven dangerman of the highest class. I never got to the bottom of his personal problems and I didn't really want to, but I knew he was a good match-up for me. Any man who could knock out Mickey Ward must have something tasty in his fists and the tapes I watched of Phillips underlined what I already knew – he was good.

I was becoming increasingly confident that I could challenge Tszyu and he was the only one I really wanted. Although I didn't think I was quite ready for him at that point, I did regard him as my ultimate goal, as he was the No.1 in the division and still was up until the day I beat him.

Phillips beat former world champion Kelson Pinto shortly after I got the better of him, so to those who thought he was washed up, I would say I don't think so. I would accept his best days were probably behind him, but he wasn't a walkover and, as I was to find out, he could still kick like a mule.

He had been on good form going into our fight, having dropped a majority decision to Sharmba Mitchell immediately before facing me. Americans, as we know, are not short on confidence and, sure enough, before we met in the ring, he was giving it all that about teaching the new kid on the block a lesson. I was nervous that night in Manchester because I knew I was stepping up another level in front of a massive crowd and from the very first round I knew Phillips was in great shape. You only had to look at him to see how well defined he was. He began by giving me a taster of his best shot, the right hook, and I felt it.

I decided to respond in kind and for the rest of the opening three minutes I was in control, landing some terrific body shots. I then poked a left hook out which had Phillips in a bit of bother. You could see his defence was momentarily disorganized, so I went charging in.

I thought I had Vince finished in the second round. He took some heavy punishment around the body, whereas concern was starting to grow in my corner, as once again my eye had opened up. It wasn't one particular punch that did the damage, but what had started as a small nick developed into a full-blown tear by the end of the fight. I needed plastic surgery afterwards and it once again showed I was vulnerable to cuts. I suppose you could say I am just a nasty little bleeder! I am sure Phillips gained some momentum because of the cut and in the fourth he caught me with the best shot I have ever tasted.

It is, to this day, the single hardest blow I have ever been hit with and, for a few seconds, my legs went to jelly. This was in a different league to the second shot I had taken from Magee. This was potentially disastrous. So what did I do? I did what all good boxers are taught; I clung on for dear life. Thankfully it didn't take long and within about ten seconds my head started to clear and I came back to planet Earth again. Mind you, for those ten seconds I was in the land of nod, with just instinct keeping me up.

Tszyu was probably a bigger puncher than Phillips, but during our battle I either got lucky or used my ability, depending on which way you look at it, because he never really caught me on the point of my chin where all the damage is done. Phillips definitely did. I had been bossing the rounds and giving him a good going-over, but in the fourth I got a bit sloppy. Then, wham! I was in cuckoo land. It was an upper cut, which I hadn't really seen coming, and the next thing I knew my knuckles were nearly grazing the canvas. Phillips went for the kill, as he knew he had hurt me. He tried to finish me off, but in doing so he used up so much energy there was nothing left later in the round. If he had caught me with another shot straight after his upper cut, I would have been in a shit-load of trouble, but in going all out for the finish he used up every ounce he had left. Vince blew a gasket and couldn't keep up that tempo and, slowly, my scrambled brain came back.

I was a bit more circumspect after that, but I knew my boxing skills would win the day because I had watched Phillips countless times on video and seen that he couldn't keep going, not at 39 years of age. When he had beaten Tszyu he had swarmed all over him, but I didn't think he had as much left in the gas tank for me and I was right, even though he was always dangerous.

In the fifth round I tagged Phillips with two cracking lefts to the body which caused him to gulp in deep intakes of breath, and in the next round a left to his ribs had him gasping for air again. Try as I might, Vince, who was from the same Florida town as the legendary Roy Jones Jnr, was taking everything I threw at him. In the eighth he caught me again, this time with a banging right upper cut. I then made the problem a lot worse by walking into his straight right, which was pretty stupid of me. It was time to knuckle down again, and I did. I upped my work rate and started moving around the ring a bit more, knowing that a pair of 39-year-old legs would struggle to keep up with me.

The crowd sensed this was not going to be a Hatton KO night and, although I tried my best in the last round to stop Vince, I couldn't land the killer punch. I caught him with a few decent combinations, but he just stood there in front of me, winced and then carried on.

My stock went up further both at home and in the States after that fight and I knew it was a good win, with the judges giving me almost all the rounds. They scored the fight 119–109, 120–107, 120–108, which underlined my supremacy, even though I couldn't knock Phillips down. There was even more drama going on outside the ring – both before and after the fight.

In the changing rooms before we clashed, Vince had been distraught. He was about to put his life on the line against a nasty fucker like me in front of about 15,000 fans. But I found out from Vince that he had accepted a low payment for the fight as he felt it was his last chance to get into the big time. I spoke to my mate Paul Speak later, and he mentioned that, before the fight, Vince had been told the purse was so low because there was no interest from American TV. But when Vince got to the arena he would have had to be Stevie Wonder not to notice there were Showtime trucks and personnel everywhere. When he found out Showtime were showing our fight, he went bonkers. Paul Speak went off to visit Vince's changing room before we were due to meet, to check on the way his hands were being wrapped as we are entitled to do. Paul was told not to go into the dressing room but could see Vince pacing around in his underpants. Next thing he knows, Vince is fully dressed and walking along the corridor to the exit of the arena. He was clearly going and was shouting out that people were trying to rip him off and that he should be getting a lot more money. Paul and Andy Ayling, from Sports Network, persuaded him to come back. Little do the 15,000 fans who were there that night know how close the fight was to being off. After the fight Vince tried to persuade me to help him out with his purse. But all I could say to him was there was jack shit I could do about it other than sympathize.

After that fight, I had a rare bit of spare time on my hands and I was able to focus on what was going on around me. I had time to ponder what had happened when I fought Vince Phillips and, looking back on that night, I suppose it is fair to say this – it was the beginning of the end for Frank Warren and Ricky Hatton. I had seen another side of Frank.

Boxers have a lot of time for each other and I sat in the

dressing room with Vince Phillips, covered in bruises from head to toe, who had just given everything his body could give in the ring, trying to comfort him. He was shitting his pants about the money. It left a nasty taste in my mouth. If the people watching that fight in the arena had known, I think they would have thrown their spare change into the ring.

* * *

I decided to take a bit of a mini-break in order to try to give my cut a chance to settle, so it would be nearly six months before I went back in the ring. I have made a few mistakes in my life and perhaps one of the most embarrassing was the debacle that was *Superstars*, which happened at around this time. Basically, I should never have done it, but who cares? My attitude is, what is done is done, no point in worrying about it now. But, let's face it, I was bloody awful – I think I managed one of the lowest ever scores. There were a few reasons for my disaster, but the main one was that I just did not take it remotely seriously, which is strange for me because I am very competitive in the ring. In fact, I am more than competitive. I can't stand the thought of losing. I'm the fittest kid on the planet, but, as you know, when I wind down, I like to wind down properly.

My dad came bounding into the house one day and said he had got some amazing news. I had been invited by the BBC to compete in their new series of *Superstars*. Dad remembered the original series and he said the whole nation would come to a halt to watch the programme. He told me it was massive, would do wonders for my profile and I would win it and make boxing look great. I was a bit unsure at first, but Dad was adamant it would be great for me and I always listen to his opinion. I decided it sounded like a bit of fun so I would do it. I was interviewed about four months before filming began and made the following comment: 'I think I can win the whole competition.' Er, big mistake.

I took part in *Superstars* a few months after I fought Vince Phillips and, because I had needed cosmetic surgery on the cut above my right eye and so wasn't in training, I was well out of shape. I must have been two and a half, or even three, stones over my fighting weight. People who only see me in fights might think I walk around like that all the time, but, of course, that's not true. I balloon. I can't help it. It is the way my body works and so, when I appeared on *Superstars*, I was like a little barrel.

It took me about ten seconds to realize I was in big trouble. First up was the 100 metres. I have never been much of a sprinter, but I am not slow either, so I fancied my chances a little, especially as a 50-something ex-West Indian cricketer called Richie Richardson was in my heat. I burst out of the blocks and the next thing I knew I was seeing this former cricketer blasting past me as if I was standing still. Jesus, I knew I was in the deep end then. I came last in the sprints and it went downhill from there. One of the sports was golf and, bearing in mind I have never picked up a golf club in my life, I was worse than rubbish at it. I kept whacking it miles over the water or the ball would barely trickle off my club. It was a disaster.

The competition was held at La Manga and, of course, on the first night there I went searching for somewhere to enjoy myself. I had taken Paul Speak out there with me and we got a cab into the nearest half-decent-sized town. We walked into the first bar we could find, a place called Last Orders, and we sat down. The owner, a guy called Terry, was a cockney boxing fanatic, so as soon as I walked in there he started going bananas, telling his staff I was the greatest this and that. I was a bit embarrassed, but Terry was a terrific bloke, who became even more terrific when he shouted out to his staff that if anyone charged me for a drink the whole time I was in there, they would be instantly fired. That was the beginning of the end.

When a bar owner says free drinks, that is a red rag to a bull when I am out of training. Needless to say, Speaky and I spent a few nights in Last Orders and got pretty merry. Unfortunately, it meant *Superstars* took a bit of a back seat. I hadn't taken it seriously from the start, and Terry's bar just made things worse. Three points was one of the worst ever overall scores in *Superstars*, but, while I am not proud of it, I look back on it fondly, because it was great fun. I used to be a decent footballer, but even that went wrong. Dave Beasant could have thrown his cap on a few shots that he let in, then, when my go came along, he pulled off two absolute blinders. At that point, I realized I wasn't going to be living up to my prediction and winning this thing. The last competition was the mountain-biking and, although I had been pissing around throughout the whole tournament, I really fancied my chances on the bike, as my strongest feature has always been the power in my legs. I thought I would at least win this one, so I went haring off and was well in front when a steep incline came into view. I am not an expert at changing gears and I proved it on this occasion as I attempted to go into a different gear to make the climb easier. Unfortunately, as I later found out when someone checked my gears, I had done it wrong. Basically, I had put the brakes on the bike, so nothing was happening as I was pedalling furiously away. The bike just would not go forward. Of course, I should have just changed gear properly, but I was knackered and hot and wasn't really thinking that at the time. Instead, just as my legs were about to give way, I decided to pick my bike up. I managed to get it over my shoulders and semi-sprinted across the line, collapsing as I did so and finishing fourth. It was only then that someone pointed out I had fucked up the gears. It is fair to say *Superstars* wasn't exactly a great success.

The other blokes on the programme were good fun though. Duane Ladejo won the whole shebang and I enjoyed myself with the likes of Dennis Wise, Brian Hooper, the skiing Bell brothers and Dave Beasant.

I spent the rest of the summer of 2003 relaxing and trying to get my darts skills up to speed.

I got to know Phil Taylor very well and he is one of the most fantastic people I've ever met in sport. I play in the Manchester and District League and one year we won the trophy for the best darts side. My dad and I also won the best pairs title one year, the first time a father and son had ever won it. Nice one, Dad, but none of us are a patch on Phil. Any sportsman who can win a world title for 13 years running has to be something special, but the best thing about Phil is that he is the most honest, down-to-earth bloke you could ever wish to meet. I have invited him to come down to support our darts team on numerous occasions and he has always been superb fun, great with the other locals. They treat him as one of their own and he, in turn, likes to just be one of the boys. There are no airs and graces about Phil, even though what he has done in darts is just incredible. I have had a few games with him, but it is a bit of a joke really. Phil can wipe the floor with anyone, but that won't stop him playing with all the other customers for hours on end.

Our friendship – and I consider Phil to be a really good mate – started when I was interviewed by Stuart Pike for Sky. During the interview, I mentioned I was a big darts fan and he passed it on to Phil. We got in touch and Phil came down to the New Inn and gave me a bit of a tonking. Now he goes to all my fights without fail, while I try and take in as many of his darts tournaments as I can.

Phil is a genuine legend in his own sport and, I must say, I love the way he treats everybody equally. You could be the richest bloke in the world or the old man sitting in the corner with a pint of beer, it wouldn't make any difference to Phil and that is what I like about him. I hope people say the same thing about me one day, because what is the point in being the best in the world if you are a stuck-up arsehole with it?

Nobody will ever get near to what Phil has achieved in

darts and if I have even half his success I will retire from boxing a very happy man.

Another thing about Phil is that he is generous when it comes to giving autographs and always takes his time. I am sure most people have had the experience of asking a famous person for their autograph. How many of us have stood for hours, waiting for a celebrity, just to get a scribble on a piece of paper that bears no resemblance to their name and took about half a second? I think that is just downright wrong. I take time over mine and if someone asks me to personalize it with their name or whatever, I'm more than happy to do that. In fact, I am happier, because it means they aren't selling it on eBay, but genuinely want an autograph from someone they admire. I will never get tired or pissed off with signing my name for whoever, and I mean never. The worst thing about fame is that you know you have lost it when people don't ask for your autograph any more and that's the way I look at it. It is a privilege. Some celebrities spend absolutely no time signing autographs then harp on about how important the fans are. Don't get me wrong, a lot of the celebrities I have met over the years are great role models, but, like in all other fields, a few let down the majority with their attitude.

* * *

As I'd seen Aldo Rios at ringside for my fight with Phillips, I was not exactly surprised when Frank Warren set me up with him for my next outing. Phillips had been a tough fight, so it would have been foolish to have immediately gone in with another of the same calibre. But Rios was certainly capable, even though he had spent almost all his career in the smaller lightweight division.

Rios, an Argentine, was a former South American light-weight champion and had twice fought for the world title, losing to Artur Grigorian and one of the very best fighters of the 1990s, American Stevie Johnston. He had lost to both on points and I was soon to discover why, because when we fought I quickly realized what a slippery customer he was.

I was supremely confident from the first bell, as he clearly had a smaller frame than me. I will always fancy my chances in those circumstances, as so much of my game plan is built around being able to push my opponent around the ring, setting him up for my big body shots.

Aldo was like a bar of soap in the bath that you just can't get hold of. Two years after our fight, he fought Jason Cook back at lightweight and KO'd him early on, so as well as being tricky, he also had a punch. He was no pushover.

The six months out of the ring didn't seem to have done me much harm, as I started with a bang. I clipped Rios with a terrific left hook in the opening minute and he went down like a sack. At the time, I thought this might be an easier night than I was expecting, because it wasn't a full-blown punch I dropped him with, but as the fight progressed he seemed to take my best shots better and better, which surprised me a little. Perhaps his first-round tumble was more nerves, but, as he had been in with some top names, I find that hard to believe.

Anyway, Rios took an eight-count and didn't seem that hurt afterwards. In the second, I started to get to work at close quarters and a couple of cracking body shots had him in difficulty. However, he showed his ability by catching me with a right upper cut which registered.

The middle rounds were a bit messy and I was beginning to see why Rios was considered a cagey opponent. He had good feet and I just couldn't get in there close enough to land my killer shots. He had obviously studied me on video, because every time I got him in the danger zone, he would leg it out of there.

The end came as a real surprise, because I remember thinking I would probably have to settle for a points win. You don't make that decision consciously, but whenever you fight, you always get an impression. If I am leading but my punches aren't having the desired effect, that doesn't really bother me. Don't get me wrong, I'm not exactly chuffed about it either, but I accept it. I know I can dig, but it is all about timing at the highest level. You can throw all sorts of bombs all night, but fighters at the top level don't go down easily. They train their neck muscles, as I do, to take a shot. If a fighter doesn't want to get knocked out and he knows what he is doing, it is fucking hard to nail him and that is what I felt with Rios. However, just as I had given up the ghost on catching up with him, he went.

I whacked him with a great double left combination. First to the body and then to the head, and he went down for another standing eight-count. I could see he was in trouble, but it was right at the end of the round so I couldn't dive on him.

Rios's corner pulled him out at the start of the tenth and I was relieved to get him out of the way. Not because I thought I would ever lose, but because slippery fighters are difficult to look good against. They can dodge your bombs all day, get you frustrated, then you can make a mistake. That is why you have to be a bit realistic. If the bloke opposite you isn't going to go down, don't worry about it too much and don't go chasing, because that can lead to trouble. Mind you, I say that, but every time I step into the ring I want to tear my opponent's head off with just about every punch, so bang goes that theory.

At the after-show party, Rios came up to me for a chat and congratulated me. He told me, in no uncertain terms, that I would win one of the major belts – a tremendous thing to hear from Aldo.

The body shot was the one which had eventually persuaded him to stop the fight and afterwards he told me he had had nothing left. His corner pulled him then, just as Johnny Lewis did nearly two years later, on the night I beat Tszyu.

THE AFTER-SHOW PARTY

Ben Tackie has been in the ring with some of the world's best and he was certainly my most dangerous opponent to date when I faced him in front of a huge crowd, just before Christmas 2003, again at Manchester's MEN Arena, which was beginning to become my second home.

I knew, when I was training for the fight, that this was one I could lose if I was not on top form, because Tackie was a mean kid and nothing like as defensive as Rios. In fact, Tackie was the exact opposite. A boxer who comes charging at you with very little science but a lot of balls. You don't have to go chasing for a fight with Ben Tackie.

The small African nation of Ghana can boast one of the all-time boxing greats in Azumah Nelson and, although no-one would pretend Tackie was in that league, he was as strong as an ox.

Even to this day, with the possible exception of my performance against Tszyu, I would rate the night I fought Tackie as my best display. I base that on the fact that Tackie presented me with problems I have not had before and yet I worked them out and boxed him beautifully.

The build-up to the fight was fantastic, because there was a real edge to my gym work. I knew that if I wasn't at my best I would lose and that made me far more nervous and tense than is usually the case. Tszyu and Sharmba Mitchell had both beaten Tackie on points, so for me to prove I belonged in their class, I needed to show the punters I meant business. Tackie had beaten the likes of Teddy Reid, Ray Oliveira and Freddie Pendleton, which showed he had real class. He had even knocked out Pendleton in one round, so it was obvious that he had a dig as well.

The charged atmosphere leading up to the fight was cranked up even further when Tackie was widely quoted in the newspapers as saying he would cut me up like chicken. I responded with my usual pre-fight comments – that I respect-ed him, but it would be my hand being lifted at the end.

Tackie came at me as if he was bonkers from the first round and caught me in the early stages with a terrific right hand which landed just to the side of my chin. I had to do something I have very rarely done: box on the back foot.

Anyone who has ever seen me fight and who knows how to spell boxing will be aware that my whole game plan is based around going forward, being aggressive and out-working my opponent until I wear him down. Or knock him out. With Tackie, it was totally different. I needed to show speed of thought and speed of movement and I like to think I did both.

Tackie can do a bit of everything and he is a world-class fighter, but I moved around the ring and made him miss and he used up so much energy. I could see he was getting more and more pissed off about it as the fight wore on. Ben doesn't speak much English, but he certainly knows some swear words. Every time I would connect or he would miss he would shout out 'Bastard' or 'You fucking pussy'. At first I thought it was funny, although when you are in the ring you are not exactly laughing your socks off.

I'm a firm believer that the best boxers have to think on their feet and I certainly believe the work I did that night was up there with anything I have done before or since. I boxed his ears off by dancing and moving. Stepping in with quick shots. Firing them off and getting out of Tackie's range.

It showed that I could box more than one way and if you can do that in this game, you have got a future. I suppose the other time I came near to fighting that way was against Eamonn Magee, when I realized that charging in there like a bull in a china shop wasn't going to do me any favours. It wasn't the usual Ricky Hatton 100 mph stuff and yet the crowd loved it.

I think it just goes to show that British crowds are often very knowledgeable. Alright, you meet people who can't tell an orthodox from a southpaw, but, in general, I think our crowds are brilliant, because they know a good fight and a good fighter when they see one. Although I didn't knock Tackie out, and I think you would have to run over him with a steamroller to do that, the applause I got at the end was deafening. They knew they had seen a high-class performance from me and it is perhaps the closest I have ever got to Joe Calzaghe's display against Lacy.

Some experts didn't think I could fight as well as that against top-quality opposition and the papers the next day were full of how I was improving all the time. I think a few even suggested I could beat the best in the light-welter division. Billy and I spoke after my clear points win over Tackie and he said that he never had any doubts about me, but that that fight had confirmed for him what he had always believed – that I had the ability to go to the very top.

He thought it was arguably my best all-round display and I agree with him. You can beat certain fighters by simply showing more determination, rather than using your talent, but on that night Tackie meant business and I got the better of him because I proved my skills.

The judges gave me the fight by 8, 11 and 11 points and, personally, I felt the latter two got it about right. I have watched the bout on video, as I do all my work in the ring, and I can't see where Tackie won a round. In my book it was a shut-out. The fight prepared me for taking on the best, namely Tszyu, because Tackie was a hard little nugget.

I boxed 80 per cent on the back foot, using my jab to great effect and I also gave him a few digs after the bell a couple of times, just to let him know who was boss. I think I would have beaten Tackie if I had stood there toe-to-toe and slugged it out with him, but why take the risk? He can only fight one way, whereas I can change my tactics, so why not do it that way? Sometimes you have to make it easier for yourself in the fight game and that was one night where I felt I used my brain and got the job done.

Billy and I had discussed the fight beforehand, as we always do, and we had agreed that those were the right tactics to use in those circumstances. Of course Billy has seen me fight that way for hundreds of rounds, so he knows I can do it, but I think it came as a bit of a surprise to others at ringside who had dismissed me as a one-trick pony and a bit of a brawler. That's not me at all. My performance was premeditated. When I was caught on the ropes, I got out of there quickly.

It's an old cliché, but the best form of defence is attack, so when Tackie came rumbling forward towards me with that mean look on his face, I just blasted him with a couple of my best shots, often to the body, then got out of the way. I stung him a few times, especially in the earlier rounds, and that would certainly have made most boxers think twice about coming forward and looking for me, but, fair play to Tackie, he has got bags of courage and, regardless of the beating he was taking, he was still trying to come out of the blocks like Linford Christie in every round.

However, I kept most of his attacks at bay with some great blows, especially to the body with my left hand. How he never went down, I will never know. Fucking hell, Tackie was hard and he had a head like granite. After the fight, my knuckle came up to about twice its usual size from banging on his marble head and concrete ribcage all night. He should have been screaming in pain, not calling me all the names under the sun, but, gradually, I was getting through. It was a great win for me.

I was chuffed to bits, but my happiness didn't last very long, as the chinks in my relationship with Frank Warren started to grow ever wider. It was about this time that I started realising that these small things were beginning to seriously piss me off.

Our relationship was never particularly close, even in the early days, but it was good because Frank was excellent company. Like anyone in boxing, I always respected Frank's knowledge of the sport and the fact that he delivered. He has been our top promoter for many years and you can see why, as he can talk the hind legs off a donkey. But there was a breakdown of trust and, when that goes, you should just walk away and accept it. I was certainly prepared to do that. But I was prepared to give Frank the benefit of the doubt. I remember my dad once saying to Frank that in this game it is better the devil you know, but although we tried to make it work, unfortunately, as events were to prove, it wasn't that easy.

After beating Tackie, I felt on top of the world and I was ready for anything and anybody. I was in my prime, my mid

20s, and I wanted a piece of the action at the very top level. So who did I get next? Dennis Holbaek Pedersen, that's who.

I look back on those times with a lot of sadness, because I genuinely felt like jacking the sport in. A sport which I had absolutely lived and breathed for from when I was a nipper.

I know a bit more about the sport now and I am very much aware that it is far from perfect. Sometimes things don't work out, but, at the time, I was impatient and in a hurry to fight the best. If I couldn't do that, I would begin to question the point of it all. This was strange for me, because I am a boxing nut. Even now, I go to tiddly little amateur shows just for fun and you could not stop me chatting to other fighters and fight fans for all the Boddingtons in Manchester.

But at that time something was wrong with me. I felt I was treading water. I had been a pro since 1997 and wanted something more. Maybe I was desperate for a challenge because I had loved the cut and thrust of the Phillips and Magee fights. Boxers who were worthy and dangerous opponents.

I am not ashamed to say that I thought about pulling the plug, because I had got so low. I cried about it on a number of occasions, through sheer frustration, and those closest to me knew how pissed off I was getting. Looking back on it now, I don't suppose for a minute I would have given up on boxing, but anyone who has ever felt frustrated at their place of work will know what I am talking about. Then the rumours started about how I didn't want to face the best and how I was cowering away from the likes of Tszyu.

Bollocks to that. By this time, I rated myself and I wanted

only the best against me in the ring. I knew I was ready and yet I was wading through treacle, or more specifically Dennis Holbaek Pedersen, a boxer who wasn't in my league and was also considerably smaller than me.

I was desperate to take on the elite of the 10-stone division. I told Frank so, in no uncertain terms, and I even told a few friends in the press that I was seriously fucked off about the whole thing. I wanted the big names, but Frank didn't always agree. Of course, he has been around long enough to have his opinion, but ultimately a promoter should do what his fighter wants. Not the other way round.

Pedersen was made after the Brazilian Kelson Pinto pulled out of our intended clash, but I have serious doubts about whether Pinto was ever coming. I was told every excuse in the book and, while I may never get on a winning *University Challenge* team, I know when someone is yanking my chain. Pinto, who was supposed to be coming over from Brazil, never even landed in Britain, and the reason? You take your pick. I heard everything from an injury to his mother being unwell to a fucking earthquake in Brazil.

I met Frank and his advisor Ed Simons at a hotel near Manchester airport at the beginning of 2004 to discuss Pinto and was told there was only so much in the pot available as Showtime were not interested. Pinto was a decent opponent, as he was the unbeaten WBO champion, but I felt the money I was offered wasn't enough. We walked out of the meeting. To say we were annoyed would be a massive understatement. I was so angry that even though I saw the footballer Richard

Dunne in the reception I didn't even say goodbye to him. My dad and I squeezed a few thousand more out of Frank after plenty of arguing when he rang us on the phone on the way back home after the meeting and we came to a figure, but a few weeks later, 48 hours before the fight, it was officially off as Pinto had pulled out.

When I found out it was off, and that a big Manchester crowd had paid money to see it, I didn't feel right about going into the ring with Pedersen and I let everyone know that, because I just didn't see the point in fighting him, other than for a pay day. My performance was pretty poor and Pedersen was only interested in survival. The fact that I was so pissed off may have been one of the reasons why it took me six rounds to catch up with him. He was only really a blown-up super-featherweight and was well out of his depth – not what I or any of my trainers wanted for me. To make matters worse, I had to accept a lower purse for Pedersen than the one my dad and I had negotiated to fight Pinto, which didn't exactly go down a bundle with either of us, but we had to swallow it.

I'll give Pedersen his due, he took some good blows, but by the end he was just a punching bag for me. I began slowly and by the fourth round I was getting as impatient as the crowd. My feet weren't working well, but, thankfully, just as things were beginning to turn sour and the crowd were showing their impatience, I caught him flush under the ribs with a left to the body. He went down and took a standing eight-count from Dave Parris.

It should have been all over, but in the fifth I couldn't find my range again. I tried to unload big bombs instead of fighting naturally, with the result that I looked sloppy. Billy told me to calm down and let my natural skills finish him off.

I think the crowd were as frustrated as I was, because by the sixth they could see Pedersen was throwing very little back. But Billy was right. I had to stay calm and towards the very end of the round I caught him again with a solid right cross which clearly stung. A little combination followed and Pedersen was in more trouble, which was when the referee moved in to stop the action. Although Pedersen complained, it was plain to all concerned that he was only going to suffer more damage.

It was a fight I would like to forget quickly, but if that was bad, the next one plumbed new depths.

Mike Stewart had lost to Sharmba Mitchell on a wide points decision in the same Manchester ring on the night I fought Pedersen, so I fancied either of those, if it wasn't to be Tszyu. There was a lot of talk about Mitchell, who was a former WBA light-welterweight world champion, but I ended up with Carlos Vilches.

Joe Calzaghe was headlining in Manchester at the MEN Arena two months after I fought Pedersen and Frank told my dad he wanted me on the bill. I was one of his main cash-providers, because I put thousands of bums on seats and it often seemed I was expected to fight whoever he wanted. I had just come off weeks of training and my hand, which had been badly damaged in the fight with Pedersen, had blown up again, as it often does, so my initial response was, 'Absolutely no chance. It can't be done.' My dad told Frank it was highly unlikely I'd be ready in time, but Frank encouraged my dad to give it our best shot and see what happened.

I knew that my hands, my bread-and-butter as a fighter, were not going to be fully ready. I would also have to lose weight quickly and, although that could be done, it wasn't anything like ideal. Posters had gone up during this period advertising both me and Joe under the headline 'Judgement Day'. So when Joe picked up a hand injury and had to pull out a few weeks before the fight my presence became crucial for Frank.

I wasn't happy about the situation at all and I knew full well why my name was on the fight posters – to sell tickets. It's not, as they say, rocket science. The worm was beginning to turn and our relationship was worsening. Those close to me knew that. They knew I didn't feel right about this one and yet Frank persisted. He begged and begged and said he had an opponent for me who I could beat with my eyes closed. He said would I do him this one favour and next time he would get a big name. He started pestering my dad so much that it was really pissing my mum off. But eventually I decided to fight for my dad.

On 12 June, just over two months after Pedersen, I was in the same MEN Arena. I fell out with my dad over it and Billy didn't even turn up to the main press conference in protest against the decision. Dad is still upset about what happened. He persuaded me, after much pushing from Frank, I am sure, that two pay days in two months wasn't the worst thing in the world. He admits now he made a mistake, which is typical of

Dad as he is as honest as anyone I know – I have seen Dad worry himself to death if he thinks he has overcharged somebody £5 for a piece of carpet.

Dad just felt we should do Frank a favour, but you could tell he was unhappy about the whole thing. I took the fight against Billy's wishes and I would gladly turn back the clock, as he was right and I was wrong to be persuaded to go in against Vilches. I was rubbish that night. The Manchester crowd, through sheer loyalty, which I can only thank them for, again turned up in amazing numbers, but I didn't do them justice. I was shite. I was blowing like an old man after about six or seven rounds and told Billy I had nothing left in me. Billy knew I was knackered. He can tell when I am coasting and he said he knew I was suffering. I went through the motions and got the job done. By the end, I think some of the crowd had even started to leave, which has never happened before or since at any of my shows. Vilches was never going to beat me in a million years and I won on a massive points margin, but I fought like a third-rater. My dad came up to me with tears in his eyes and said, 'Sorry, son, I will never ask you to do anything like that again.' I said, 'Don't worry about it,' and just gave him a hug as I could see he was hurting.

I showed immense loyalty to Frank Warren that night and, looking back on it now, I wish I had stuck with my initial instincts and stood firm. But Frank can be a very persuasive man and his efforts eventually won the day. Of all the things Frank has said since we split up, the one about questioning my loyalty sticks in my throat more than any other. Loyalty?

Don't make me laugh. In boxing? If I had lost two or three fights in a row in my early career I would have been dropped like a stone by Frank. That is the way the sport works and fighters accept that. I should have turned to Frank and said I wasn't fighting, full stop. After all, it is me putting my neck on the line in the ring. I know people will say they don't know why I was moaning but if I had trained properly I could have put on a proper show. Whichever way you look at it I saved the show and made sure other fighters didn't lose their pay days as well. I allowed myself to be persuaded against my wishes and all I can say now is this: it won't happen again. I had ballooned up to around 12 stone four weeks before Vilches and losing two stone in a month is not clever. If I hadn't got down to 11 stone within a week, the fight wouldn't have gone ahead. The British Boxing Board of Control would never have allowed it, as they now monitor fighters' weights. It would have done me a big favour if they had called it off, but as it was I lost a stone in a week. Needless to say, losing so much weight by sweating it out through hard work in the gym cost me dear when it got to the fight. I was knackered. I was drained by the seventh round onwards and I have absolutely no excuse for the punters who paid good money to watch me.

* * *

The Vilches business left a nasty taste in my mouth. Frank is very determined when it comes to getting his own way. It is either his way, or there is the road, son. He has argued he did a great job with my career and, up to a point, I would agree with him, but all these little things kept chipping away inside my head and they became big things. I just felt we had a master and servant relationship by the end and I couldn't live with that.

Don't think for one minute I didn't have some great times with Frank, because I did. I'm the first to admit that he did a decent job in the early and middle stages of my career. It's just that I think he feels he has to control his fighters much more than I wanted. Obviously, other boxers accept that as part of the deal when it comes to having the biggest promoter in the country in your corner, but I got more and more pissed off with it over the years. I'm not a difficult person to get on with, but I'm not an angel. With Frank, I just lost confidence in him and I started to feel he was doing what was best for Frank Warren and not his fighter.

At the time the view my dad and I took was better the devil you know. But my dad was conscious even then that there were to be no more long-term deals and we would, in future, be negotiating on a fight-by-fight basis. That meant we could walk away if the need arose. Knowing what I know now, I would have left him earlier. I felt I was an easy touch for Frank for ages. When it came to negotiating for my purse, there was none. For years, he told me what I was getting and I accepted it. My dad started helping me out when the money coming in began getting a bit better, but I didn't even use a solicitor or an agent to argue my case, I just largely accepted what Frank told me was the going rate.

Without stating the obvious, I wouldn't have known a

solicitor from fucking Adam. My world doesn't involve solicitors. I was happy not using one, because I was happy just being a fighter and doing something that I loved for a living. I almost had to pinch myself every morning when I realized I was getting paid to box. It felt like a joke. But then, over the years, it slowly dawned on me that serious money was being made by Frank and Sports Network. I was just the fighter, the bloke who put his life on the line every time he went in the ring.

* * *

Frank did at least provide me with a decent opponent next up, but then my granny would have been an improvement on Pedersen and Vilches! Mike Stewart was a hard nut from America who had taken Sharmba Mitchell the distance on the Pedersen undercard. I knew he was going to be a good test for me.

Knowing that I was facing a challenging opponent made me a lot more geed up leading to the fight. I knew Stewart had been in there with the best, so if I could stop him, it would look good on my record.

I boxed well that night in Manchester, in front of another massive crowd, and I think I began to make the doubters take notice again. He had never been stopped as a pro and was renowned for a granite chin. Granted he wasn't exactly the best mover since Sugar Ray Leonard, but Stewart could fight. I was determined to get my career back on after the Vilches no-show, and I did.

Even before we touched gloves I detected that this could be an early night. I don't know why, as he was a very good pro, but I just felt I couldn't lose. There was a real snap to my punches from the first bell. I banged Mike to the canvas twice in the first round and genuinely thought he was ready to go. One of the shots I hit him with is one of the sweetest I have ever delivered – a left hook to the body which would have flattened a horse. He went down for a standing eight-count and I poured on the pressure.

Mike was throwing very little back at me, so my confidence hit the roof. I blitzed him with shots from all angles and, just as the round was ending, I saw a lovely little gap as he backed onto the ropes. Mike was so busy protecting his ribs, he neglected to defend his head and a straight right knocked him down again. Once more, there was an eight-second standing count from the referee.

I felt I could not miss and in the second I really should have finished him off. Mike had his nickname, 'No Joke', written on his shorts, and he was hardly laughing as I ripped into him. A meaty left to the body had him going again, but it was right at the end of the round and I didn't quite have enough time to follow it up.

I was a bit annoyed with myself when I sat on my stool, as I knew Mike was there to be finished, and yet I hadn't ended the job. Billy summed it up perfectly by telling me to just keep the same rhythm going, not to get too excited and the knockout would come. He was right, of course. I produced some effective work over the next couple of rounds, without having Stewart in any real trouble, but by the fifth he had recovered well. You could see why he had a reputation for being durable and tough, because he could take a punch. Even though Mike was throwing very little in my direction, he was certainly a very tidy fighter.

Just as it appeared I couldn't get through his defences, it was very quickly all over. We were cuddling each other close to the ropes, when a short left of mine appeared to drain him of all his reserves. It is a strange thing in boxing. You can pound away for round after round and feel a stoppage is never going to come, then, all of a sudden, a fighter will just go. It is almost as if his body is saying, 'Look, I've done my best and now I have had enough.'

Earlier in my career the same thing had happened when I fought Krivolapov. I had blasted away for what seemed like half my life, when suddenly he had just had enough. His body had said no more. The same was the case with Stewart. The punch I caught him with to set up the end was nothing out of the ordinary, but his eyes were suddenly glazed over and I could sense he had gone into survival mode.

I moved forward, trying to choose my shots and finish him off. It was a belting ending. Three lefts, one after the other, bang, bang, bang, all landed on his whiskers and I knew there was no way he was coming back from that. Stewart sat on the canvas and looked up at the ref and his eyes said it all.

Dave Parris counted him out and I went nuts. That was much more like it after the Pedersen and Vilches disasters. I had got myself back on track. It was a spectacular TKO and one which must have sent a warning to all the other 10-stone operators in the world. It wasn't a matter of 'if' I would win, but 'when' that night, as I was seriously charged up. I knew I had beaten Stewart far more convincingly than Mitchell had.

The Stewart fight had been billed as a final eliminator for the IBF title, held by Tszyu, and I went to see Frank Warren shortly afterwards. I told him I wanted Tszyu. I wasn't interested in hanging around in the comfort zone any more.

I hoped the fight could have been made there and then, or at least, failing that, Frank could have got me in the ring with Mitchell or even the then WBA champion Vivian Harris. Frank said he would let me know.

I got Ray Oliveira, another decent fighter, but not the one I wanted. When I found out, I let Frank know I was getting more and more cheesed off with the fights I was getting. Oliveira was high-class, but he was 36. I was in my prime and wanted to be pitted against the top man.

Billy and my dad were disappointed as well, and had to calm me down. They both convinced me that Oliveira was at least a step in the right direction and it was billed as a possible warm-up fight for Tszyu. Oliveira had previously beaten Vivian Harris and he was a seriously good fighter who had never been stopped in his career.

I accepted that I had to get the job done and, after a couple of weeks off to relax and wind down, I went into training like a man possessed. Just before Christmas 2004 I was ready and I wanted Oliveira badly, to prove, yet again, that I was ready for the big one.

As it was, I beat Oliveira all over the place. I was angry, and not with Ray Oliveira, who was a smashing bloke. I just took out my frustrations on him and knocked him all over London's packed-out ExCeL Arena before stopping him in the tenth round.

It was a fight which I dominated from first bell to last and Ray never really got a foothold. I lay down my marker in the first round by showing Oliveira the kind of work rate he could expect and I knew I was getting through. A couple of lefts to the body told him all he needed to know about my power and yet Ray was difficult to pin down. He was a proper pro in that he knew the areas where I could cause him trouble and he would get on his bike if ever I got close. Whenever I tried setting myself up for a left to his body, he would leg it out of the way. Very clever and very wise.

He showed all his experience early on when I caught him with a peach of a right hand and he simply went down on one knee and took an eight-count from the referee. He was gambling on losing the points, but hoping that I would run out of steam. It was never going to happen.

By the fourth round, a welt had appeared around his left eye and I set about targeting it. In the sixth, a crashing right hook opened up a cut over the same eye and he was beginning to look a mess. Ray wasn't responding with much but he was always throwing enough in every round to keep the fight interesting.

He certainly didn't hit me with anything too hard that night and yet it was a slow-burner of a fight for me. I knew I was up against class and so I had to bide my time and wait for the right moment to come along. As the latter rounds started unfolding, the gap between our work rates was growing and I started to feel it was only a matter of time.

In the tenth, I caught him with a solid left to the head and Ray complained to the ref I had hit him in the back of his neck. This was my chance, because a fighter who complains is a fighter in big trouble. I pounced on him. A snapping upper cut knocked his head back and I went in to finish him.

As Ray backed off on the ropes, I let loose with a flurry of shots, but it was an overhand right to the side of his head which caused him to go down. Oliveira was holding his ear and with his eye seeping blood there was no way back.

The ref rightly called it off and afterwards I discovered Ray had suffered a perforated ear drum.

Ray was nice enough, when asked after the fight, to praise me to the hilt. He had absolutely no doubts that I could live with and beat the very best in the world and in the dressing room he said the same thing to my face. Michael Watson also came into my dressing room after the fight which was a real honour. He came in as a fan and I was delighted to see him, but I'm sure he won't mind me saying that his presence alone underlines the dangers involved in the fight game.

* * *

There were a few surprises in store for me after that fight. Firstly, I found out that there had been a discrepancy between what I had been told my purse was and what I was actually

© PAUL SPEAK

above: With Matthew taking part in our usual pre-fight breakfast ritual down at the Butty Box. It might send my nutritionist bonkers, but it is now ingrained in my preparation.

© PAUL SPEAK

above: With my biggest and best fan James Bowers and his Mum. James has been with me for years and I just wouldn't feel the same without his smiling face around.

© PAUL SPEAK

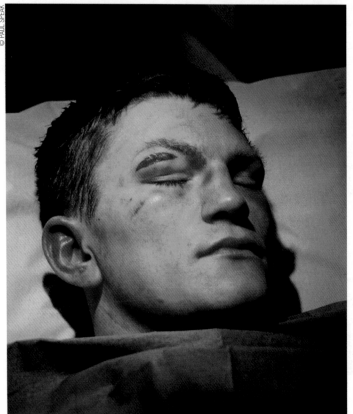

© PAUL SPEAK

above: On the Hattersley estate with two of my other boxing pals, Ensley "Bingo" Bingham and Carl "The Cat" Thompson, who beat Chris Eubank in an epic encounter.

left: It takes a surgeon to knock me out! Some of the cuts I have suffered have been bad, but this one, from the Vince Phillips fight was like a railway sleeper above my eye.

© PUNCH PROMOTIONS

right: A family affair, with brother Matthew and my son Campbell, who definitely has the right pose for a boxer.

below: My mum Carol and dad Ray on our annual cruise holiday. I owe them both so much and the fact I live only a few hundred yards from their house means barely a day goes by when I don't speak to them.

© PUNCH PROMOTIONS

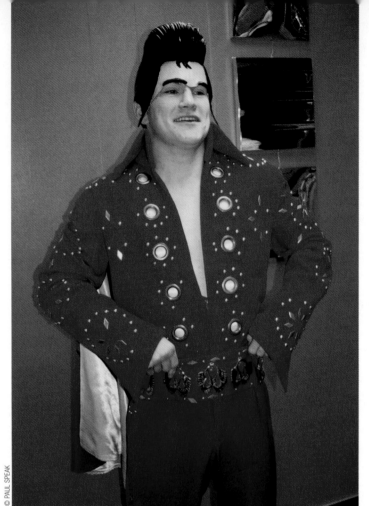

© PAUL SPEAK

left: The wonder of me.

below: Del Boy Hatton is the name, complete with sheepskin coat and flat cap. In the back is a blow up doll! The three-wheeler, made for the TV series, is parked in my garage at home and I still drive it around Manchester. The looks I get from passers-by are priceless.

© MANCHESTER EVENING NEWS

above: The day after beating Kostya Tszyu we held a shit shirt competition at my old local, the New Inn. Cheers!

right: Ricky "Hitman" Hatton in gangster gear. This was for a promotional shoot with Sky and I reckon I just about pulled it off.

© MARK ROBINSON

© PAUL SPEAK

above: Me and Joe Calzaghe are both aiming a playful punch at Frank Warren. Later in my career, I would exchange verbal blows with my former promoter.

© PAUL SPEAK

above: With one of my first boxing coaches Paul Dunne, who – like my other amateur trainer Ted Peate – is still very much a close friend.

© TOM CASINO SHOW TIME

above: Tearing into Vince "Cool" Phillips. I beat him by a wide points margin, but he hit me harder than anyone before or since and that includes Tszyu.

left: Ben Tackie takes one to the jaw from a cracking right hand. My victory over the Ghanaian has gone down as one of my best performances in the ring. I fought a different way that night to prove I am not just a brawler.

© TOM CASINO SHOW TIME

right: Kostya Tszyu was a legendary champion and the way he took defeat was a lesson to all sportsmen. If I ever lose, which I hope I don't, I will try to display the same attributes.

© MARK ROBINSON

above: Carlos Maussa took a hell of a beating before I finally caught up with him. With one of the best single punches I have ever delivered.

right: Apart from my son's birth, the greatest moment of my life. As I wear the IBF light-welterweight world title belt for the first time having just beaten Tszyu. The T-shirt says "There's only one Ricky Fatton" – a reference to *The Sun*'s love of the fact that I balloon in weight between fights.

going to get. I'm not an expert on numbers — I leave the figures to my dad — but I do recall it was something around the £25,000 mark. This became apparent when I spoke to my dad after the fight. Frank Warren was in America with Danny Williams so we tried to speak to Ed Simons, but he was nowhere to be seen. Later that night we got a call from Ed asking if I could make my way to a different hotel as Sky television were expecting me to do a commentary on the Williams–Vitali Klitschko fight taking place in the early hours in Las Vegas.

I was furious. Absolutely boiling. To make matters even worse, if they could be any worse, I was sitting in my hotel having a pint with my family and friends when I got a phone call asking me if I wanted to come to the after-show party at a five-star hotel near the venue. An after-show party? I hadn't been invited to any after-show party. I was the top boxer in Britain, drawing the biggest crowds in the country and I hadn't been invited to Sports Network's after-show party, at which they were showing the Danny Williams–Vitali Klitschko fight live from Las Vegas. Un-fucking-believable. Both me and my dad were fuming and had no intention of going but we then took a call from Sky commentator Adam Smith. He seemed pretty astonished we knew nothing about the party. After a few minutes to think things through, we decided if we didn't go we would be letting down both Adam and Sky, with whom we had a very good relationship. Sky had not done anything wrong and I like a lot of the people that work there, not just the main commentators.

Of course, my initial reply was something along the lines of, 'You can stick your shebang where the fucking sun doesn't shine.' When we eventually got to the do, Amir Khan was there and was with his entourage, in the hotel, a five-star job, whereas I was staying somewhere considerably less flashy. It was almost as if Amir was getting the star treatment as he even had a private suite and I was off the red carpet. I was even more annoyed when it became apparent people were being charged £75 to attend the function and it was being advertised that I would be there.

It sounds very nit-picky of me and I don't wish to come across that way. I can lay my head down on a concrete pavement after a fight, as long as there's a bar nearby ready to stay open until the early hours. But you can imagine how I felt. The little things were all adding up to big things and, slowly, all the confidence and belief I had in Frank Warren were being drained away by daft things like this. I am not the type of person who needs, or even wants, special treatment, but at the same time I had been the main attraction in front of a sell-out crowd of 12,000 and there I was sitting in a small hotel bar and being told of an after-show party down the road that I hadn't been invited to.

Eventually I said yes, but that I would have to bring some mates with me as I wasn't going anywhere without them. By the time Adam got round to interviewing me on my opinions on the Williams fight for Sky, I was already a few beers into winding down. I didn't really fancy Danny to beat Klitschko and yet, like everybody who watched that fight, I was massively impressed with the heart and balls Danny brought to the table. Danny is a much better fighter than he gives himself credit for, but on that night Klitschko proved he was the best of a fairly modest bunch in the heavyweight division. But Danny had given it his all and that's really all you can ask.

I travelled back to Manchester the next day very happy with my performance against Oliveira, which I think underlined yet again my credentials to fight the best, Kostya Tszyu. But I wasn't too chuffed in other respects. The slow eating away of my trust in Frank Warren had started to get on top of me a bit, but at that point I was still very much prepared to play ball with him.

That willingness to let bygones be bygones didn't last very long, though. He delivered in getting me the fight I wanted, Kostya Tszyu, but his actions after the best night of my life left me little choice but to turn elsewhere. And that was when the fun really started. It was on this night that Dad and I decided enough was enough; we had to get some outside help in. During the evening Dad got to know Gareth Williams, who was to become our solicitor. He had been a guest of Frank Warren's at the fight because at the time he was representing Amir Khan. This was the night when Dad and I realized that the discrepancy in my purse meant we needed proper legal advice.

THE BADDEST MAN ON THE PLANET

The first time I met Kostya was when I travelled out to see the Australian versus Zab Judah after I had beaten Eamonn Magee. It turned out to be a cracking trip, with just me and Billy enjoying a good fact-finding mission. Kostya had been the best in the division for so long and I had watched him for hours on end on tape – so much so, in fact, that I was almost sick of the sight of him.

I spoke to Kostya for the first time in my life in the foyer of a hotel after he had beaten Judah. As usual me and Billy had gone out there to enjoy ourselves and this we did in the usual manner, so quite what Kostya thought when some little bloke with a funny accent came over to him, telling him we were going to meet one day in the future, heaven knows. I imagine he thought, 'What a dickhead,' and I would probably have been the same. I introduced myself very politely. 'Hi, I am Ricky Hatton from Manchester.' He looked at me and didn't have a fucking clue who I was.

At the time of the Judah fight, I wasn't quite ready to take Kostya on. My chance, when it came, was at exactly the right time.

I think the people who got knocked out by him were the ones who were too much in awe of his power. They tended to back away and that is surely the worst thing you can do against Kostya. He lines you up. He paws you with his left jab and he sets you up. If you pull away there is every chance he will clock you. He did that to Sharmba Mitchell and Judah and stacks of others. I watched all the videos and I knew they were fighting him the wrong way. It takes a lot of bottle to keep going forward with somebody who punches that hard, but I knew that was the way to do it.

I knew I had the tactics to beat him, but when I finally came to fight him Billy got a bit pissed off, because when he did happen to catch me with his right hand I just kept dropping my hands and looking at him as if to say, 'You have got to do better than that.' Billy kept saying, 'You don't have to show everyone how tough you are! I think we get the picture now! Stop dropping your fucking hands.'

I knew his big shots were coming. Billy said, 'You know

what is happening, Ricky. He is trying to catch you cold with that right hand. You can get out of the way of it if you want!' But if I had stood there and pulled away it would have been curtains. He was catching me, not with a straight right hand, but a roundhouse shot. He wasn't knocking me out because I was taking the leverage out of his punch.

It is either a very foolish tactic or a very brave one and I think I will plump for a bit of both. The right hand he knocked out Mitchell and Judah with was a straight one, right down the pipe. Against me, he had to loop it and that is what took the sting out of the shot. Mind you, if I had made a split-second miscalculation I would have been on the deck counting stars.

Kostya is a thinking fighter and he uses his brain. You only need one punch to land and it is all over. Because that is the way he is, he doesn't train at a hot pace. He trains for five hours a day. You couldn't get anyone fitter than him, but he does like to box at a tempo. Slow it down, speed it up, slow down. Pick your shot. He only needs that one chance. My response was to try to force the pace all the time to make him work harder than he wanted to.

Even if I lost five of the first six rounds I knew I would not be bothered, because I wanted him blowing out of his arse. I started off well, like a house on fire. Kostya must have thought, 'I have got to do something here,' so he upped the pace. He won rounds three, four, five and six. They were all good rounds for him but I wasn't too bothered because he was working a lot harder than he wanted to. I was banking on rounds nine onwards, when I thought I would have him.

I have watched the tape of the fight over and over again and you can hear Johnny Lewis saying, 'Kostya, you have got to catch this little fucker with your right hand at the start of the round. You have got to stop him coming forward. We have got to nail him.' He knew what was going on.

I had to be very sure of my own ability to fight the way I did. I am not a show-off and I am not big-headed at all, but I know I can fight. Because I fought the fight at 100 mph, a lot of people would say that there were no tactics in there, that I just relied on my will and my bottle. But that is just not true. If you look carefully at Tszyu's fights, you'll see that he will only throw 20 or 30 shots in a round. He just waits and sets you up, then bang, it is all over. I thought, 'I don't want him throwing 30 punches in a round. I want him to double that.' I wanted him to do things he is not used to. As it was, the tactics worked a treat and in the latter rounds I dominated our fight, before Lewis pulled his man out.

If I had to describe my technique as a fighter in general terms, I would say this: I am a counter-puncher. Always have been and probably always will be. When I fought Eamonn Magee there were two counter-punchers in the ring, which is probably why I got nailed, because I went chasing after him in the early rounds.

What I mean by a counter-puncher is that I respond to what a fighter throws at me. If my opponent tries one thing, I will respond with something better, because in delivering the punch he has made himself vulnerable. That is what I am all about in the ring. Watch my fights and you will see what I mean. The best thing you can do in fighting is always make your opponent think and the day I stop doing that, I will be in trouble.

I suppose the obvious step forward for me after Tszyu was to go for the fighter who has now become recognized as the best operator in the world, pound for pound, although my opinion of Floyd Mayweather, while I accept he is massively talented, is that he has never been tested by someone like me.

People say to me, 'I think Floyd Mayweather would give you a licking,' and my reaction is, 'That's your opinion, mate, not mine.' To be able to beat me you have got to have some serious firepower to keep me off and, no matter how much talent he has got, I don't think Floyd could do that. Tszyu couldn't and there is no way Kostya is a lighter puncher than Mayweather.

Floyd has got great hand speed and some brilliant combinations, but I will stand by this belief: if anyone can beat Floyd Mayweather it is me. He has got the kind of style which would give me problems, but for how long? How long could he keep me off him? For the first four to six rounds it might be tricky, but if I persevered, and I would, I think I would end up getting to him.

I am a pressure fighter, someone who goes forward looking for a scrap. I will keep going at that crazy tempo all day long. Nothing will stop me. I will be in your face throughout 12 rounds, unless you make me think, 'This is something I've not come up against before.' Nothing scares me.

Actually, when I say nothing scares me, I am not, strictly speaking, telling the truth. Cats scare the shit out of me. I know I have a reputation as a fearsome fighting machine to uphold, but cats put the wind up me. It all started when I was a little kid and got badly scratched by a cat. Ever since then I can't stand to be near them. Some of my mates have got cats and if there's one in the room I won't go in until it's been kicked out. It is either me or the cat!

When I was training for the Kostya Tszyu fight, I had to get accustomed to being up at night because the fight was scheduled for 2 a.m. So I was out jogging one morning, at about 1 a.m., when I nearly crashed into a fox doing its night-time prowling. I don't know who was more scared, me or the fox. A fox I could just about handle, but cats, forget it.

Floyd could bring a tabby into the ring, otherwise he would have to hit me with something very meaty, because if he didn't I would keep going after him for the whole 36 minutes. And I wouldn't let up for a second.

Power isn't the only important thing in boxing, though. Timing is crucial too. Floyd has got bags of timing and accuracy, so even in the last round you would have to watch him like a hawk, because a split second is all it takes. It would be a great fight, with two very contrasting styles. Lovely, silky, smooth hands against a fighter like me who isn't just a slugger, but likes to get stuck in straight away. Don't get me wrong, I wouldn't go into a fight with Floyd like a headless chicken, but I would want to ask him questions about himself, not the other way round. That's what I did with Tszyu and it worked. More importantly, I knew it would work. Similar tactics would be the way around Mayweather, but I am not kidding myself. He is a class act.

I saw Arturo Gatti immediately after his fight with Mayweather when 'Thunder' took a right pasting. Arturo is a fantastic bloke and someone who I have a lot of respect for, as he is the genuine article, a real ring warrior who attracts some of the biggest crowds in America with his old-fashioned brawling style. His trilogy against Mickey Ward has gone down in history and Gatti is a true great. However, and I've told him exactly what I am saying now, he played straight into Mayweather's hands when they fought.

Gatti sat back and tried to dance. His tactics were terrible, because nobody can out-move and out-jab Mayweather. Gatti needed to get in close, rough him up and make Mayweather brawl. Instead Arturo tried to use his skills to dab away at Mayweather. Bad idea. I wouldn't beat Mayweather in a month of Sundays that way, because it would just be playing to his strengths. Mayweather wouldn't like my body shots, no-one in the world would, so that is what I would have to bring in to play. Arturo, by fighting at a distance and keeping Mayweather at bay, got murdered. Mayweather had time to pick his shots and he does that better than anyone around.

When we meet in the ring, I am sure I will try to make Mayweather think about things he has not faced before. That is when fighters are vulnerable and Mayweather is the same as any other boxer, he won't like facing the unusual in the ring. Stand in the middle of the ring for Floyd and you are dead meat.

I have met Mayweather, although I don't think we

understood each other. It was at ringside when he beat Gatti in Atlantic City in June 2005, just a few weeks after I had stopped Tszyu, and I was pleasantly surprised at how small he looked. I sized him up and I think he caught me! He said something which I didn't understand, but I knew it wasn't a compliment, so I fired back with some good old-fashioned Mancunian language. We both stood there until a few bouncers came over and then he walked around the back of the seats, eyeballing me the whole time. If he thinks that sort of shite will work with me, he has got another think coming.

Mayweather is one of the all-time greats and until I face him I won't be finished with boxing, but he started life as a super-featherweight and, just before winning his first world title, he went the distance with Tony Pep. I cut Pep in half. That doesn't necessarily amount to a string of beans, but it shows that I would be a bit of a test for Mayweather.

Mayweather's list of victories is hugely impressive – Gatti, Judah, DeMarcus Corley, Sharmba Mitchell, Jose Luis Castillo, Jesus Chavez, Carlos Henandez, Angel Manfredy and Diego Corrales to name but a few – as is the fact that he has gone up from super-feather to welter. So there's no doubt that I would be facing one of the very best fighters of the last few decades. It will happen someday and when it does, Floyd, I'll be ready.

Floyd's attempt at menace outside the ring doesn't work, in my opinion. Well, it doesn't work with me anyway. Just look at Lennox Lewis – he could not have scared anyone with his talk before a fight. Lennox was not my cup of tea at all as a

THE HITMAN — MY STORY

fighter, but that is not to say he wasn't the best heavyweight in the world and a high-class boxer. It is just that he would not be one of the names I would pay to watch if I had the choice.

I respect him and his achievements. After all, he became the undisputed heavyweight world champion and you cannot ever take that away from him. He was supremely talented and had a magical jab, but exciting? Not for me. Others think differently and, fair play, everyone has their own opinions. The Americans always took the piss out of our heavyweights but they didn't with Lennox. They didn't really take to him either, mainly because he was better than any of theirs and, let's face it, he wasn't Mike Tyson, was he? Tyson, in his early years, had an aura of nastiness about him, whereas Lennox was very methodical. He would wear down opponents with that fabulous jab and well done to him.

The British heavyweight pool certainly became a lot smaller after he retired. I watched Audley Harrison against Danny Williams just before Christmas 2005 and was stunned by what I saw. I don't think I have ever seen a fighter so scared in all my life. Audley just ran and ran. He did himself no favours by saying what he was going to do to Danny before the fight. It was all the usual stuff. I am going to knock him out, roast his bollocks in the ring and all that rubbish you get these days. There is nothing worse if you cannot then back it up. You are just there to be shot down and, boy, did Audley get shot down. Muhammad Ali could do it because a) he was funny and b) he backed it up, but Audley just looked daft.

One fighter who still makes the hairs on the back of my neck stand up is Michael Gerard Tyson. What a machine he was in his early years. Unfortunately, that comment says it all: his early years. Unknown to us at the time, when he fought Buster Douglas and lost in 1990 he was already on the downward slope, as his lifestyle caught up with him.

But Tyson in that early period was utterly devastating. He could throw some serious stuff and yet his defence was also high-class, with the constant side-to-side head movements taught to him at Cus D'Amato's gym in the Catskills.

I still consider myself to be the luckiest kid in the world to have fought on a Tyson undercard, when he took on and demolished Julius Francis in Manchester. Joe Calzaghe had just served up a mediocre fight with David Starie, although, to be fair to Joe, his opponent ran away all night, so when I came on it was fireworks all the way. I blasted out my opponent inside a couple of rounds and the MEN Arena went nuts. Nothing is bigger than fighting on a Tyson card and I will never forget it. Of course, by then Tyson was a mere shadow of himself when he was at his peak, but he was still far too menacing for someone like Francis.

Tyson had great boxing skills in those early days. Lovely fast hands, quick reflexes and thunder in his fists. He burned through the likes of Trevor Berbick, Tony Tubbs, Pinklon Thomas, Michael Spinks and Larry Holmes, then, all of a sudden, it went sadly and horribly wrong.

The Tyson who lost to Danny Williams in 2005 was not the Tyson of the early years and no-one should pretend he was. I think even Danny accepts that, although he fought a terrific battle, beating Tyson after taking some early punishment.

I suppose I should lay my cards on the table here and say that while Tyson was his own worst enemy, he also got some bad breaks in his life, which must have upset his equilibrium. First of all, he was a street kid from the worst neighbourhood in New York. Then he goes to a gym under the leadership of D'Amato and dedicates himself to boxing, only for Cus to die. A year later and his other mentor Jimmy Jacobs also dies. Bill Cayton was his manager, but Tyson never had a strong relationship with Cayton, who was basically a money man. You can understand why Tyson started to go off the rails, especially when his marriage to Robin Givens broke up so publicly after about a year. Then Don King came into the equation and you have got all the ingredients for a person who could go badly wrong and that is exactly what happened. Looking on the outside, Tyson was a disaster waiting to happen.

He had no proper support behind him but, as all adults do, he made his own choices. They just turned out to be bad ones. What would have happened if D'Amato and Jacobs had lived is anyone's guess. Mike might have gone the wrong way anyway, but I have my doubts. He had a solid base there which was taken away from him and, bearing in mind his upbringing, I have got some sympathy for him.

I can't begin to justify some of the things he has done with his life, but I think he was a very young man when he became the most famous sportsman in the world and it would have been difficult for a lot of kids thrown into that environment with no guiding light to lead them. There are stories about him attempting suicide, which obviously suggests he hasn't got a great opinion of himself. The story of his career is a sad one.

On the night of the fight in Manchester I told Tyson and his entourage to fuck off. Not the wisest thing I have ever done. My pal Paul Speak was driving me and Dad to the Midland Hotel, where I was going to drop my stuff off and attend a weigh-in. Speaky pulled the car up in the parking space outside the hotel and I was just about to get out when the driver behind started honking his horn, over and over again. I wound down the window and gave him some verbals, only for Crocodile, Mike Tyson's main cheerleader, to come out of the car. I wound up the window very quickly and bolted for the hotel door. Unknown to me, we were parking in Tyson's reserved space, but, thankfully, I don't think they understood broad Mancunian and I got away with it. Frank Warren introduced us later that night and he was very polite, as he was to all boxers.

Years later, I was in the lobby of a hotel in Las Vegas with my then girlfriend, who was having acting lessons in Los Angeles, when I spotted Jeff Fenech, the Australian boxing hero who used to train Tyson.

We got chatting and I told him how much I admired Tyson's ability in the ring and the next thing I know Fenech is telling me to hang around for two minutes. He picked up his mobile phone, chatted away for a few seconds, then handed it to me. The person down the line said, 'Hi, this is Mike Tyson. Is that Ricky Hatton?' I nearly dropped a bollock, I was so chuffed. We had a natter on the phone for a while and he called me 'the body-punching kid who fights like a Mexican'. By the time I handed the phone back, I could hardly get my head through the hotel door.

Getting back to Tyson's legacy, some will argue that, even in his prime, he never beat much in the way of opposition. His best victory arguably came over Larry Holmes, who was way over the hill by then. But I wouldn't necessarily read too much into that. Firstly, there was nobody very significant out there for Tyson to fight at the time. He blew away the best of the rest. Secondly, just because a fighter knocks somebody over who is not too highly rated, that is not to say he will lose when he steps up in class. Just look at me. The Ricky Hatton that ground out a dull win over Carlos Vilches or Dennis Holbaek Pedersen would never in a million years have beaten Tszyu, according to most ringside observers.

In those early years, I reckon Tyson would have blown away anybody bar Ali, and that includes Liston, Rocky Marciano and Joe Louis. Having seen tapes of all these fighters, I think the amount of menace he brought into the ring when he was in his early 20s and was really focussed would have been enough to win. Ali, though, may have worked him out, just as he worked out much bigger and stronger fighters throughout his career. Ali used his brains in the ring and, in his prime, had the fastest hands there have ever been. Tyson was murderous, but whether he could have out-thought Ali is a different matter. He wasn't called 'The Greatest' for nothing. Ali always came up with an answer and I think he would have done the same against Tyson. But it would have been close.

Tyson has become something of a byword for how to self-destruct and it is well known that when he drank or took stronger substances he was a wild man. One thing I can say with great certainty is that I will never be remotely tempted by anything stronger than a beer. Of course I am aware that drugs are available when I go out. You would have to be pretty stupid or blind or both not to notice, but I have never had any inkling at all to get involved in anything other than beer. I cannot understand why anyone else would either. The thing with having a few beers is that it is such a sociable pastime. You can meet your pals and have a great time while gradually getting a bit merry. The idea of taking something which would send me out of my fucking tree doesn't appeal and never has. I just can't see the point. The whole idea of going out is to have a good time and to remember having a good time, not to be found in some gutter so off your tits you don't even know your name.

When I go out with my pals the only things on our minds are whose round is it next and what about the football and the ladies. That is the be-all and end-all. If someone asked me, 'Are you OK? Do you want to try a bit of this?' I would reply, 'No thanks, I am out with my mates, just having a few beers.'

Just as I will never put on an act with my pals, I also don't act any different with the press boys. I find the minute a camera comes along a lot of boxers seem to instantly turn into livewires, which I find pretty false. I've never felt the need to do that. Floyd Mayweather will come out with all the crap under the sun just to sell tickets, but if you are looking for me to do that, you will be waiting a long time.

I'm quite pally with the majority of the press lads and I respect some of their opinions. They often ring me up to ask if they can do an interview and 99 per cent of the time I have no problem with that. It is a little more difficult nowadays, because obviously I am no longer a young upstart from Manchester, but a world champion, and as such I do get a lot more media requests. However, I try to accommodate the press as much as I can, as I believe they generally do a good job and I get on well with them. Some of the press blokes are genuine mates and I think they want only what is best for boxing, like anybody who loves the sport.

The only bad press I have really received over the years has been in the *News of the World*, specifically in Frank Warren's column. One accusation that hurt was the one about me being greedy. He's got to be having a laugh.

Of course, money is part of boxing, but I would say the glory has always been the bigger prize for me and always will be. Obviously, at the level I am at now, I am earning a good living, but what I really want is what every fighter wants – the belts. I am convinced I would still fight if there wasn't any financial incentive. You can't say you are not interested in the money because, of course, with the glory comes the big cash, but as long as I have got a pound more that I can spend, I'm not that bothered.

I'm still not satisfied, far from it. There are always challenges out there in boxing, because when you have beaten one opponent, another will be coming up from behind, ready to bite you on your arse. There is much more I can do and, with the likes of Mayweather, Castillo and Corrales, there is still a heck of a lot to aim for.

THE BREAK-UP

Just before Christmas 2005, I was heading down to London with three friends to watch one of my best boxing pals Paul Smith fight on Frank Warren's show, the disastrous Audley Harrison versus Danny Williams clash. At the time, Paul was still training with Billy Graham – he has since left him to fight for Frank Warren – so I wanted to support him, but, after discussing it with everybody, I decided it was best not to go to the show because of all the friction between me and Frank. However, I still decided to travel to London as I was down to appear on the BBC's prestigious Sports Personality of the Year awards show the following day.

We went down to London and booked ourselves into our hotel before dashing off to do some shopping. On Saturday night, after watching the boxing, the four of us decided to go to a lap-dancing club called Spearmint Rhino. So we all piled in there and were just getting stuck into our first pints when a club employee came up to us and told us Frank Warren was coming. There was a reserved table in the club which I presumed was for him. The owners asked if we wanted to stay and I said I didn't mind at all. I wasn't going to cause a scene or anything. In fact, I would not have said a dicky bird to Frank unless he had come over to me. I honestly didn't even think about leaving. We were having a great time and my mates were loving it, so why leave?

For whatever reason, Frank didn't turn up, so that was the end of that. No confrontation, but there would not have been one anyway, as I would have preferred to walk away.

My real problems with Frank had started a few months before, when I had won the Kostya Tszyu fight. Frank knew I was out of contract and he knew he had to negotiate another deal for me. I would never in a million years have fallen out with him over a few pennies, or even a few tens of thousands, but the offer he made to me after the Tszyu fight was unacceptable. I could not believe it.

Dad and I travelled down to London and there was Frank and Ed Simons. He made us an offer and my dad said we had received much better ones.

I have absolutely no regrets about us falling out, because no-one in their right mind would have accepted the offer, especially in a business like boxing where you are only a couple of fights away from being yesterday's man.

I had thought for some time that Frank regarded me and my family as an easy touch and I based that opinion on previous history. Essentially, whatever Frank offered for fights we just shook hands on it. We knew he was making vast amounts of money from the promotions, but it didn't really matter because I was also doing well out of it.

At the level I am now, I earn a good living, but I would struggle to find anyone who says I don't deserve it. My primary ambition for the rest of my career is to be able to retire with the IBF, WBA and WBC titles on my mantelpiece. That is my motivation, not how much cash I am going to make. I don't suppose Wayne Rooney or Steve Gerrard would give up football if they didn't get paid, and I am no different. Having said all that, I am not stupid and I won't have the piss taken out of me.

As I've said, Dad handles my finances and in the past it was dead simple. He would say, 'For this fight you have been offered this amount,' and I would say, 'Yeah, good, it sounds OK. Get it done.' The Hattons are an honest, genuine family and we never gave the question of money much thought.

Maybe Frank Warren saw that side of us as a weakness. Frank would sort out the fight and tell me what I was getting. That was that. He wouldn't tell me what he was making or where it was coming from. Frank has a strong personality and is a forceful man with a cracking business brain for making money. He is the best in the promotional business, whereas I am a boxer. Show me a balance sheet and I wouldn't know where to fucking start.

But I am not entirely daft, either, when it comes to money. Over the years, Billy, my dad, my brother and everyone else I knew moaned and groaned a few times, but we always accepted it, even though we knew Frank was making big money out of it all. Fair play to him. He was promoting the shows so he had a right to make that money. But by the same token I had the right to fight for whoever I wanted, provided I was a free agent. There came a time when the differences between us became too great.

Throughout all my problems with Frank, Sky television have been brilliant to me. People say to me now, 'But you could be fighting on terrestrial television with ITV, in front of audiences in the millions,' but I always say I haven't done too badly with Sky.

It is true, ITV have a cracking boxing set-up and everybody who has the best interests of boxing at heart will agree that their return to the sport has been a massive boost. Obviously, one day I may fight on ITV and I would love to. I grew up in the great days of Nigel Benn, Frank Bruno, Chris Eubank and Steve Collins, when the whole country seemed to come to a standstill for boxing and I would love for that to return.

I would have no problems at all working with ITV and I have commentated for them many times. Jim Rosenthal is a fantastic bloke who everybody in the sport has a lot of time for, as is Barry McGuigan, one of the friendliest people I have ever met. ITV's head of sport, Mark Sharman, brought them back into boxing and I don't know anyone who doesn't want them to succeed. I know I do.

Of course, ITV get great viewing figures, which Sky Sports cannot possibly match. But I think we have to remember that when the BBC and ITV pulled out of boxing in the past, it was Sky who picked up the baton and ran with it. It was Sky who kept boxing on television when the others weren't interested. A while ago, the BBC came back to the sport with Audley Harrison, but look what a cock-up they made of that. I don't think for a minute ITV will make the same mistakes, but you just don't know what is going to happen in the future, do you? All I know is that Sky have been there from day one for me and they helped put me on the map, to the extent that I was selling out 22,000-seater arenas in two hours, with the tickets going faster than for the Tyson fight in Manchester. So we, as a team, must have been doing something right.

The return of ITV to the sport has brought back an element of competition to boxing and that is great. In America in recent years, the TV companies have started calling the shots more and there are now a lot more great match-ups. There have been some vintage fights recently, involving all the top names like Oscar de la Hoya, Mayweather, Bernard Hopkins, Winky Wright and Jermaine Taylor. The Mickey Ward–Arturo Gatti trilogy was an all-time classic, as were the fights between Marco Antonio Barrera and Erik Morales and Jose Luis Castillo and Diego

Corrales. I hope that happens in Britain, because competition is good for boxing. It should lead to better shows, which means the fans get better value for money.

I was surprised when Gareth telephoned me after the Tszyu fight and said that it was all over the internet I had signed a deal to box for Frank Warren on ITV. Gareth asked me if I knew anything about it. I told him I didn't and it was agreed Gareth would contact ITV and let them know I had no contract with Frank Warren. If they wanted me to appear on ITV they would have to speak to me first and no-one else.

I didn't think Frank should even be discussing my future plans with the outside world until we had come to another deal, which, I might add, I fully expected us to do at the time. He was talking about my future and yet we had not even had any real discussion about it. It was the cocksure way he was doing it which made me sit up and take notice. It was as if I was the last person he would speak to about the finer details of the matter. I was just the boxer. All I had to do was sign on the dotted line.

For eight years I had taken this attitude that Frank knew best. He would present me with a contract and I would sign it, until the last couple of years when I was on a fight-by-fight deal. No discussion about what he was making and what I was making, just the contract. End of story. It shouldn't be like that. What other industry would conduct its business like that?

I was told by one reporter that Mark Sharman had said he had a contract with Frank Warren for me to fight for him. To which I remember replying, 'Frank might have a contract with Mark, but he hasn't got one with Ricky Hatton.'

I am convinced Mark thought Frank Warren still had a deal in place. He certainly appeared surprised when he was told there was no contract, and quite rightly so, as I am sure he thought I was a done deal. I have since been told by Gareth that he spoke to Mark Sharman and left him in absolutely no doubt that no contract existed between me and Frank Warren. Without blowing my own trumpet, I would have been the biggest catch for ITV. I put more bums on seats than anybody, including Amir Khan and Joe Calzaghe.

I never wanted it to come to this. I had started my career with Frank Warren and Billy Graham and I wanted to end my career with Frank and Billy. We had some great times, but unfortunately I am now left only with Billy.

A few friends told me I should not risk going to court to face Frank if it turned nasty and, bearing in mind I had never been in a courtroom in my life, it was not something I wanted to do. But when the offer for my next fight after Tszyu came along, I knew there was trouble brewing.

Frank only had to get near to what I had been offered by other promoters in order for me to accept it, because I just didn't want a battle. I didn't want to take Frank on, because he had done lots of good things in my career. Like I said, I would not have left Frank for money unless it was a ridiculous amount. Unfortunately, it was a ridiculous amount. Frank's offer was hundreds of thousands of pounds less than I was being tentatively offered elsewhere.

It was then decided in a series of meetings with Dad and Gareth that we would put the feelers out properly and see what other concrete offers we could get from other promoters. I soon realized that the majority of the money I could make would be from the TV companies. Gareth spoke to Sky's boss Vic Wakeling and he said they were prepared to put together a deal to keep me. Having just a straight deal with a TV company made sense because the money generated would come to me and there would be no fighting for percentages.

I was happy to go down this avenue but after considerable thought we decided we still needed a promoter to arrange a fight and it was at this time I started speaking to promoters both in Britain and America. The one thing that was agreed was that we would only sign a one-fight agreement. I know my dad was quite keen for this part of the deal, so that he could compare what we got to what Frank Warren had been offering.

Shortly after beating Tszyu, Carlos Maussa surprisingly got the better of Vivian Harris to win the WBA light-welterweight title. I was determined to try and get a crack at Maussa as this would unify two of the belts. Dad and Gareth spoke to Main Events in America and it was around this time that Dennis Hobson approached us.

Dennis Hobson from Sheffield was offering substantially more and said he could set up a unification fight with Carlos Maussa for his WBA belt. I listened to Dennis. I was the person in the ring putting my life on the line and I was out of contract. I had every right to listen to every offer that came

my way. I was adamant, though, that I wanted Maussa. Firstly,
he had just beaten Vivian Harris to win the WBA belt.
Secondly, it meant I would have another world title which
would keep the momentum going, and thirdly, I knew I would
beat him. I didn't want a straightforward fight. I wanted
another world champion and eventually I got it. I agreed in
principle to fight for Dennis but at the 11th hour Oscar de la
Hoya's Golden Boy Promotions also offered me a good deal
which came in £200,000 above Frank's offer. Having gone
quite far down the line with Dennis Hobson I decided the
best course of action was to go with him, especially as time
was dragging on and I was keen to fight as soon as possible.
Dennis also seemed a straight and genuine bloke, and I
needed that level of trust back. Full marks to Oscar de la
Hoya, though, he showed his interest and invited me to Las
Vegas for the Jermaine Taylor-Bernard Hopkins fight. I met
Oscar and was very impressed with him and in fact, at one
stage I was 95 per cent sure I would accept his offer. But
Dennis promised to deliver and we were prepared to wait for
him to put together a deal, which he did.

Frank knew I was speaking to other promoters and that is
when it really started to turn bitter. I understand he wrote to
all the major TV companies and promoters in Britain and
America telling them he had a contract with me and
threatened to sue any of them if they spoke to me. At this
time there was not one peace offering from him. It was just,
'Accept this and get on with it.'

Around this time Frank Warren was still speaking to my

dad but his offers were not matching up. My dad said it was not enough, simple as that. We never heard another peep from Frank until I got a solicitor's letter through my letterbox in Hyde saying unless we accepted he had a valid contract with me he would start proceedings against us for breach of contract. What fucking contract? We didn't have one. Frank was telling everyone and his wife he had a written agreement with me, but where was this agreement? Where was this contract? If he had one he would have whipped it out and that would have been that, but he didn't. Later on, he changed his story and said it was a verbal agreement with my dad. What complete horse-shit. My dad would never have verbally agreed to a contract with Frank Warren without discussing it with me first. Verbal agreement, as Jim Royle would say, my arse. When we got the letter both Dad and I were worried as we had never had anything like this happen to us in our lives. What made matters worse was the fact that Gareth was in Dubai on holiday. Fortunately Dad managed to contact him and he reassured him that he would sort it out when he got back. In fact, his exact words were, 'It is a load of bollocks, don't worry about it.'

Frank then accused me of being greedy in his column in the *News of the World*. He said he had made me £6 million in the ring from 39 fights and now, just as I was making some serious money, I had pulled the plug on him. The whole basis of the piece was how Frank had been wronged by a greedy, ungrateful, selfish little tosser like me, who would never have made it in boxing without his faithful, guiding hand.

I found his comments unbelievable. I don't really want to go into detail about what I have earned from boxing, but, believe me, it is nowhere near £6 million. Billy gets 10 per cent of what I earn and my dad looks after the rest. That's all I know.

Basically, Frank was plastering my private business all over the newspapers. He wouldn't in a million years want readers to know what he earns. I am sure he would say it was his own private matter and nobody else's. Why should I be any different? I don't go around asking people how much they earn, but all of a sudden the rules of common decency don't apply to Ricky Hatton because he has not accepted a contract which was worth hundreds of thousands of pounds less than he could have got elsewhere. Where is the fairness in that? Frank was just using his newspaper column to get his own back. But I am a nightmare to fight in the ring and I was not about to become an easy touch out of it. I think any normal person would have reacted the same way I did. By turning the other way.

I certainly didn't want a row with Frank and I definitely did not want to end up in court with him. I would have been perfectly happy walking away and saying, 'Thanks, but I am moving on now.' I said maybe we could stay friends and do business in the future, but Frank is a powerful man and powerful men have big egos. I think I dented his ego, because here was the kid who had made his debut in front of a couple of hundred fans in Widnes taking him on.

At the time I had made 15 WBU world title defences and I

can only imagine how much Frank made out of those fights. I always boxed in front of big crowds in those defences and it was always on live TV, so the figures must have been pretty good. Without putting too fine a point on it, I was Frank's biggest name. That's why he got the hump when I left him, because I was his regular business. The easy touch had turned around and bitten Frank on the arse.

Boxers are brave souls in a brutal sport, which is why it takes a lot to make me question a fellow fighter. We are the ones in the ring doing the entertaining, so why shouldn't we get paid top dollar? Of the 22,000 in the arena that night I fought Tszyu, I don't think there would be a single person who would say that I didn't earn my wages. They got entertained on a memorable night, but I am the one in there with Tszyu knowing that any little slip and my lights would be out.

What is important to me is that people understand that I am not a greedy bastard. I have never had anyone accuse me in my life of being greedy apart from Frank Warren. So where does the truth lie? I'll let you decide.

The row with Warren has opened my eyes to the way boxing works. It is a business just like any other. If I had lost two or three fights in a row Frank would have dropped me like a stone and every other top promoter out there would have done the same thing. As any boxer will tell you, if they lose a fight or two, they're on 50 per cent of what they were on previously; if they lose three in a row they're on the scrap-heap. Promoters chase the latest hot prospect and I understand and accept that. It goes with the territory. But talk from Frank about loyalty in boxing makes me want to laugh. Loyalty! You have got to be joking. Loyalty doesn't exist in boxing. It is a job. You get in there, do your best over a very short career and get out again. Most boxers in this country hardly earn a bean. They do it for the love of the job and a few free tickets to shows here and there.

The fact that I just happen to be a better fighter than average doesn't change the rules at all. I was loyal to Frank for years.

So, I decided to break away from Frank and I got significantly more for my next fight. I may as well tell you the figures before tax, seeing as my private finances have been all over the papers. Against Tszyu, my earnings were £1 million and against Maussa, a considerably smaller attraction, I got £1.9 million. For the Tszyu fight the live gate was 22,000 and for the Maussa fight it was 12,000. I accept that Tszyu would have had to have been paid very well in order to persuade him to come over to Britain and that would have affected my earnings, but, still, the figures don't add up. How can I have earned nearly double for fighting a far less glamorous opponent? I hope people realise that whatever purse offer I get I will be lucky if I end up with half that amount. You have to pay for trainers' expenses, sparring partners, air travel, accommodation, food, and then there are obviously taxes. I appreciate to the average person it sounds like winning the lottery and I accepted a huge amount of money, more than my mum and dad could ever have earned for years of hard graft, as boxing is classed in the same mould as the entertainment industry. I hope people also realise that it took me 15 years of hard work to get to this level.

The Tszyu fight was also very successful on pay-per-view on Sky, which will have generated a lot of money, especially as it was the fastest-selling ticket in British boxing history. But the figures don't lie.

As a free agent I was, and still am, entitled to earn as much money as I can during the short time I am in this career and so, I ask you, would you have turned down hundreds of thousands of pounds just to stay loyal? Would you have stayed loyal to somebody who announced you were fighting on ITV even though there was no contract between you? Would you have stayed loyal to somebody who made you a pathetic offer then sent you a letter threatening legal action? This was the person who had looked after my career and had seen me put my life on the line countless times, but when Frank Warren could not get his own way, regrettably legal action followed.

Dennis is an up-and-coming promoter who has done an excellent job with Sheffield's IBF light-heavyweight world champion Clinton Woods, getting him some great fights over the years, including Roy Jones Jnr and Glencoffe Johnson. I found him ambitious, great company and keen to be helpful. He runs a very professional outfit and I was happy with what he was telling me.

My relationship with Frank Warren was officially over. The little things had grown into big ones and the trust had gone. When that happens, you have got to just walk away. I went from being disappointed about Frank's reaction when he sent me the legal letter, to feeling seriously annoyed when the threats kept coming.

All I wanted was to leave him and go my own way. I didn't want to be the first Hatton ever to go to court, but eventually we realized we had to defend ourselves. We are not the sort of people to cower down to anyone. People kept telling me that we could not take on Frank Warren. A stack of reporters and friends told me Frank had an army of lawyers and would beat us. Frank Warren went on record saying he would stop the Maussa fight and some newspapers were reporting that the fight would not take place.

It was around this time I started spending more time with my solicitor than my trainer, which can't be right. Gareth remained confident about our case and repeatedly told me Frank Warren could not stop the fight. Then a bombshell dropped as Gareth phoned me on a Friday in late September and told me Frank had started injunction proceedings to stop the Maussa fight, but again he told me not to worry. Easier said than done, bearing in mind this is my job.

Despite his assurances I was concerned the fight might not take place and worried whether all the weeks in training would be for nothing.

A few weeks later, also on a Friday, I got another call from Gareth. He had just been told Frank Warren was no longer proceeding with the injunction. This was just three days before the injunction was set to be heard on the following Monday. My dad and Gareth went down to London and a judge formally dismissed the injunction. He ordered Frank

Warren to pay £40,000 towards my legal costs, which I understand came to about £80,000.

The first the judge knew about the injunction being withdrawn by Frank Warren was when he read about it in Saturday's *Times* newspaper. Thankfully, me and the judge had a weekend when we could both concentrate on other things. The case is due to be heard in October 2006.

It was the start of countless legal arguments and I try to stay as far away from them as possible. In fact, I don't even want to go into great detail about them because, while I am happy to outline why my relationship with Frank Warren turned sour, I am sure nobody is really interested in the countless court cases inflicted on us by him.

I wouldn't threaten legal action against anyone unless pushed to the very limit. What exactly is Frank trying to prove? I don't understand what his motivation is for spending thousands of pounds on taking me to court, because, whatever happens, I will never fight for him again. That much is not in any doubt.

Before I signed with Dennis Hobson, I had a few chats with Clinton Woods and he told me that he had never had any problems at all with his promoter and could not recommend him highly enough. After losing to Roy Jones, Clinton could have gone backwards, but Dennis kept him in there, and continued to do so even after he lost to Johnson. Eventually, all the hard work by boxer and promoter came off as Clinton won the IBF light-heavyweight title against Rico Hoye in another great night for British boxing.

A lot of the credit for that must go to Clinton, but some of it has to go to Dennis Hobson as well, because he kept his fighter in there with the big boys.

Dennis was very clear about the terms of the promotion in Sheffield, where I was to fight Carlos Maussa for the WBA light-welterweight belt. He spelt it out in language even an idiot like me could understand, basically saying if the live gate is this, I will get that. I know one thing: the money from the TV contract alone, before any gate receipts were added up, was more than I had been offered by Frank Warren.

Dennis had no difficulty in telling me how much he was making from the fight and he also told me how much Maussa was getting. But with Dennis it was just dead simple. This is what you are getting as a guaranteed figure and this is what you are getting with add-ons.

I sat down with Gareth and he advised me that it was a watertight deal so we told Dennis that if he could deliver, I would be there fighting for him against Maussa in November. I had got the fight I wanted, against a light-welterweight champ who owned the WBA belt. I also got paid very well, win, lose or draw. And I wasn't thinking of the latter two.

I had no problem with leaving Manchester for the fight. I had received a fair amount of criticism for fighting so often in Manchester, but, from day one, I have never had a problem with boxing at other venues. I love fighting in front of my home crowd, but, equally, it doesn't really bother me if I am elsewhere. I don't want to sound ungrateful about this –

Manchester is my home and my best moments as a pro have happened there, in front of thousands of daft Mancunians, all having a great night out – but when you are actually in the ring it doesn't make naff all difference whether I am in Manchester or Morecambe. You hear the crowd when you walk into the ring and after that, you just concentrate on getting the job done.

I had fought in Newcastle and London fairly recently and now I was going to be performing in Sheffield, Dennis Hobson's home patch. Frank Warren had secured an exclusive deal with the MEN Arena in Manchester, so that was a non-starter and, to be honest, it didn't really bother me. I knew the people who loved to come to my fights wouldn't think twice about going to Sheffield and I was lucky enough to know that they would follow me anywhere. The only downside to the build-up for the fans was Frank's injunction to try to get the fight stopped, which I suspect made a lot of people think twice before shelling out a lot of money for hotels and an event they did not know would go ahead. I can't blame them for that, because I would have been the same.

The Hallam Arena, as it turned out, was sold out, which just goes to show what a fantastic set of fans I am lucky enough to have. I was absolutely determined to repay them with a cracking performance.

In the weeks prior to the fight I had been getting more and more wound up with Frank Warren's regular snipes at me in the *News of the World*. Funnily enough, it is a paper I read, as it is good on boxing and has Fred Burcombe writing for it, a bloke who I have a lot of time for. But every week, Frank's column just droned on about how he had been hard done by and this was why and that was why. In fact, I started reading Frank's column to my son Campbell for his bedtime stories and all I can say is, it worked a treat; he went out like a light.

I kept quiet most of the time, but in the press conference before the fight I said I had heard enough. All I wanted was for Frank Warren to get on with his life and let me get on with mine. Regardless of all the threats made about cancelling the show, my supporters packed the place out. A lot of credit for that must go to Dennis Hobson, who stuck by his guns and, as I have found out, is not intimidated by anyone. It is like water off a duck's back to him. It was a difficult time for Dennis and my head was also in bits, but we came through it together.

I told a lot of press boys and my friends that I was blanking the whole situation out of my life, but, as Mum and Dad would tell you, I would go home and the conversation invariably got round to Frank Warren and what he had done. He was constantly on my mind and I kept asking myself what I had done wrong.

All I heard from Frank's corner in the build-up to Maussa was what a money-grabbing, ungrateful little shit I was and my response was to refuse to allow that to affect my boxing. I suppose Frank's plan had worked in some ways. He had wound me up and I knew that. But I also knew that I was a professional fighter and that other boxers had suffered similar run-ins in their careers. I just had to show some bollocks, get him out of my mind and beat the crap out of Maussa. I wanted people to be reading about me unifying the belts, not what Frank Warren had to say.

I got talking to Billy and all my other trainers and advisers and they were all in agreement: if I lost to Maussa, Frank Warren would be pissing himself laughing. I used our row as an extra incentive, but, believe me, when I was in that ring in Sheffield I felt I was fighting Carlos Maussa and Frank Warren. I wanted to take Maussa's fucking head off.

As for training, that went fine. I was worked up, but it didn't do me any real harm in the gym. A few nights I had trouble sleeping, but I am a pretty deep sleeper anyway, so generally I was OK.

But it had bothered me and I was dying to lash out. In the fight, my carelessness nearly cost me dear. The tone for the evening was set when I came out of the changing rooms to a different tune than 'Blue Moon' for the first time. I decided on the day to play the old hit 'Gonna Get Along Without You Now' and I don't really think I need to explain why. In fact, I started crying when I got into the arena as everything had got on top of me. We also thought about using Sister Sledge's awful song 'Frankie' but quickly ditched that idea! I went into the fight nowhere near as relaxed as I wanted to be and I got caught. Twice.

The first time was a clash of heads that I felt was deliberate on his part. My lanky opponent had a very odd style and one of the strangest things about it was that when he moved forward, he dropped his head and kind of charged in. Like an idiot, I threw a punch and the next thing I knew my head had been sliced open. The second cut, another bad one, was my fault. I threw a left shot and he stumbled in and, like a stupid beginner, I left my head out to dry. Again, Maussa saw his chance to use his head and, whack, my eye was cut. By leaving his head in the firing line, then moving forward, I had been cut badly twice in the opening exchanges. The first one was a head butt Denis Law would have been proud of. The second was as much my fault as his.

I wasn't going to start crying about it, as this is boxing, not playing in the sandpit. I suppose if you can do it and get away with it, then fine. Maussa got away with it and was brilliant with his head. The rest of his boxing skills weren't quite so sharp and never at any time in the fight did I feel that I might lose. I don't think I even lost a round and I knew as the rounds wore on that Maussa was getting weaker.

The referee, Mickey Vann, never even gave my eyes a second glance and, although they were badly cut, I don't think there was ever a suggestion that the fight would be stopped. Mick Williamson, the best cuts man in the business, did a fantastic job on them. After the fight, I had to have four stitches above the right eye and nine above the left, which made it double figures in total. But the cut I suffered against Jono Thaxton was far bigger and deeper.

Within an hour of me coming out of the ring, Mr Hodson, a plastic surgeon at the Sheffield Infirmary, had already started work on my injuries, I can only thank Dennis Hobson for getting him and the plastic surgeon, who didn't even charge me for the work.

The only drama in the fight was the cuts I suffered, because I was pissing every round. This was a Ricky Hatton fight at its best, a show where you did not know what was going to happen next. I knew from the crowd's reaction that they were loving it. I suppose the cuts problem just underlined the fact that my fights are always exciting, edge-of-the-seat stuff, but could I have done without it, sure I could. But then I wouldn't be Mr Entertainment!

I didn't feel as though Maussa was making much headway in the rounds that followed the early exchanges and I felt as though I was leading by a long margin, despite the fact that his odd style made it difficult to catch up with him. The force of his punches wasn't anything special and Maussa wasn't causing me any major problems, but, of course, that is when a fighter can often screw it up, by getting too cocky and over-confident. I wasn't going to let that happen.

By about the sixth round the cuts, thanks to Mick, had pretty much cleared up, although I had a bit of a chuckle at the end of one round when Mick told me the cuts were fine now because I didn't have any blood left in my body. In a sense the cuts made me a little more cautious, which, bearing in mind my mood before the fight, was exactly what I needed.

What I did make sure of was that I didn't leave my head anywhere near the danger zone, as I had already found out how good Maussa was with his bonce. I think the cuts spurred him on for a little while and he kept trying to throw big overhand shots, without much success.

I think against Maussa I showed again that I have become

technically a much better fighter and I have matured in the ring, as I felt very relaxed about it all. I was busy working Maussa and his horrible, awkward style out. I could still see Frank Warren on Maussa's shoulders and as a result I was a bit over-eager and fired up, but having been in there with Kostya Tszyu, I also felt very confident about my ability to beat Maussa.

Maussa was a bit like Phillips and Tony Pep in that he was so lanky and I think his extra height made me miss a few times when I had him lined up. I kept catching him at the end of a punch and not with the really meaty part of the swing, but he was constantly on the back foot and I kept telling myself to be patient, it will come. Maussa was expending loads of energy avoiding me and I was getting closer to nailing him in every round. I missed with one shot, which would have taken his head off, by about two inches.

Then the end came in the ninth round and, boy, was it fucking sweet. Maussa kept circulating to the right when he threw a right lead. Then he would go to the right again. I noticed this happen a couple of times and while the fight was progressing I locked it away, ready to pounce.

Maussa fired a right at me and I feinted to move right, but instead took a step to the left. It was beautiful as it opened him up as a target, so what did I do? Exactly what I had trained for for weeks. I took a run up to him and threw everything I had at his whiskers, the same punch Floyd Patterson used to call his gazelle punch. This time the angles were perfect and I caught Maussa flush on the chops. He dropped like a stone and not for one second did I think he had a cat in hell's chance of getting up. I went to a neutral corner and Maussa, to give him credit, managed to get one of his gloves onto the middle rope, but that was about as much as he could muster. His body had had enough. The punch I had caught him with was too good. As soon as the ref called it over I jumped with joy, happy in the knowledge I had won two world titles in two fights.

It had taken Miguel Cotto eight rounds to stop Maussa, one better than me, but that fight had been stopped on cuts, whereas I had demolished him. I had truly bashed him up and, in my book, had not lost a round. The fact that I had beaten Maussa much more impressively than one of my rivals made me even more chuffed with the night's work.

Vivian Harris had thrown a lot of shots at Maussa and they had had no effect, so to KO someone with a granite chin like that was a great feeling and a massive weight off my shoulders. I felt I was proving again that I was the No.1 light-welterweight in the world. There could surely now be no disputing the fact that I was the best, having beaten Tszyu, the widely recognized No.1 and then Maussa, the WBA champion.

After the fight I had my cuts properly treated by a plastic surgeon, who we had decided to employ on the basis that if you deal with cuts immediately after they have opened, using a specialist, the long-term damage should be minimal.

That night at the after-show party, which on this occasion I was invited to, I celebrated in traditional style until the early hours and I felt I deserved it.

THE WELTERWEIGHT

What a year 2005 was! And that Christmas, the celebrations at my new house were legendary! After the Maussa fight I decided I needed to unwind, so I threw a party at my new home, just a few hundred yards from where I had lived with Mum and Dad. It was for family and close friends, to say thank you for their support. At the age of 26 I thought it was about time I flew the coop and so I bought a slightly run-down house in Gee Cross, just outside Hyde, and set my building mates to work! Lofty, a long-time friend of the family and the person who first sponsored me during my amateur days as a boxer, got his boys to work and what a job they did on it. My house has been described as every bloke's dream home.

Basically it is like a tardis. From the outside it doesn't look too flash, but it seems to get bigger and bigger once you get inside. First up, I have a garage, which houses my Del Boy Reliant Robin three-wheeler. The car is full of Del Boy stuff, from Only Fools and Horses right down to the blow-up doll in the passenger seat and the furry dice. It is actually taxed, otherwise I wouldn't be able to drive it, but it has the 'tax in post' sticker on the dashboard. Fortunately it also works. There is one garage near me which sells old four-star petrol so whenever it needs filling up I just go around there for a spin.

I love taking it out for a drive and I always wear my Del Boy sheepskin coat whenever I let it loose on the roads of Manchester. Obviously, the looks I get when I am driving around are priceless. You get kids stopping in the street with their eyes popping out and the mums and dads look like they have seen a ghost. Unfortunately, many of the locals know me, so it doesn't have quite the same effect with them. I take the car out of the garage and it is just, 'Oh, here comes Ricky again, driving around pretending to be Del Boy.'

I love everything about the programme and can recite whole episodes word for word. What a boring sod I must be! I have even got a poster signed by all the principal actors, which is quite hard to get hold of, as Lennard Pearce, who played Grandad, signed very few authentic mementos of his time in the series.

My garden is fairly small, but it is big enough for a row of terracing from Manchester City's old Maine Road ground. Like any daft City fan, it was just something I had to have!

My home is a shrine to signed memorabilia. I have my favourite movie posters signed by the actors and actresses and my favourite sports heroes are everywhere. There's a trophy cabinet with all my cups and belts, of course, and I also have the original signed boxing gloves and wraps from my days as an amateur all the way through to my professional career. I don't really know why, but I am a memento nutcase and always have been.

My place is like walking into a sporting version of the Hard Rock Café, as there isn't a wall which has got any space free. I have already mentioned my Wayne Rooney and George Best memorabilia, but I have got stacks of stuff from other celebrities. A lot is to do with Manchester City, of course, but there are loads from others, ranging from Ali to Madonna, Robert de Niro to Elvis Presley.

But I suppose it is fair to say that it is the games room which makes blokes want to move in with me the next day. I have a darts board, reclining chair, a pool table and, of course, a personal fridge in which to put my cold drinks. In fact, I have even got a bottle of whisky which was made especially for me when I beat Carlos Maussa with the words 'Ricky Hatton – World Champion' written on the side instead of 'Famous Grouse'! I don't want to sound ungrateful, because it was a cracking present, but I don't really drink whisky.

In one corner of the games room is the famous Ricky Hatton

karaoke machine, which comes out on special occasions. Christmas at my home is always open house and, boy, was the one in 2005 a humdinger. Basically, everyone I know and a few others came round and we got stuck into a few shandies. When we had had a few – and on this occasion even my dad enjoyed a couple of beers – the karaoke box came out. Everyone was belting out their favourite tunes and the neighbours must have thought Glastonbury was going on next door. Fortunately, my neighbours are very understanding and I think, although for obvious reasons I am not sure, they joined in.

I managed to murder a few Frank Sinatra numbers and then Elvis Presley got a bit of a pasting. There is a sign outside my home saying 'Welcome to Heartbreak Hotel – reserved parking – Elvis' which always gives people a chuckle. While I don't think I am the worst singer in the world, I am certainly not the best either, but with a couple of beers inside me, it doesn't seem to matter. I bought so much booze I think the last of it went three months later, but we certainly drank enough that Christmas to keep the local Threshers in business for a couple of years.

I had earned a proper party after beating two world champions and, with my family and friends celebrating with me, it was a really happy time.

For a while I could forget the problems I had been having with Frank Warren, but I knew they would resurface again after the New Year. In January I got a call from Gareth telling me I had to attend a federal court in New York to give evidence. Proceedings had been brought against me by Soulamayne M'Baye, alleging that he should have fought Carlos Maussa instead of me.

I spent a week in New York, again spending more time with lawyers than with my trainer, only this time it was in America. It was still the same legal bullshit to me.

Once again, despite all the grief, we had a successful outcome. The case was stopped on the first morning, although I did have to give evidence to the court, which was far worse than anything I have ever experienced in the ring.

At the time I was falling out spectacularly with Frank Warren. He had just taken up a promotional deal with M'Baye, who at the time was the WBA's No. 1 challenger.

My dad was worried I was spending a week in New York when I should have been starting up another training camp, but he was sure I would be looked after by Gareth, who was considered a good influence.

However, one night Gareth must have regretted being with me as we went for a meal in Times Square. We decided to have a few pints then went outside to check out another bar when completely without warning a stranger ran up to Gareth from behind, punched him and ran off before either of us could do anything. Gareth's attacker, who didn't try to steal money or jewellery, left my solicitor looking more like a boxer than me. He had broken his nose and left him with a nasty cut above his eye. Needless to say, on the plane coming home the stewardesses assumed I was the trainer and Gareth the fighter.

As the year turned, I spent an hour or so a day in the gym,

just getting a bit of a sweat going, safe in the knowledge that I wasn't looking at another fight until around April or May, in order to let the cuts I had suffered against Maussa heal properly.

I was enjoying life to the full before the annual Hatton family cruise in January 2006. Anything from a dozen to 20 of us go away every year to unwind and this year was no different. It is usually the whole Hatton clan, plus a few close friends, and we always have a whale of a time. Cruising in the Caribbean is not for everyone, but it is perfect for me, even though it is fair to say I don't exactly tan easily! I basically go a bit pinker, that's all, but it is very relaxing and I love sitting around the pool deck doing bugger all for a change. Needless to say, the evenings are a bit more lively.

I got back in late January and the preparations were already being made for my next fight, this time in America. We had been negotiating for a while with a number of US organizations and promoters and, after lots of talks, I ended up going with HBO – the massive American Home Box Office TV company.

HBO's boss, Kerry Davis, badly wanted me on his channel and was prepared to pay big money for me to fight for them. It was all very flattering for a kid from a very run-of-the-mill Manchester suburb and, after plenty of negotiations between HBO and Dennis Hobson, my dad and Gareth Williams, we came up with a deal. Unfortunately, like many deals, it hit a few snags on the way. It seemed all the prospective opponents HBO had come up with were either not available, injured or not interested. We went through a whole list of them.

Essentially, HBO were not interested in putting me in with a massive name like Mayweather or Gatti yet. They wanted to build me up, which was fair enough. What they wanted was for my first headline fight in America to be a taster of what was to come. But they also wanted me to take on someone useful in order for the fight not to be dismissed by critics as an easy option. I was perfectly happy with this, as the days when I was put in a ring with opponents who were not in my league were now over.

We tried a number of fighters, but the one my management put forward, Australian-based Naoufel Ben Rabah, my No.1 mandatory challenger for the IBF light-welterweight title I had won in beating Maussa, was not acceptable to HBO as they believed he wasn't box office enough. We went through many names before settling on Carlos Baldomir, the experienced Argentine who had just beaten Zab Judah for the linear welterweight title. It seemed like a good idea, but then the fight was off before it even started as Baldomir began talking telephone numbers to take me on.

Next up was Juan Lazcano, who seemed to fit the bill perfectly. He was highly ranked, he was good and he was acceptable to all sides. Then, about seven weeks before the fight, he got injured and the deal was off.

The last name on HBO's list for their next available date – 13 May – was Luis Collazo, the New Yorker of Puerto Rican background who was the reigning WBA welterweight champion, having beaten Jose Rivera on a close decision in 2005. It seemed Collazo was pretty much the last option I had.

Collazo was a southpaw – the last I had fought were Eamonn Magee and Joe Hutchinson – and tough. He was taller than me, with a longer reach, and I knew it was going to be a difficult battle. Little did I know how difficult. Billy Graham didn't fancy it from the start and I could understand why. He argued that I made the 10 stone limit easily, so why move up to 10 stone 7 lbs? I would be giving my opponent an immediate advantage. It made sense. Every fighter has a natural weight and mine seemed to have settled at 10 stone. I had fought at that weight throughout my career, was comfortable with it and I felt like a light-welter.

Nobody put a gun to my head, so I weighed all the options and basically it came down to this: either I fought Collazo or I would be forced to sit by and wait for the next available opponent to come along, which could be months later. After much thought, I decided to go for it. It was either that or I would miss the 13 May date. I didn't want to do that as the Maussa fight had taken place in November and I have always been a boxer who likes to go to work on a regular basis.

As it turned out, Collazo probably gave me more problems than any fighter has ever done in my career.

It was easily as hard as the Kostya Tszyu fight because of Collazo's style. He was a counter-punching southpaw, which I was always going to find difficult to deal with. Any boxer who fights like me needs a Collazo like a hole in the head, but at the same time, what sort of champion are you if you only face fighters who are made for your style? I could not live with that. I would never be prepared to say no to a certain style of fighter, purely on the basis that it would be advantageous for me to steer clear of him. If I did that, what right would I have to claim I was the best in the world?

There was a lot of talk before the fight that it was an opponent who was thrust on me, which was not the case. He was the only person who all sides were happy with and who was available, but I wouldn't go into the ring against anyone I didn't think I could beat and I certainly felt I could get the better of Collazo, even though I knew it would be a bruising night.

It was my debut as a headliner in America and, in a perfect world, I would not have wanted that style of fighter, but I was put in a position where other opponents had pulled out, so I felt I had to take it.

A few weeks before the fight, the venue was moved from Foxwoods casino in the middle of nowhere in Connecticut to the Boston Garden, where the famous Boston Celtics play basketball. I had gone to Foxwoods a month or so before facing Collazo for a press conference and I was glad it was moved. Foxwoods is a great casino, but as for its surroundings, let me put it this way, it is alright if you're into squirrel-watching, otherwise you are knackered. There was nothing there at all. It was stuck in the middle of a field, miles from anywhere.

I know my supporters would travel to the other side of the world to see me, but I would rather they got somewhere a bit livelier for their money.

Boston was much better – a proper city with plenty of

bright lights and, more importantly, Irish pubs. It would be the first big world championship fight in Boston for 25 years, since Marvin Hagler, who came from nearby Worcester, fought Vito Antuofermo for the middleweight title. I found it strange that such a huge city had waited so long to stage another big fight, but then the casinos in Atlantic City and Las Vegas and New York's Madison Square Garden now seem to have something of a monopoly on big fights.

My training went as well as planned for Collazo, except, of course, there was one main difference. I would be moving up to welter. Kerry Kayes was happy that I would be fine at the weight as, although I make the 10 stone limit easily, I always go into the ring on fight night weighing 11 stone 2 lbs. But as anyone in boxing will tell you, you should take time to build up to a higher weight, sometimes by taking a couple of easier fights to adjust. Straight after the weigh-in, I will eat like a horse and on the morning of the fight I will always have my usual full English fry-up of sausages, bacon, eggs, mushrooms, beans, fried bread, black pudding, tea and toast. I spoke to the hotel beforehand about my special needs on the day of the fight and they managed everything apart from the black pudding, as there is no such thing in America! The hotel staff looked a bit stunned when I told them what black pudding consisted of.

Anyway, everything had gone as smoothly as I would have hoped and I had made the 10 stone 7 lbs limit on the nose with no problems, as did Collazo. In the press conference before the fight, he whipped out a six-pack . . . of Guinness that is. He said he had heard I liked a drop of the black stuff. I thanked him for the gesture and said we could share them after the fight, only to be told by Luis that he didn't drink!

I wasn't taking the fight lightly, though, as some people have suggested. You can't cut corners in boxing and I wasn't about to start at the age of 27. I had trained as hard, over 10 weeks, as I had for any match-up and I was ready for anything Luis Collazo could throw at me. I trained just as intensively as I usually do, but I had less time as I had to appear at a court case in New York against Frank Warren.

Collazo had won his title by beating Jose Rivera, who a week before we met had managed to win the WBA light-middleweight title, so I was facing a difficult task.

Unfortunately, in the lead-up to the Collazo fight I had to relinquish both world titles I had won against Tszyu and Maussa, which is a terrible shame. In an ideal world you want to win and lose your titles in the ring, but boxing is far from an ideal world. I had to give up the titles because I was moving up a weight and therefore not fighting the relevant mandatory challengers.

It pissed down with rain all week in Boston, so I stayed cooped up in my hotel room most of the time, bored shitless. I was getting very restless. We went to a baseball game in Boston to see the Red Sox, but it all seemed very odd and after a few minutes we got up and left. Basically, I was just dying to get the fight over and done with because I knew it was going to be a hell of a night. And I was right – it was a blood and guts battle from start to finish.

The journey to the arena was made in the kind of weather Manchester would have been proud of. It absolutely poured down, to the extent that on the Sunday, the day after the fight, a state of emergency was announced in many parts of Massachusetts as they had endured so much rain.

Paul Speak put up the English flag with my name written on it and I played my usual Stone Roses and Oasis music full-blast in the training room. About two hours before I was due on, I was delighted when my brother Matthew managed to secure a split decision points win over a tough opponent.

Half of Manchester seemed to come into my changing room that night, which I loved. It sounds daft, but I think it is great when my pals come into my dressing room before my fights, and start telling me to put on a show. Other fighters would hate it, but I have always enjoyed it, so why change now?

My time was coming and I was ready. This is when it hits you. These are the moments when you realize you have to earn your living. And I love those minutes before a big fight. I walked to the ring to 'Blue Moon' in front of about 7,000 fans, most of whom were cheering for me. Collazo came out ten minutes later and I was desperate to get down to business. There was a two-minute period of silence for former world heavyweight champion Floyd Patterson, who had died during the week, and then it was time to get down and dirty.

I was pumped up and I could see Collazo, who seemed a blur of tattoos, fancied his chances as well. He was a decent person, who I liked when I spoke to him before and after the fight, but this was our living. This is what we do to look after our families.

Within 12 seconds of the bell I had him on the floor with a peach of a left hook. It was a great connection, right at the end of my swing. Collazo didn't look in any real trouble, just shocked, but I knew I had to drive home my advantage. I went after him and I felt I was getting through in both of the first two rounds, but then, as the fight unravelled, I knew Collazo was coming more into it. Some of his shots were very hard and very hurtful, so I had to just hit back with some of my own. I felt I had wrestled out a pretty good lead by the middle rounds, but I wasn't boxing with my usual rhythm and I knew Collazo was throwing me around the ring with his bigger physique. I definitely felt his extra power at welterweight, even though when I got in the ring I was slightly heavier than him. Usually, I can throw my weight around and no boxer has been able to out-muscle me, but I couldn't really do that with Collazo as he was just too big and strong.

However, I was pretty confident, as I felt I was two or three rounds ahead going into the middle and later rounds, but I would be the first to admit he was having some success as well. When he caught me with a few shots, I would always try and counter them straight away because I didn't want him catching up. Collazo would then rally a bit, so I would respond. It was like that – a sort of cat-and-mouse game – for round after round, but I knew I was just edging it, thanks to the start I had enjoyed.

I dug him in the stomach a few times with my trademark

body shots, but the punches seemed to have little effect, so I concentrated more on the head.

I wanted to pull away that little bit more and Billy told me to start upping my work rate to ensure we were not on the bad end of a wrong decision. Collazo was a clever fighter, though, because throughout our battle he would use different tactics. At first he would open up and welt me with a few, then he would go on the move, pawing at me with his jab, then back again. He was a lot better than people gave him credit for and I can confidently predict he will be around at the top level for many years to come.

The strength of his shots regularly swung my head from side to side and in the 12th round I was in trouble. He caught me with a cracking combination and, while you could see I had my faculties with me all the time, I was holding and grabbing, knowing that he was landing some heavy stuff. I think the way I handled it, to hold on to him, close the gap and weather the storm, showed that even while I was shipping a few blows, I was still in control of myself.

It was not just in the last round either that he hurt me. He caught me with several big shots throughout the fight and the weight of the punches was a shock to me. I wasn't in any real trouble of going down in the 12th round, but I was surprised by how much harder he hit. I felt stronger than him, but I could sense the difference. It was significant.

I think as a champion you have to recover from adversity. Since becoming a fighter, I have been knocked down and come back. I beat Ben Tackie by boxing his ears off on the back foot. Years before, in Detroit, I came back and won after being given one round to finish off my opponent. Against Collazo, I feel I managed to get the 'W' next to my name by doing it a different way again.

As a champion you have to be able to deal with everything which is thrown at you and I feel I have done that over my career. I think that makes me a true champion in every sense of the word.

The fact that I had to put up with so much from Frank Warren's continual legal challenges before the Maussa and Collazo fights has made me, I believe, a much stronger person. I was dealing with a major problem in the ring, but an awful lot outside of it as well.

Collazo threw everything at me at the start of the last round, but by halfway through I felt I was recovering and so I let him have a few of my own. I caught him with a cracking right hand towards the end, which I know shook him and, when the bell went, I felt I had done enough, even though he had won the 12th.

The ring was packed with people and Collazo's corner were saying they had nicked it, but throughout the fight I had been getting information back to me that I was always a couple of rounds ahead. Just before the announcement was made, I found out I had won and so I leant through the ropes and shouted at Steve Collins, the former world champion who was there for the fight, that I had done it. He gave me the full clenched-fist salute and I knew it was in the can even before the MC, Michael Buffer, hollered out the words, 'And the new . . .'

Buffer went through the scorecard and I had won it 115–112, 115–112 and 114–113 – a unanimous decision. I knew it had not exactly been vintage Ricky Hatton, but I had come through a nightmare of an opponent on foreign soil and won the WBA welterweight title on the first occasion that I had moved up to 10 stone 7 lbs. Not even Floyd Mayweather could claim that.

I had some fairly heavy bruising around my left eye and before leaving the ring I made sure I told Collazo what a cracking fighter he was. Naturally, he looked disappointed and he was constantly asking for a rematch. My only response was to say that we had just fought 12 amazing rounds, so let's sit on that for a few days before deciding our futures.

Collazo had given me my toughest fight to date and, when I went back to the dressing room, I could feel it. I had a banging headache for about an hour. It slowly wore off, but I could feel I had been in a war. My arms and chest ached and, if I was in a bad state, I knew Collazo would be feeling the same way because I hit him with some serious stuff. Kerry gave me some of his super magic shakes which are packed full of energy and vitamins to help me recover.

The plastic surgeon inspected me after the fight and said to me, with a stern expression on his face, 'Ricky, you have broken your nose.' I laughed and said, 'Get away. I think you'll find I first broke it when I was about 13!'

The surgeon, called Sheldon Savignon, is famous for having all sorts of celebrity clients and despite the fact he had no real work to do, I was once again grateful to my promoter for having him there, just in case.

Steve Collins came in and said he had me three rounds ahead going into the final round and asked me what the fuck was I doing trying to knock Collazo out in the last 30 seconds of the fight. I just said, 'I am daft as a brush, but that is the way I box. I always like to finish in charge!'

After a couple of hours, I went to the after-fight press conference and said I would take a rematch with Collazo, but only if all things were agreed between all parties. Don King, Collazo's promoter, seemed to take the defeat OK, but even he was pressing me to say I would immediately agree to a rematch. Bearing in mind it was straight after the fight, I wasn't in a mood to agree to anything. All I wanted was to wind down with a few beers at the post-fight party.

King is a funny bloke, I will give him that, and after the fight I found out he was waving a little Union Jack flag when Collazo was knocked down in the first round. As the fight wore on and Collazo came into it, out came the American and Puerto Rican flags. Typical Don! At the end, when the scores were announced, guess what? Yep. Out came the British flag again.

King cracked his usual jokes about meeting the Queen if we could get the rematch on in Manchester and I just said what I believed was the truth, that I had done enough to win it. Mind you, I would be the first to accept it was very close and Collazo taught me what I probably already knew – that my natural weight was 10 stone.

At the press conference, there were some accusations that it was a dirty fight and that I was a dirty boxer. I said that in future I wouldn't try to hold him and smother him, but what I would do is just stand there and let him hit me. I don't think the Americans, who, let's face it, are not exactly big on irony, got the joke. It wasn't a dirty fight at all, in my opinion. It was boxing and sometimes it gets a bit messy in there. Luis wasn't an angel and I would be the first to admit that neither am I in the ring.

The press boys accepted it was a close fight and some of them had Collazo winning, but the judges had the best view and they were unanimous, so there is not much else that matters. There were some suggestions that HBO wanted me to win and the judges were in their pocket, but these theories always exist in boxing and they are just plain rubbish. Judges give their scores on what they see and most of the time they are in agreement. All three were in agreement on this occasion, so I didn't see where the controversy was. I felt I had always had my nose slightly in front and the judges agreed with me.

By the time I got to the after-fight party it was already 1.30 a.m. and the hotel we were in stopped serving at 2 a.m., so we all went back to my hotel, the Hyatt, and got stuck into the mini bars. I needed to be surrounded by friends and family and they all agreed it was a ballsy performance by me. Even Billy, who hadn't wanted the fight in the first place, was relieved and Kerry told me I had gone from being a good champion to a great one. His logic was that I had won when it would have been easier to lose and I thank him for saying that.

I don't know about being a great champion, but I know you have to find a way sometimes and I managed that.

While I wound down with a few beers after the fight and met the English press Sunday lunchtime, it was Sunday evening when the fun really started. After so many weeks in the gym I let my hair down properly, knowing that I had done the job. The sad part was that I knew that if I were to move back down to light-welter I would have to relinquish yet another belt, but unfortunately I believe that is the way boxing is going. Belts and titles are what all boxers are chasing after when they first start fighting. All I was interested in as a little kid was becoming a world champion, but nowadays it is not so simple. The TV companies, certainly in America, are no longer that interested in belts. Sure, if there is a belt on the line they will take it, but it is not the be-all and end-all. HBO were pleased Collazo had a belt, but it didn't mean that much to them either. They felt he was the right fighter for me and the fact that he had a WBA title was good news, but not essential. It is increasingly going that way in the US as the TV companies feel they have been held to ransom too often in the past by the various sanctioning bodies.

It is strange, though, because the one ambition you have as a young fighter is to be called a world champion, but then, when you get it, the politics of boxing is such that it doesn't mean that much. There are so many belts that the public are confused, so what the TV companies say is, 'Sod the belts, we just want the best fights.' I have some sympathy with that, because all the paying public wants to see are the best boxers fighting the best boxers and if that is the only way it can be done, fair enough.

That is the way boxing is going nowadays and I can't see it changing. I would have preferred to take on my world title mandatory challengers, but nobody was prepared to pay for it, so that left me with little option. I had had to shed blood to win the world title against Kostya Tszyu and, to a lesser extent, against Maussa, so it was a massive shame that I had to give them up voluntarily. Any fighter worth his salt would say the same thing. I imagine everyone who loves boxing thinks along the same lines as me: that it would be great for the sport to have a single world champion in all the weight divisions.

I returned to Manchester for a few days to recover and then I took Campbell to Florida for a holiday. I felt I had earned it and it was great to spend some time with my little boy. I hadn't conquered America by any stretch, but I had shown that I meant business.

While Collazo wasn't exactly my best performance it wasn't my worst either and, bearing in mind the legal disputes we had been having with Frank Warren, some people were surprised I had even managed to step into the ring at all. But I had beaten Collazo and, if Campbell ever has any kids, I can sit my grandchildren on my knee and bore them with tales of how I was a three-time world champion at two different weights and had beaten the linear world title holder in Kostya Tszyu.

THE SPORT I LOVE

T he man in the street goes to work, be it in a factory or an office. I go to a gym. That is the main difference between me and every single person reading this book. There are other differences, of course. Most people don't do their jobs in front of thousands of people, but essentially that is it. I don't consider myself special in any way, just different. I happen to be better at my job than other fighters, but that doesn't make me special.

Since the age of about 11, the only thing I have ever been any good at has been boxing. I suppose I was OK at football, but other than that I wasn't much good at anything else. Even when I had that brief period of going fishing, I can't ever remember catching any fish! Boxing takes up my whole life. I am in the gym every day, even if I am not preparing for a fight.

If I didn't go down the gym every day it would feel very strange. My brother Matthew is the same. About midday we always surface in the gym, have a chat in the changing rooms then get down to business, taking the piss out of each other all the time.

I suppose a lot of fighters make unwise comebacks because they go from one extreme to the other. One minute they are in the gym, training religiously, the next it is all taken away from them and, understandably, they miss it. They then make comebacks which usually, although not always, are a wrong move.

Boxing has given me such a great life and I will forever be grateful for that. I absolutely love the sport and, yes, if my boy Campbell wants to take up fighting, I will definitely let him, because I am a firm believer that the positives in the sport outweigh the negatives. Boxing has made me a very happy person and has opened up many new experiences for me. I can even inflict my after-dinner speaking talents on the nation!

I never wanted to be second best at boxing. From the day I first started getting serious and laced up a glove, I only ever wanted to be No.1. Second place doesn't interest me. I don't have a clue why I was given the natural talent to be good at boxing, but I am not going to waste it. Some fighters aren't like that, but I was from the day I stopped pissing around and began to realize I was lucky enough to have some natural ability. Billy tells me he knew I was going to be a world champion from the minute I first stepped into his gym. I don't know about that, but I know I wanted to be a world champion and was prepared to do just about anything to make it.

I have learnt over the years that the sport can be a force for so much good. I go to gyms all the time where there are kids who without boxing would be fucking about on the streets, nicking milk bottles off doorsteps and making a nuisance of themselves. They have too much energy. What better way is there to get kids to use up their extra energy than getting them down the gym? Or out playing football or cricket or any sport for that matter.

Boxing has set me up very well for the rest of my life and it all started with a scrawny kid going to a kickboxing class because he worshipped Bruce Lee! Without any doubt, when I finish I will remain in the sport in some capacity. I get a massive buzz from helping to train my brother Matthew or doing his corner for a fight. We have another lad in Billy's gym, Birmingham's Matthew Macklin, who is going to go a very long way and, again, I love training with him and helping him in any way I can. Being a trainer and making a champion can be almost as good as being a fighter and I know Billy loves his job. When I pack up as a pro, I already have plans to open up a gym in some part of Manchester and use it to try to develop the champions of tomorrow. Passing on my knowledge to youngsters is very rewarding and it is something I would like to pursue, because I feel the experiences I have had, when passed on, would be invaluable. When you have been fighting for over 15 years, you do pick up things about boxing and, without wanting to sound like a know-it-all, I like passing that on. I wouldn't want to make any young fighter a Ricky Hatton clone, because everyone has their own style which works for them, but I do know how you should throw a left hook and where your feet should be for a right upper cut. These things can be taught.

I would also like to do lots of TV work, commentating on fights and so on, because I find that very enjoyable and it is a great way of keeping in touch with what is going on in the sport.

Some fighters, when they finish, walk away from the sport and never see the inside of a gym again, but I won't be doing that under any circumstances. Like most people, my time needs to be used effectively, otherwise I go stir crazy. I don't need telling that ex-boxers have often endured huge problems when they have hung up their gloves, but I feel it is the ones who don't use the extra time on their hands properly who are in the biggest danger of messing up their lives.

I come from a good family and although I am not exactly looking forward to the day I finish, I know that when the time comes the people I have had around me all my life will stick around me. If they don't, they will miss out on my karaoke nights!

Boxing is a very hard game and I have had over 40 fights. That is over 40 times I have got myself to the absolute peak of fitness. It is a lot and I have achieved a great many of the goals I set for myself. Beating Tszyu and becoming *The Ring*'s Fighter of the Year will always be my outstanding achievements, but there are still ambitions I want to fulfil before I become a boring old fart.

Topping the bill at Madison Square Garden or Las Vegas is something I am desperate to do and that time will come soon.

Floyd Mayweather is currently ranked by all the best judges as the best pound-for-pound boxer in the world, but when I beat him they will have to think again. Maybe it will be The Hitman at the top of the pile.

I know that fight will happen one day and I hope as many fans as possible can make it there for what I can promise will be a memorable night.

My supporters have been incredible throughout my career, from the coachload who came to my first pro fight against Colin McAuley, to the thousands who watched me beat Tszyu, Maussa and Collazo to win world titles. I cannot thank them enough and I can only hope that I have given them value for money. The memories they have given me are priceless. When people come up to me and say I have made Manchester proud, which they do all the time, I feel very humble. I know boxing is an expensive sport and some fans have had to beg, steal and borrow to get to my shows and I can only thank them for what has been an incredible journey so far. If you ever see me on the street, or round about, I am always approachable for a chat. That will never change.

I see a lot of myself in the people who come to watch me fight and maybe that is why it has been so much fun.

Even though I was having my own private war with Frank Warren, I went to Joe Calzaghe's fight against Jeff Lacy on Warren's promotion because I just had to be there. I am a world champion, but I am also just a fight fan and the chance to see two great athletes take each other on was too tempting to miss. After the incredible show Joe put on, I'm very glad I went. So who are the Calzaghes and Hattons of the future? Amir Khan hasn't had his chin properly tested yet, but it is plain for everyone to see that he has a lot of talent. Is he a world champion in the making? In my opinion, yes he is, but there is a long way to go yet.

Manchester's John Murray reminds me a lot of myself in that he has a fantastic work rate, throws some mean body shots and has a style not dissimilar to my own. John is a rapidly improving fighter who has had a couple of tough battles already in the pros and has come through them. He looks a fine prospect and has an exciting, attacking style which I love to watch.

Steve Foster Jnr is developing very well, as is Kevin Mitchell, who has been earmarked for years as a potential champion. Mitchell has dynamite in his fists and now needs to go up to the next level. If he can tighten up his defence, he could go all the way. My gym mate Matthew Macklin has come on in leaps since using Billy Graham and in recent fights has looked amazing as he has blown away one opponent after another. He is certainly twice the fighter he was when he lost a very close one to Andrew Facey in 2003. Under Billy, I think he could become a world champion. I watch him every day at close quarters and I could not be more impressed by Matthew's dedication and, above all, his ability. My own brother Matt, after very little amateur experience, is now learning his trade in the pro ranks. He is becoming a good fighter who could go all the way.

There are plenty of others and of course, there will be future champions who will come from nowhere to surprise us all.

The sport has its fair share of problems, but the return of terrestrial TV in the form of ITV has been a godsend. While I would never take anything away from Sky, who provide brilliant coverage, the fact that there is now some healthy competition must be good for fight fans.

I'm extremely happy with Sky and although ITV could transmit my fights to far bigger audiences, being famous was never a particularly important part of being a boxer for me. I have never sought fame and I don't really want it. I accept a measure of it is part and parcel of being a top fighter and I have got no problem with that, but given a choice between being recognized by half the population and being anonymous, I would choose the latter any day of the week.

Winning fights and proving myself in the ring are far more important to me than chasing fame. Although I did take part in BBC's *Superstars*, more for a laugh than anything else, I absolutely promise you will never see me on the likes of *Celebrity Big Brother*.

I can't understand the current obsession with all things celebrity. Half the people I read about in the paper I haven't a fucking clue what they have done to become famous. I think it is sad. Some people chase fame. They think it is important because it can get them into better restaurants. Fame is nothing and, as for celebrity, I don't understand it and I want nothing of it.

I would much rather cheer on somebody who has, through hard work, achieved something in their lives, be they a footballer, swimmer, tennis player or whatever.

I want to live my life as normally as possible and, outside the ring, I think I do that. In the part of Manchester where I live I don't get any special treatment, not that I would want it anyway. I know a few footballers who live in monster mansions in Cheshire behind ten-feet-high walls and I wouldn't want that either. It is just not me.

I suppose I simply prefer normality, if there is such a thing. I know I am a lucky bloke and never is that rammed home to me more than when I spend time with a lovely little lad called James Bowers. You may have seen him on TV before my fights, because he always brings in my belt.

James is a smashing kid who has always got a smile on his face. About six years ago I noticed he started coming down my gym. He used to just sit in the background and watch for hours on end. You could see he was happy as Larry just to be there. One day I told him to come over and have a chat and James was a nervous wreck. I could hardly get a word out of him.

He laughed a lot and I told him to come down the gym whenever he wanted to watch me train. It would always be open house for him. It didn't take a genius to notice that James had a few scars on his head and I found out from his mum that he has a condition which is known as water on the brain. Not being a medical expert, I don't know exactly what that means, but essentially James suffers from black-outs when there is too much pressure on his brain.

When we first met I was told James had only three months to live. A few weeks later I was telephoned by the doctors, who told me to prepare myself for a shock, so I naturally assumed James had passed away. In fact, his young mother Julie had died of pneumonia. A while later, the doctors rang me again and said that one of the operations that James had had was miraculously starting to work. I like to think Julie was sitting up there looking down on her son and was in his corner looking after him.

I have got to know James very well over the years. Just before I fought Tony Pep I thought it would be nice to make his day, so I asked him if he would like to take my British title belt into the ring and show it to the fans. He could hardly control himself he was so excited.

James brought the belt into the ring and since then it has become something of a tradition. He is always there and so far he has been a very lucky mascot.

The only fight he has missed in recent times was my victory over Collazo. The doctors advised that, because of his condition, it would be very unwise for him to fly to America. James came to tell me himself and started crying because he thought he was letting me down. What a silly kid! I nearly began crying myself and I said we would all miss him in Boston, but he was letting down nobody. I made him promise to watch the fight and I called him soon after beating Collazo.

I don't know what to say about James other than this: he's just a lovely boy who has been unlucky enough to get an illness. But I know he can't stop smiling because he has got a pal who boxes for a living. It sounds a bit corny, but the fact that me and my coaches and family can make James a little happier means a heck of a lot to all of us.

Although I am still young at heart, I feel, as I get older, that I am learning about life and what it is all about. Don't worry, I'm not going to get philosophical, but, like everybody does, I am changing as I get older.

Perhaps my finest achievement as an amateur was winning the bronze medal in the world junior championships when I was 17 years old. I haven't mentioned it so far because for years I blotted it out of my life as I was so incensed about what happened all those years ago in Cuba. I qualified to fight in the world championships, which in itself was an achievement for a British fighter. I went to Cuba, the home of amateur boxing, to see how far I could go. The crowd seemed to love my style. I knocked out my first opponent in the first round and my second in the second round and, the next day, I picked up a paper and saw the headline: 'We have found the little Tyson – Ricky Hatton from England.' I was chuffed to bits.

I was down to face a Cuban next and anyone who knows anything about amateur boxing will be aware that the Cubans are the kings. Purely on this basis, I shouldn't have even bothered going to the arena, but I had seen the Cuban fight and I knew I could have him.

In the end, I beat him very convincingly and the crowd even cheered for me when my hand was raised. Remember all those grainy black and white pictures of the old days in boxing? That was what it was like. The arena was like a chicken coop. Small and packed with a couple of thousand mad Cubans, all smoking fat cigars and getting pissed on the local brew.

As I walked out of the arena, having beaten the local boy, one punter even made the 'slit throat' gesture and shouted that I was going to be killed in my bed that night. Not what you would call Queensbury rules! My next fight was against the second favourite, an American. When I beat him the majority of the crowd forgave me for getting the better of their fellow Cuban and afterwards they gave me all the support in the world.

I had seen off the favourite for my weight class and was paired against a Russian in the semi-finals. I don't think he laid a glove on me. I slaughtered him all around the ring and even though I could not stop him, there was never any doubt about the result. Except there was. When the result came through at the end, it was his hand being raised by the ref and not mine. Boos rang around the arena and all kinds of stuff was thrown into the ring in protest. I was crushed. I could not believe it. I later found out that only one of the judges voted for my opponent, but he did so by such a massive margin that it cancelled out my aggregate score with the other judges. There were claims that bribery was involved and there was an investigation but that was no consolation to me. In the other semi-final, a German lad also got robbed. It was Jurgen Brahmer, who had already beaten me in the amateurs and was the last person to KO me. We both stood on the bronze podium during the medal ceremony knowing it should have been us on the top levels.

They announced my name and the audience went bonkers. The cheering seemed to last for ages before they eventually got around to the gold medal winner, the Russian. As soon as they started to announce his name the crowd started booing and, again, that lasted for yonks. I felt a bit sorry for the Russian lad, as it was hardly his fault.

Despite the loss, it was a great experience to see what boxing was like in Cuba and I came back from there with mixed feelings. I had not won the gold medal, but I had not done anything wrong and the crowd had showed who they felt was the real champion.

That bronze medal went in the bottom of a drawer for years, underneath my socks and pants, until very recently. A friend of mine was making a montage of all my amateur days – badges, medals, boxing forms, etc – and asked if he could have the bronze medal. I thought about it for a while and, although the defeat still hurt, I decided that nearly ten years is a long time to be bitter about something. I said yes and it hangs on my wall now.

The point of this story is that, as I've said, I've changed over the years. It is an indication that I can now accept what has happened in the past, without beating myself up about things I had no control over.

We all change over the years, but at the same time I like to think I have stayed the same person in many respects. Beer and boxing may not seem the most ideal bedfellows, but so far I have not done too bad.

After beating Collazo, I got a call from Freddie Flintoff asking if he could come down the gym and do some sparring with me for a TV series he was doing. I said no problem, as I've met Freddie a few times and he is a terrific bloke.

I got him in the ring and it was clear he had done a bit of boxing before, as he knew how to throw his punches from his legs, not his shoulders. He admitted he had tried it as a kid, but had then got hooked on cricket. He still watches all the big boxing shows on television and attends them in person if he can.

Freddie was a right laugh and his reputation as one of the nicest people you can ever meet is well and truly justified. There is no edge to him at all. He is just a big bear of a bloke who seems to get on well with everyone.

Freddie and I did a bit of filming and I joked that in a few weeks I would be ready to take him on, at his weight! Mind you, I would need to grow about two feet. We agreed to go out on the town and have a few beers.

I can now safely vouch for the fact that Freddie is great company. I thought I was pretty high-class when it comes to enjoying myself, but Freddie is in the Premiership too. I can't begin to remember all the conversations we had, but let me just say that it was one of the most enjoyable evenings I have ever had and hopefully there will be many more.

I don't want to sound like a celebrity name-dropper, but Wayne Rooney fancies taking me on in the gym as well. Just before the World Cup, Wayne rang me to say he wanted to come down to my gym after the finals and give me a good old-fashioned arse-kicking! Being a Scouser he is not slow to come forward with his opinions, so I said, 'Any time, son.'

Wayne used to box as a kid and he joked that he would come to Manchester and take my belt off me. I told him he eats too many chips and there was no way he would get it around his waist! We laughed our tits off on the phone for ages and, even though he plays for the wrong team in Manchester, he is a great lad. I can't wait to spar with him and I know we will be big mates as he has a cracking sense of humour.

The ability to laugh at yourself is such an important thing. Take this little story, which happened to me three years ago.

I had been chasing this girl from Ashton-under-Lyne for a long time and was getting nowhere. Eventually I plucked up the courage to speak to her in the pub and, lo and behold, as the night wore on, I knew I was getting somewhere. As the pub was closing, she asked me if I wanted to go back to her place for a coffee.

I said, 'Sure, no problem,' and clicked my heels. She said that if I wanted to come back, maybe there was something I could get from the gents toilets to make the night a bit more memorable.

So I went into the bog and bought the required you-know-whats from one of the machines.

I was a bit tipsy, but we walked back to her place and, eventually, after a bit of petting, went upstairs. I thought everything was going smoothly until she told me now was the right time to get out what I had bought in the toilets earlier.

I rummaged through my trouser pockets and found that instead of condoms, I had bought some mints. Oh dear. I told her there were three machines in the toilet – one for toothbrushes, one for mints and one for condoms and I had obviously got the wrong one.

She said no probs. Simple solution. There was a 24-hour garage just a couple of hundred yards across the road. I could go there and get some condoms and we could still salvage the night. I thought it sounded a great plan, but even though I looked everywhere for my shoes, I couldn't find them. I pulled up my trousers and she lent me her fluffy slippers so I could go down to the garage.

I walked down the street, found the garage easy enough and bought the condoms, but then came the hard part. I had completely forgotten which house she lived in. Fuck. Bollocks. I walked around and around and started whistling to see if she would hear me. I was walking for what seemed like hours in her slippers, whistling along the road and hoping she would open up her bedroom window and beckon me in. I think I woke up a couple of grannies, but not her! Eventually, I realized I was completely lost in the middle of nowhere without the foggiest idea where I was or where she lived.

Luckily enough, I found a main road and hailed a late-night cabbie. But without her address I didn't have a clue where to direct him, so I told the driver to take me home instead. I think he noticed the slippers, but took the risk.

I went to bed and woke up thinking it was all a bad dream, until I saw the slippers at the end of my bed.

About a week went by and I went into the girl's usual pub again to see if I could make amends. Sure enough she was there. As I tried to explain and apologize she looked at me and said just two words. The second was off.

Ricky Hatton. A world champion. And, in the words of Del Boy, what a prize plonker!

Ricky Hatton's Statistics

ABBREVIATIONS KEY

DQ	Disqualification
KO	Knockout
PTS	Points
TKO	Technical knockout
UD	Undisputed
W	Win
Wld	Win, lose, draw record

Sex	Male
Nationality	British
Alias	The Hitman
Birth Name	Richard Hatton
Home Town	Manchester, England
Birthplace	Stockport, England
Rated at	Welterweight
Date of Birth	06.10.1978
Age	27
Reach	65"
Stance	Orthodox
Height	5' 6"
Trainer	Billy Graham
Manager	Ray Hatton
Promoter	Frank Warren 1997–2005
	Dennis Hobson 2005–

W 41 (30 KO's) | L 0 | D 0 | Total 41

Date	13.05.06
Hatton's weight	147 lb
Opponent	Luis Collazo
Weight	147 lb
W/d	26-1-0
Location	TD Banknorth Garden, Boston, MA, USA
Result	W UD 12 12
Referee	John Zablocki
Judge	Don O'Neill 115-112
Judge	Paul Driscoll 115-112
Judge	Leo Gerstel 114-113

WBA Welterweight Title
Collazo down in the 1st round

Date	26.11.05
Hatton's weight	139½ lb
Opponent	Carlos Maussa
Weight	140 lb
W/d	20-2-0
Location	Hallam FM Arena, Sheffield, England
Result	W KO 9 12
Referee	Mickey Vann
Judge	John Coyle
Judge	Ruben M. (Dr) Garcia
Judge	Guy Jutras

IBF Light Welterweight Title
WBA Light Welterweight Title

Date	04.06.05
Hatton's weight	139¾ lb
Opponent	Kostya Tszyu
Weight	140 lb
W/d	31-1-0
Location	MEN Arena, Manchester, England
Result	W TKO 11 12
Referee	Dave Parris
Judge	Manuel Maritxalar 105-104
Judge	Alfred Asaro 106-103
Judge	Don Ackerman 107-102

IBF Light Welterweight Title
Corner retirement

Date	11.12.04
Hatton's weight	139½ lb
Opponent	Ray Oliveira
Weight	139½ lb
W/d	47-9-2
Location	ExCeL Arena, Docklands, London, England
Result	W KO 10 12
Referee	Mickey Vann

Judge   Dave Parris
Judge   Karl Rogers
Judge   Reg Thompson
WBU Light Welterweight Title

Date   01.10.04
Hatton's weight 139¼ lb
Opponent   Michael Stewart
Weight   139¾ lb
Wld   36-2-2
Location   MEN Arena, Manchester, England
Result   W   TKO   5   12
Referee   Dave Parris
WBU Light Welterweight Title
IBF Light Welterweight Title Eliminator
Stewart down twice in round one, once in round five

Date   12.06.04
Hatton's weight 139¼ lb
Opponent   Carlos Wilfredo Vilches
Weight   139½ lb
Wld   41-4-2
Location   MEN Arena, Manchester, England
Result   W   UD   12   12
Referee   Darryl Ribbink
Judge   Reg Thompson 120-107
Judge   Karl Rogers 119-108
Judge   Tony Walker 119-108
WBU Light Welterweight Title

Date   03.04.04
Hatton's weight 139¼ lb
Opponent   Dennis Holbaek Pedersen
Weight   140 lb
Wld   44-2-0
Location   MEN Arena, Manchester, England
Result   W   TKO   6   12
Referee   Dave Parris
Judge   Mickey Vann
Judge   Glenn Feldman
Judge   Howard Goldberg
WBU Light Welterweight Title

Date   13.12.03
Hatton's weight 139½ lb
Opponent   Ben Tackie
Weight   139 lb
Wld   24-4-0
Location   MEN Arena, Manchester, England
Result   W   UD   12   12

Referee   Mickey Vann
Judge   Tony Walker 118-110
Judge   Jean-Louis Legland 120-109
Judge   Edward Marshall 120-109
WBU Light Welterweight Title

Date   27.09.03
Hatton's weight 139¼ lb
Opponent   Aldo Nazareno Rios
Weight   139¼ lb
Wld   35-2-0
Location   MEN Arena, Manchester, England
Result   W   TKO   10   12
Referee   Mickey Vann
Judge   Howard Goldberg
Judge   Jean-Louis Legland
Judge   Reg Thompson
WBU Light Welterweight Title
Rios down in the first and ninth rounds
Corner retirement

Date   05.04.03
Hatton's weight 139½ lb
Opponent   Vince Phillips
Weight   140 lb
Wld   44-7-1
Location   MEN Arena, Manchester, England
Result   W   UD   12   12
Referee   Ian John Lewis
Judge   Howard Goldberg 119-109
Judge   Reg Thompson 120-107
Judge   Des Bloyd 120-108
WBU Light Welterweight Title

Date   14.12.02
Hatton's weight 139½ lb
Opponent   Joe Hutchinson
Weight   138¼ lb
Wld   25-3-2
Location   Telewest Arena, Newcastle, England
Result   W   KO   4   12
Referee   Ian John Lewis
Judge   Karl Rogers
Judge   Reg Thompson
Judge   Tony Walker
WBU Light Welterweight Title

Date   28.09.02
Hatton's weight 139¾lb
Opponent   Stephen Smith
Weight   139½lb
Wld   31-1-0
Location   MEN Arena, Manchester, England
Result   W   DQ   2   12
Referee   Mickey Vann
Judge   Des Bloyd
Judge   Howard Goldberg
Judge   Glenn Feldman
WBU Light Welterweight Title
Smith DQ'd after his trainer ran into the ring to protest a cut caused by an apparent elbow. Smith down twice.

Date   01.06.02
Hatton's weight 139¾ lb
Opponent   Eamonn Magee
Weight   139¼lb
Wld   23-2-0
Location   MEN Arena, Manchester, England
Result   W   UD   12   12
Referee   Mickey Vann
Judge   Des Bloyd 116-111
Judge   Glenn Feldman 116-111
Judge   Howard Goldberg 115-112
WBU Light Welterweight Title
Hatton down for first time as a pro in the first round

Date   09.02.02
Hatton's weight 139½lb
Opponent   Mikhail Krivolapov
Weight   139½lb
Wld   34-2-0
Location   MEN Arena, Manchester, England
Result   W   TKO   9   12
Referee   Mickey Vann
Judge   Des Bloyd
Judge   Tony Walker
Judge   Glenn Feldman
WBU Light Welterweight Title

Date   15.12.01
Hatton's weight 139½lb
Opponent   Justin Rowsell
Weight   139½lb
Wld   31-1-2
Location   Conference Centre, Wembley, London, England
Result   W   TKO   2   12
Referee   Mickey Vann

Judge	Reg Thompson				
Judge	Karl Rogers				
Judge	Tony Walker				
WBU Light Welterweight Title					

Date	27.10.01				
Hatton's weight	139¾lb				
Opponent	Freddie Pendleton				
Weight	139¾lb				
Wld	47-25-5				
Location	MEN Arena, Manchester, England				
Result	W	KO	2		12
Referee	Mickey Vann				
Judge	Karl Rogers				
Judge	Reg Thompson				
Judge	Tony Walker				
WBU Light Welterweight Title					

Date	15.09.01				
Hatton's weight	140lb				
Opponent	John Bailey				
Weight	139½lb				
Wld	19-7-2				
Location	MEN Arena, Manchester, England				
Result	W	TKO	5		12
Referee	Mickey Vann				
Judge	Reg Thompson				
Judge	Karl Rogers				
Judge	Ian John Lewis				
WBU Light Welterweight Title					
Bailey down four times					

Date	07.07.01				
Hatton's weight	139½lb				
Opponent	Jason Rowland				
Weight	139½lb				
Wld	25-1-0				
Location	Velodrome, Manchester, England				
Result	W	KO	4		12
Referee	Mickey Vann				
Judge	Karl Rogers				
Judge	Howard Goldberg				
Judge	Reg Thompson				
WBU Light Welterweight Title					

Date	26.03.01				
Hatton's weight	139lb				
Opponent	Tony Pep				
Weight	139lb				
Wld	42-7-1				

Location   Wembley Arena, London, England
Result   W   TKO   4   12
Referee   Mickey Vann
Judge   Terry O'Neill
Judge   Reg Thompson
Judge   John Poturaj
Vacant WBU Light Welterweight Title

Date   21.10.00
Hatton's weight   139½lb
Opponent   Jonathan Thaxton
Weight   139lb
Wld   19-5-0
Location   Wembley Conference Centre, London, England
Result   W   PTS   12   12
Referee   Paul Thomas 117-113
Vacant British Light Welterweight Title

Date   23.09.00
Hatton's weight   139¾lb
Opponent   Giuseppe Lauri
Weight   138¼lb
Wld   19-1-0
Location   York Hall, Bethnal Green, London, England
Result   W   TKO   5   12
Referee   Bartolome Torralba
Judge   Jean-Louis Legland
Judge   Dave Parris
Judge   Paul Thomas
WBA International Light Welterweight Title
WBO Inter-Continental Light Welterweight Title

Date   10.06.00
Hatton's weight   140lb
Opponent   Gilbert Quiros
Weight   140lb
Wld   11-2-0
Location   Fox Theater, Detroit, MI, USA
Result   W   KO   2   12
WBO Inter-Continental Light Welterweight Title

Date   16.05.00
Hatton's weight   140lb
Opponent   Ambioris Figuero
Weight   140lb
Wld   8-1-2
Location   Spectrum Arena, Warrington, England
Result   W   KO   4   12
Referee   Roy Francis
Judge   John Coyle

Judge   Paul Thomas
Judge   Mickey Vann
WBO Inter-Continental Light Welterweight Title

Date   25.03.00
Hatton's weight 139¼ lb
Opponent   Pedro Alonso Teran
Weight   139 lb
Wld   13-2-0
Location   Olympia, Liverpool, England
Result   W   TKO   4   12
Referee   John Keane
Judge   Phil Edwards
Judge   Howard John Foster
Judge   Keith Garner
WBO Inter-Continental Light Welterweight Title

Date   29.01.00
Hatton's weight 141¼ lb
Opponent   Leoncio Garces
Weight   141½ lb
Wld   10-2-0
Location   MEN Arena, Manchester, England
Result   W   TKO   3   8
Referee   Mickey Vann

Date   11.12.99
Hatton's weight 139 lb
Opponent   Mark Winters
Weight   139 lb
Wld   13-2-1
Location   Everton Park Sports Centre, Liverpool, England
Result   W   KO   4   12
Referee   Dave Parris
Judge   John Coyle
Judge   Paul Thomas
Judge   Mickey Vann
WBO Inter-Continental Light Welterweight Title

Date   09.10.99
Hatton's weight 139¾ lb
Opponent   Bernard Paul
Weight   140 lb
Wld   21-8-4
Location   Bowler's Arena, Manchester, England
Result   W   TKO   4   12
Referee   Dave Parris
WBO Inter-Continental Light Welterweight Title

Date	17.07.99
Hatton's weight	142 lb
Opponent	Mark Ramsey
Weight	145 lb
Wld	15-25-5
Location	Doncaster Dome, Doncaster, England
Result	W PTS 6 6
Referee	Mickey Vann 60-56

Date	29.05.99
Hatton's weight	139 lb
Opponent	Dillon Carew
Weight	138 lb
Wld	10-3-2
Location	North Bridge Leisure Centre, Halifax, West Yorkshire, England
Result	W TKO 5 12
Referee	Roy Francis
Judge	Dave Parris
Judge	Paul Thomas
Judge	John Coyle

Vacant WBO Inter-Continental Light Welterweight Title

Date	03.04.99
Hatton's weight	140 lb
Opponent	Brian Coleman
Weight	144 lb
Wld	17-72-7
Location	Royal Albert Hall, Kensington, London, England
Result	W KO 2 10

Date	27.02.99
Hatton's weight	140 lb
Opponent	Tommy Peacock
Weight	139 lb
Wld	9-0-1
Location	Oldham Leisure Centre, Oldham, England
Result	W TKO 2 10
Referee	Keith Garner

Vacant British (Central Area) Light Welterweight Title

Date	19.12.98
Hatton's weight	141 lb
Opponent	Paul Denton
Weight	141 lb
Wld	7-9-2
Location	Everton Park Sports Centre, Liverpool, England
Result	W KO 6 8
Referee	Keith Garner

Date	31.10.98			
Hatton's weight	142 lb			
Opponent	Kevin Carter			
Weight	139 lb			
Wld	1-2-0			
Location	Convention Center, Atlantic City, NJ, USA			
Result	W	KO	1	6

Date	19.09.98			
Hatton's weight	140¼ lb			
Opponent	Pascal Montulet			
Weight	140 lb			
Wld	10-19-3			
Location	Arena Oberhausen, Oberhausen, Nordrhein-Westfalen, Germany			
Result	W	KO	2	6

Date	18.07.98			
Hatton's weight	140 lb			
Opponent	Anthony Campbell			
Weight	unlisted			
Wld	12-14-4			
Location	Ponds Forge Arena, Sheffield, England			
Result	W	PTS	6	6

Date	30.05.98			
Hatton's weight	143 lb			
Opponent	Mark Ramsey			
Weight	141 lb			
Wld	13-18-4			
Location	Whitchurch Leisure Centre, Bristol, England			
Result	W	PTS	6	6

Date	18.04.98			
Hatton's weight	141 lb			
Opponent	Karl Taylor			
Weight	142 lb			
Wld	14-36-3			
Location	Nynex Arena, Manchester, England			
Result	W	TKO	1	6

Date	27.03.98			
Hatton's weight	141 lb			
Opponent	Paul Salmon			
Weight	unlisted			
Wld	4-12-0			
Location	Telford Ice Rink, Telford, England			
Result	W	KO	1	4

Date	17.01.98
Hatton's weight	141½ lb
Opponent	David Thompson
Weight	142 lb
Wld	7-20-3
Location	Whitchurch Leisure Centre, Bristol, England
Result	W KO 1 4

Date	19.12.97
Hatton's weight	141 lb
Opponent	Robert Alvarez
Weight	145 lb
Wld	2-2-0
Location	Madison Square Garden, New York, USA
Result	W UD 4 4
Result	40-36	40-36	39-37
Judges	unlisted

Date	11.09.97
Hatton's weight	140 lb
Opponent	Colin McAuley
Weight	138 lb
Wld	8-48-3
Location	Kingsway Leisure Centre, Widnes, England
Result	W TKO 1 4
Corner retirement	
Pro debut for Hatton	

Index